PYTHON SCIKIT-LEARN
FOR BEGINNERS

SCIKIT-LEARN SPECIALIZATION
FOR DATA SCIENTIST

AI PUBLISHING

© Copyright 2021 by AI Publishing
All rights reserved.
First Printing, 2021

Edited by AI Publishing
eBook Converted and Cover by Gazler Studio
Published by AI Publishing LLC

ISBN-13: 978-1-7347901-8-4

The contents of this book may not be copied, reproduced, duplicated, or transmitted without the direct written permission of the author. Under no circumstances whatsoever will any legal liability or blame be held against the publisher for any compensation, damages, or monetary loss due to the information contained herein, either directly or indirectly.

Legal Notice:
You are not permitted to amend, use, distribute, sell, quote, or paraphrase any part of the content within this book without the specific consent of the author.

Disclaimer Notice:
Kindly note that the information contained within this document is solely for educational and entertainment purposes. No warranties of any kind are indicated or expressed. Readers accept that the author is not providing any legal, professional, financial, or medical advice. Kindly consult a licensed professional before trying out any techniques explained in this book.

By reading this document, the reader consents that under no circumstances is the author liable for any losses, direct or indirect, that are incurred as a consequence of the use of the information contained within this document, including, but not restricted to, errors, omissions, or inaccuracies.

How to contact us

If you have any feedback, please let us know by sending an email to contact@aipublishing.io.

Your feedback is immensely valued, and we look forward to hearing from you. It will be beneficial for us to improve the quality of our books.

To get the Python codes and materials used in this book, please click the link below:

www.aipublishing.io/book- sklearn-python

The order number is required.

About the Publisher

At AI Publishing Company, we have established an international learning platform specifically for young students, beginners, small enterprises, startups, and managers who are new to data science and artificial intelligence.

Through our interactive, coherent, and practical books and courses, we help beginners learn skills that are crucial to developing AI and data science projects.

Our courses and books range from basic introduction courses to language programming and data science to advanced courses for machine learning, deep learning, computer vision, big data, and much more. The programming languages used include Python, R, and some data science and AI software.

AI Publishing's core focus is to enable our learners to create and try proactive solutions for digital problems by leveraging the power of AI and data science to the maximum extent.

Moreover, we offer specialized assistance in the form of our online content and eBooks, providing up-to-date and useful insight into AI practices and data science subjects, along with eliminating the doubts and misconceptions about AI and programming.

Our experts have cautiously developed our contents and kept them concise, short, and comprehensive so that you can understand everything clearly and effectively and start practicing the applications right away.

We also offer consultancy and corporate training in AI and data science for enterprises so that their staff can navigate through the workflow efficiently.

With AI Publishing, you can always stay closer to the innovative world of AI and data science.

If you are eager to learn the A to Z of AI and data science but have no clue where to start, AI Publishing is the finest place to go.

Please contact us by email at:
contact@aipublishing.io.

AI Publishing Is Looking for Authors Like You

Interested in becoming an author for AI Publishing? Please contact us at author@aipublishing.io.

We are working with developers and AI tech professionals just like you, to help them share their insights with the global AI and Data Science lovers. You can share all your knowledge about hot topics in AI and Data Science.

An Important Note to Our Valued Readers:

Download the Color Images

Our print edition books are available only in black & white at present. However, the digital edition of our books is available in color PDF.

We request you to download the PDF file containing the color images of the screenshots/diagrams used in this book here:

www.aipublishing.io/book- sklearn-python

The typesetting and publishing costs for a color edition are prohibitive. These costs would push the final price of each book to $50, which would make the book less accessible for most beginners.

We are a small company, and we are negotiating with major publishers for a reduction in the publishing price. We are hopeful of a positive outcome sometime soon. In the meantime, we request you to help us with your wholehearted support, feedback, and review.

For the present, we have decided to print all of our books in black & white and provide access to the color version in PDF. This is a decision that would benefit the majority of our readers, as most of them are students. This would also allow beginners to afford our books.

Get in touch with us

Feedback from our readers is always welcome.

For general feedback, please send us an email at contact@aipublishing.io and mention the book title in the subject line.

Although we have taken extraordinary care to ensure the accuracy of our content, errors do occur. If you have found an error in this book, we would be grateful if you could report this to us as soon as you can.

If you are interested in becoming an AI Publishing author and if you have expertise in a topic and you are interested in either writing or contributing to a book, please send us an email at author@aipublishing.io.

Table of Contents

Preface 1
    Book Approach 2
    Who Is This Book For? 3
    How to Use This Book? 3

About the Author 5

Chapter 1: Introduction 7
    1.1   What Is Machine Learning and Data Science? 7
    1.2   Where Does Scikit-Learn Fit In? 8
    1.3   Other Machine Learning Libraries 9
        1.3.1   NumPy 9
        1.3.2   Matplotlib 9
        1.3.3   Seaborn 10
        1.3.4   Pandas 10
        1.3.5   TensorFlow 11
        1.3.6   Keras 11
    1.4   What's Ahead? 12

**Chapter 2: Environment Setup and
                  Python Crash Course** 13
    2.1   Environment Setup 13
        2.1.1   Windows Setup 13
        2.1.2   Mac Setup 19
        2.1.3   Linux Setup 24

		2.1.4	Using Google Colab Cloud Environment............27
	2.2	Python Crash Course..31	
		2.2.1	Writing Your First Program..31
		2.2.2	Python Variables and Data Types..............................35
		2.2.3	Python Operators...38
		2.2.4	Conditional Statements...44
		2.2.5	Iteration Statements..47
		2.2.6	Functions..48
		2.2.7	Objects and Classes...50
	Exercise 2.1...53		
	Exercise 2.2..53		

Chapter 3: Data Preprocessing with Scikit-Learn............ 55

	3.1	Feature Scaling.. 56	
		3.1.1	Standardization... 56
		3.1.2	Min/Max Scaling...60
		3.1.3	Mean Normalization...62
	3.2	Handling Missing Data.. 64	
		3.2.1.	Handling Missing Numerical Data............................ 65
		3.2.2.	Handling Missing Categorical Data..........................77
	3.3	Categorical Data Encoding...83	
		3.3.1	One Hot Encoding..83
		3.3.2	Label Encoding...90
	3.4	Data Discretization..92	
		3.4.1	Equal Width Discretization...92
		3.4.2	Equal Frequency Discretization................................ 98
	3.5	Handling Outliers...103	
		3.5.1	Outlier Trimming.. 104
		3.5.2	Outlier Capping Using Mean & Std........................108
	Exercise 3.1... 111		
	Exercise 3.2... 112		

Chapter 4: Feature Selection with
Python Scikit-Learn Library....................... 113

4.1 Feature Selection Based on Variance 113
4.2 Feature Selection Based on Correlation 117
4.3 Feature Selection Based on Recursive Elimination 121
4.4. Feature Selection Based on Model Performance 123
Exercise 4.1 125
Exercise 4.2 126

Chapter 5: Solving Regression Problems in Machine Learning using Sklearn Library 127

5.1 Preparing Data for Regression Problems 128
    5.1.1 Dividing Data into Features and Labels 131
    5.1.2 Converting Categorical Data to Numbers 132
    5.1.3 Divide Data into Training and Test Sets 135
    5.1.4 Data Scaling/Normalization 135
5.2 Single Output Regression Problems 136
    5.2.1 Linear Regression 137
    5.2.2 KNN Regression 140
    5.2.3 Random Forest Regression 142
    5.2.4 Making Prediction on a Single Record 145
5.3 Multi-output Regression Problems 146
    5.3.1 Linear Regression for Multiclass Output 148
    5.3.2 Random Forest for Multiclass Output 149
    5.3.3 Direct Multiclass Output Regression with Wrapper Algorithms 151
    5.3.4 Chained Multiclass Output Regression with Wrapper Algorithms 153
Exercise 5.1 156
Exercise 5.2 156

Chapter 6: Solving Classification Problems in Machine Learning using Sklearn Library 157

6.1 Preparing Data for Classification Problems 157
    6.1.1 Dividing Data into Features and Labels 159
    6.1.2 Converting Categorical Data to Numbers 160
    6.1.3 Divide Data into Training and Test Sets 163

      6.1.4   Data Scaling/Normalization 163
  6.2   Solving Binary Classification Problems 164
      6.2.1   Logistic Regression 164
      6.2.2   KNN Classifier 168
      6.2.3   Random Forest Classifier 170
      6.2.4   K Fold Cross-validation 172
      6.2.5   Predicting a Single Value 172
  6.3   Solving Multiclass Classification Problems 174
      6.3.1   One-vs-Rest for Multiclass Classification 177
      6.3.2   One-vs-One for Multiclass Classification 179
  6.4   Solving Multilabel Classification Problems 181
  Exercise 6.1 186
  Exercise 6.2 186

Chapter 7: Clustering Data with Scikit-Learn Library 187

  7.1   K-Means Clustering 187
      7.1.1   Clustering Dummy Data
              with K-Means Clustering 189
      7.1.2   Customer Segmentation
              Using K-Means Clustering 194
  7.2   Hierarchical Clustering 208
      7.2.1   Hierarchical Clustering Example
              using Dummy Data 210
      7.2.2   Clustering the Iris Plant Dataset 218
  Exercise 7.1 223
  Exercise 7.2 224

Chapter 8: Dimensionality Reduction with PCA and LDA using Sklearn 225

  8.1   Principal Component Analysis 225
  8.2   Linear Discriminant Analysis 231
  8.3   Singular Value Decomposition 236
  Exercise 8.1 243
  Exercise 8.2 244

Chapter 9: Selecting Best Models with Scikit-Learn 245

- 9.1 K Fold Cross-validation...245
  - 9.1.1 Prediction without Cross-validation 246
  - 9.1.2 Prediction with Cross-validation.............................248
- 9.2 Hyper Parameter Selection..251
- 9.3 Model Evaluation via Validation Curves................................255
- 9.4 Saving Models for Future Use 260
- Exercise 9.1..265
- Exercise 9.2..266

Chapter 10: Natural Language Processing with Scikit-Learn 267

- 10.1 What is Natural Language Processing 267
- 10.2 Spam Email Detection with Scikit-Learn............................. 268
  - 10.2.1 Installing Required Libraries 269
  - 10.2.2 Importing Libraries 269
  - 10.2.3 Importing the Dataset...270
  - 10.2.4 Data Visualization 271
  - 10.2.5 Cleaning the Data 275
  - 10.2.6 Convert Text to Numbers 276
  - 10.2.7 Training the Model 277
  - 10.2.8 Evaluating Model Performance..............................278
  - 10.2.9 Making Predictions on Single Instance 280
- 10.3 IMDB Movies Sentimental Analysis 281
  - 10.3.1 Importing Libraries 281
  - 10.3.2 Importing the Dataset...282
  - 10.3.3 Cleaning the Data 283
  - 10.3.4 Convert Text to Numbers 285
  - 10.3.5 Training the Model 286
  - 10.3.6 Evaluating Model Performance..............................287
  - 10.3.7 Making Predictions on Single Instance 288
- Exercise 10.1..289
- Exercise 10.2.. 290

Chapter 11: Image Classification with Scikit-Learn 291
- 11.1 Importing the Dataset 291
- 11.2 Dividing the Dataset into Features and Labels 294
- 11.3 Dividing Data into Training and Test Sets 295
- 11.4 Data Scaling/Normalization 295
- 11.5 Training and Making Predictions 295
- 11.6 Evaluating the Algorithm on Test Set 296
- Exercise 11.1 298
- Exercise 11.2 299

From the Same Publisher 300

Exercise Solutions 303
- Exercise 2.1 303
- Exercise 2.2 304
- Exercise 3.1 304
- Exercise 3.2 305
- Exercise 4.1 306
- Exercise 4.2 307
- Exercise 5.1 308
- Exercise 5.2 309
- Exercise 6.1 311
- Exercise 6.2 312
- Exercise 7.1 313
- Exercise 7.2 314
- Exercise 8.1 315
- Exercise 8.2 316
- Exercise 9.1 318
- Exercise 9.2 319
- Exercise 10.1 321
- Exercise 10.2 322
- Exercise 11.1 324
- Exercise 11.2 325

Warning

In Python, indentation is very important. Python indentation is a way of telling a Python interpreter that the group of statements belongs to a particular code block. After each loop or if-condition, be sure to pay close attention to the intent.

Example

```python
# Python program showing
# indentation

site = 'aisciences'

if site == 'aisciences':
    print('Logging to www.aisciences.io...')
else:
    print('retype the URL.')
print('All set !')
```

To avoid problems during execution, we advise you to download the codes available on Github by requesting access from the link below. Please have your order number ready for access:

www.aipublishing.io/book-sklearn-python

Preface

Thank you for your decision to purchase this book. I can assure you that you will not regret your decision. Python's Scikit- learn library is one of the most widely used libraries for data science and machine learning. With Python's Scikit-learn library, you can perform almost all the data science and machine learning related tasks such as data visualization, feature engineering, classification and regression, text and image processing, and so on. This book is a beginner's gateway to Python's Scikit-learn library. After reading this book, you will be able to perform common data science and machine learning tasks, such as predicting the price of a certain item, predicting whether or not a banknote is fake, recognizing an image, classifying public sentiments, and much more. You will also learn how to perform data preprocessing and feature engineering tasks, such as handling missing values, converting categorical data into numerical and vice versa, etc. While this book is aimed at beginners, it can also be used by expert programmers as a reference to perform various machine learning and data science tasks.

§ Book Approach

The book follows a very simple approach. It is divided into 11 chapters. Chapter 1 provides a very brief introduction to data science and machine learning and the use of Python's Scikit-learn library for machine learning. The process for environment setup, including the software needed to run the scripts in this book, is explained in Chapter 2. Chapter 2 also contains a crash course on Python for beginners. If you are already familiar with Python, you can skip chapter 2.

Chapter 3 explains various data preprocessing techniques, while chapter 4 details how to perform feature selection with the Scikit-learn library. Chapters 5 and 6 contain introductions to supervised machine learning approaches like regression and classification with the help of the Scikit-learn library. Chapter 7 explains unsupervised machine learning, where you study different clustering approaches using the Python Scikit-learn library. Dimensionality reduction approaches in Scikit-learn have been discussed in the 8th chapter of this book. Chapter 9 explains various model selection techniques in Scikit-learn. Finally, chapters 10 and 11 show how to process text and images with Scikit-learn.

Each chapter explains a concept theoretically followed by practical examples. Each chapter also contains exercises that students can use to evaluate their understanding of the concepts explained in the chapter. The Python notebook for each chapter is provided in the SharePoint repository. It is advised that instead of copying the code, you write the code yourself, and in case of an error, you match your code with the corresponding Python notebook, find and then correct the error. The datasets used in this book are either downloaded at runtime or are available in the *Datasets* folder in the SharePoint repository.

§ Who Is This Book For?

This book explains how to use Python's Scikit-learn library to perform different types of data science and machine learning tasks. The book is aimed ideally at absolute beginners to data science and machine learning. Though a background in the Python programming language and feature engineering can help speed up learning, the book contains a crash course on Python programming language in the second chapter.

Therefore, the only prerequisites to efficiently using this book are access to a computer with the internet and basic knowledge of linear algebra and calculus. All the codes and datasets have been provided. However, to download the data preparation libraries, you will need the internet.

§ How to Use This Book?

To get the best out of this book, I would suggest that you first get your feet wet with the Python programming language, especially the object-oriented programming concepts. To do so, you can take the crash course on Python in chapter 2 of this book. Also, try to read the chapters of this book in order since the concepts taught in the subsequent chapters are based on previous chapters.

In each chapter, try to first understand the theoretical concepts behind the different types of data science and machine learning techniques and then try to execute the example code. I would again stress that rather than copying and pasting code, try to write the codes yourself, and in case of any error, you can match your code with the source code provided in the book as well as in the SharePoint repository. Finally, try to answer the questions asked in the exercises at the end of each chapter. The solutions to the exercises have been given at the end of the Book.

To facilitate the reading process, occasionally, the book presents three types of box-tags in different colors: Requirements, **Further Readings,** and **Hands-on Time**. Examples of these boxes are shown below.

> **Requirements**
>
> This box lists all requirements needed to be done before proceeding to the next topic. Generally, it works as a checklist to see if everything is ready before a tutorial.

> **Further Readings**
>
> Here, you will be pointed to some external reference or source that will serve as additional content about the specific **Topic** being studied. In general, it consists of packages, documentations, and cheat sheets.

> **Hands-on Time**
>
> Here, you will be pointed to an external file to train and test all the knowledge acquired about a **Tool** that has been studied. Generally, these files are Jupyter notebooks (.ipynb), Python (.py) files, or documents (.pdf).

The box-tag Requirements lists the steps required by the reader after reading one or more topics. **Further Readings** provides relevant references for specific topics to get to know the additional content of the topics. **Hands-on Time** points to practical tools to start working on the specified topics. Follow the instructions given in the box-tags to get a better understanding of the topics presented in this book.

About the Author

M. Usman Malik holds a Ph.D. in Computer Science from Normandy University, France, with Artificial Intelligence and Machine Learning being his main areas of research. Muhammad Usman Malik has over five years of industry experience in Data Science and has worked with both private and public sector organizations. In his free time, he likes to listen to music and play snooker.

1

Introduction

In this chapter, you will study what machine learning and data science are, how they differ, and what are the steps that you need to take to become a machine learning data science expert. Since this book is about the use of the Scikit-learn library for machine learning, this chapter also briefly reviews what Scikit-learn is and what you can do with it. Finally, some of the other most commonly used machine learning libraries have also been introduced.

1.1 What Is Machine Learning and DataScience?

Machine learning and data science applications are taking the world by storm. Autonomous cars, interactive robots, personal assistants like Alexa and Siri are all applications of data science and machine learning.

The terms data science and machine learning are often interchangeably used. However, the two terms are different. Data science is a field of study that uses scientific approaches and mathematical techniques such as statistics to extract meaning and insights from data. As per Dr. Thomas Miller from

Northwestern University, data science is "a combination of information technology, modeling and business management."

Machine learning, on the other hand, is an approach consisting of mathematical algorithms that enable computers to make decisions without being explicitly performed. Rather machine learning algorithms learn from data and then, based on the insights from the dataset, make decisions without human input.

In this book, you will complete different types of machine learning projects with the help of Python's Scikit-learn library.

1.2 Where Does Scikit-Learn Fit In?

Most of the machine learning and data science models are based on statistical algorithms. You can implement machine learning models in a programming language of your choice. However, machine learning is an empirical process where you need to try and test multiple models with various combinations of parameters and datasets. Furthermore, the sheer number of machine learning models, preprocessing approaches, and model evaluation and selection criteria make it virtually impossible for an average user to implement and test everything. This is where Scikit-learn comes into play. With Scikit-learn, you have almost everything you need to implement, test, and evaluate your machine learning model.

Scikit-Learn (https://scikit-learn.org/stable/), also known as Sklearn, is one of the most widely used libraries for machine learning and data science. Scikit-learn offers comprehensive solutions for different types of machine learning problems. With Scikit-learn, you can implement supervised machine learning algorithms for classification and regression tasks.

The Scikit-learn library also offers solutions for unsupervised machine learning problems, such as clustering. With Scikit-learn, you can also perform data preprocessing tasks, such as data normalization, feature scaling, conversion between various data types, one-hot encoding, etc. Scikit-learn library doesn't only offers off-the-shelf solutions for various machine learning algorithms but also provides methods for the evaluation of various algorithms. It also allows you to select the best parameters for your algorithm and apply various methods to evaluate the robustness of a model.

1.3 Other Machine Learning Libraries

Though you will primarily be using the Scikit-learn library in this book to perform different types of machine learning tasks, in this section, you will see some of the other most commonly used machine learning and data science libraries:

1.3.1 NumPy

NumPy is one of the most commonly used libraries for numeric and scientific computing. NumPy is extremely fast and contains support for multiple mathematical domains, such as linear algebra, geometry, etc. It is extremely important to learn NumPy in case you plan to make a career in data science and data preparation.

To know more about NumPy, check this link: https://numpy.org/

1.3.2 Matplotlib

Matplotlib is the de facto standard for static data visualization in Python, which is the first step in data science and machine learning. Being the oldest data visualization library in Python, Matplotlib is the most widely used data visualization library. Matplotlib was developed to resemble MATLAB, which is one of the most widely used programming languages in academia. While Matplotlib graphs are easy to plot, the look and feel of the Matplotlib plots have a distinct feel of the 1990s. Many wrapper libraries like Pandas and Seaborn have been developed on top of Matplotlib. These libraries allow users to plot much cleaner and sophisticated graphs.

To study more about Matplotlib, check this link: https://matplotlib.org/

1.3.3 Seaborn

Seaborn library is built on top of the Matplotlib library and contains all the plotting capabilities of Matplotlib. However, with Seaborn, you can plot much more pleasing and aesthetic graphs with the help of Seaborn default styles and color palettes.

To study more about Seaborn, check this link: https://seaborn.pydata.org/

1.3.4 Pandas

Pandas library, like Seaborn, is based on the Matplotlib library and offers utilities that can be used to plot different types of static plots in a single line of codes.

With Pandas, you can import data in various formats such as CSV (Comma Separated View) and TSV (Tab Separated View), and you can plot a variety of data visualizations via these data sources.

To know more about Pandas, check this link:
https://pandas.pydata.org/

1.3.5 TensorFlow

TensorFlow is one of the most commonly used libraries for deep learning. TensorFlow has been developed by Google and offers an easy-to-use API for the development of various deep learning models. TensorFlow is consistently being updated, and at the time of writing of this book, TensorFlow 2 is the latest major release of TensorFlow. With TensorFlow, you can not only easily develop deep learning applications but also deploy them as well with ease, owing to the deployment functionalities of TensorFlow.

To study more about TensorFlow, check this link:
https://www.tensorflow.org/

1.3.6 Keras

Keras is a high-level TensorFlow library that implements complex TensorFlow functionalities under the hood. If you are new to deep learning, Keras is the one deep learning library that you should start with for developing a deep learning library. As a matter of fact, Keras has been adopted as the official deep learning library for TensorFlow 2.0, and now all the TensorFlow applications use Keras abstractions for training deep learning models.

To study more about Keras, check this link:
https://keras.io/

1.4 What's Ahead?

In this chapter, you covered a very brief introduction to machine learning and Scikit-learn. In the upcoming chapters, you will see how you can use Python's Scikit-learn library to solve different types of machine learning problems. However, before that, chapter 2 provides a crash course for Python beginners, which you can skip if you are already familiar with the basic Python concepts. Chapter 3 provides a brief introduction to feature selection with Scikit- learn, while the fourth chapter contains information about how you can preprocess your data using the Python Scikit- learn library. Chapters 5 and 6 show how you can solve supervised classification and regression problems, respectively, with the Scikit-learn library. Chapters 7 and 8 explain unsupervised learning techniques like clustering and dimensionality reduction, respectively. Model selection approaches with Scikit-learn are explained in chapter 9. The applications of the Scikit-learn library for natural language processing and image classification are explained in chapters 10 and 11, respectively.

2

Environment Setup and Python Crash Course

Various programming languages offer libraries that can be used for machine learning and data science tasks. However, you will be using the Scikit-Learn library, which is written in the Python programming language. Python is flexible and an easy-to-learn library for beginners.

In this chapter, you will see how to set up the Python environment needed to machine learning and data science algorithms with Scikit-learn. The chapter also contains a crash Python course for absolute beginners to Python. The chapter ends with a simple exercise.

2.1 Environment Setup

2.1.1 Windows Setup

The time has come to install Python on Windows using an IDE. In fact, we will use Anaconda throughout this book, right from installing Python to writing multithreaded codes in the coming chapters. Now, let us get going with the installation.

This section explains how you can download and install Anaconda on Windows.

Follow these steps to download and install Anaconda.

1. Open the following URL in your browser.

   https://www.anaconda.com/distribution/

2. The browser will take you to the following webpage. Select the latest version of Python (3.7 at the time of writing this book). Now, click the *Download* button to download the executable file. Depending upon the speed of your internet, the file will download within 2–3 minutes.

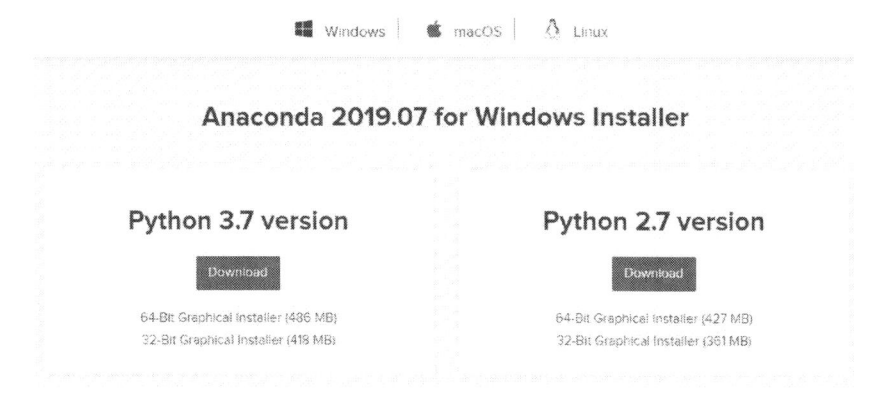

   Windows | macOS | Linux

   Anaconda 2019.07 for Windows Installer

   Python 3.7 version | **Python 2.7 version**

   Download | Download

   64-Bit Graphical Installer (486 MB) | 64-Bit Graphical Installer (427 MB)
   32-Bit Graphical Installer (418 MB) | 32-Bit Graphical Installer (361 MB)

3. Run the executable file after the download is complete. You will most likely find the downloaded file in your download folder. The name of the file should be similar to "Anaconda3-5.1.0-Windows-x86_64." The installation wizard will open when you run the file, as shown in the following figure. Click the **Next** button.

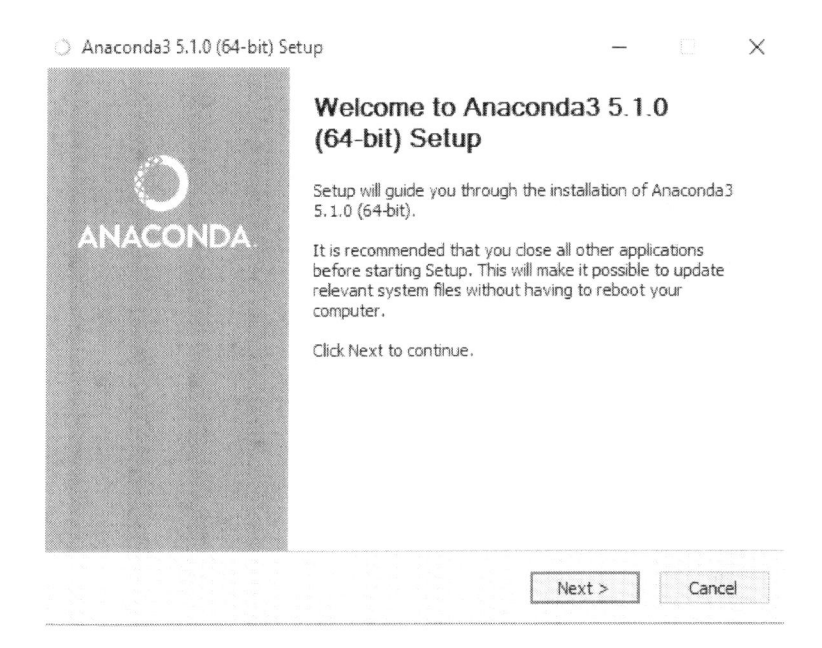

4. Now click **I Agree** on the *License Agreement* dialog, as shown in the following screenshot.

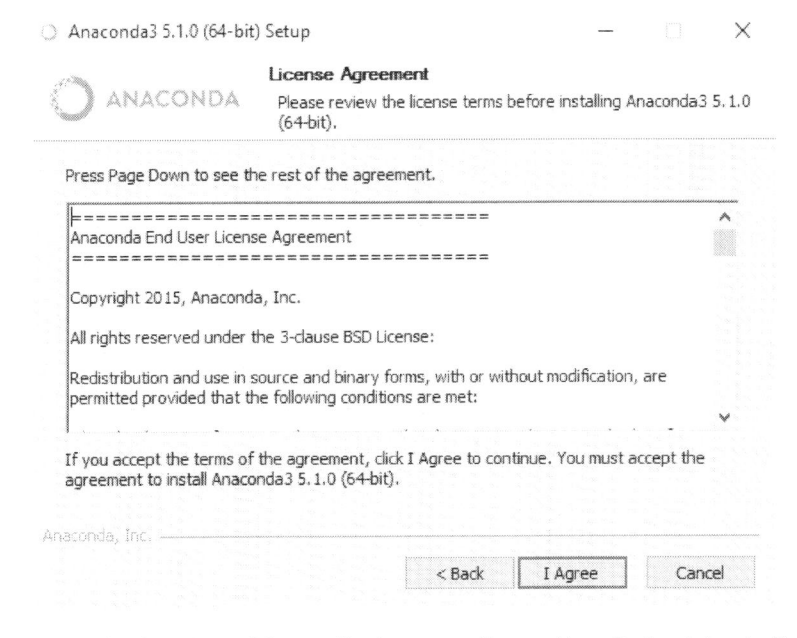

5. Check the **Just Me** radio button from the *Select Installation Type* dialogue box. Click the **Next** button to continue.

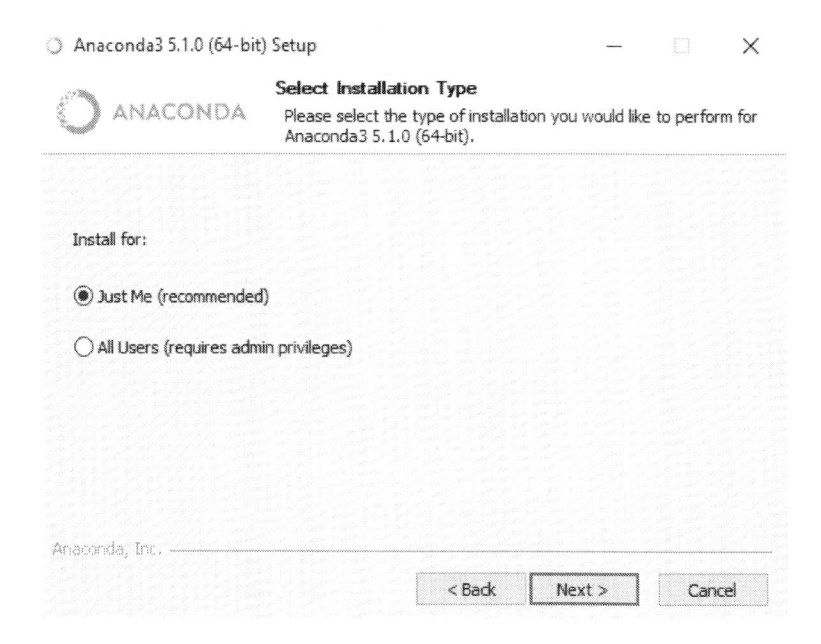

6. Now, the *Choose Install Location* dialog will be displayed. Change the directory if you want, but the default is preferred. The installation folder should at least have 3 GB of free space for Anaconda. Click the **Next** button.

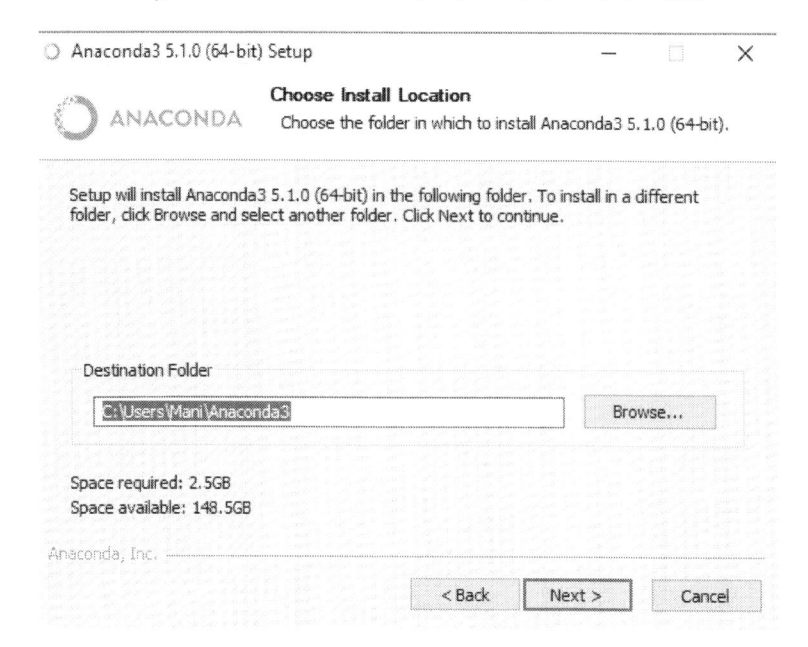

7. Go for the second option, *Register Anaconda as my default Python 3.7* in the *Advanced Installation Options* dialogue box.

   Click the **Install** button to start the installation, which can take some time to complete.

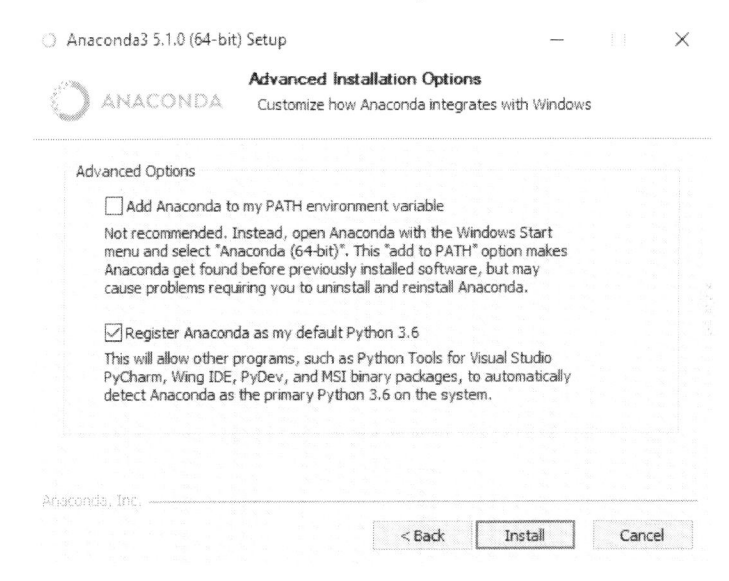

8. Click **Next** once the installation is complete.

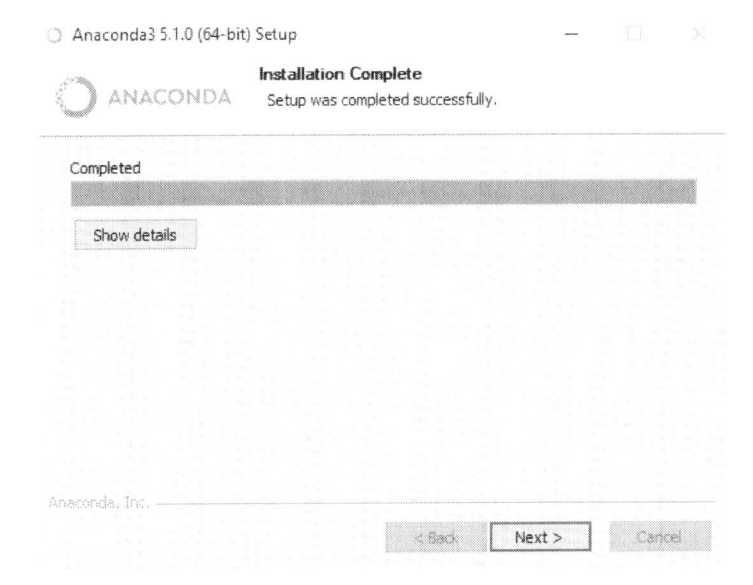

9. Click **Skip** on the *Microsoft Visual Studio Code Installation* dialog box.

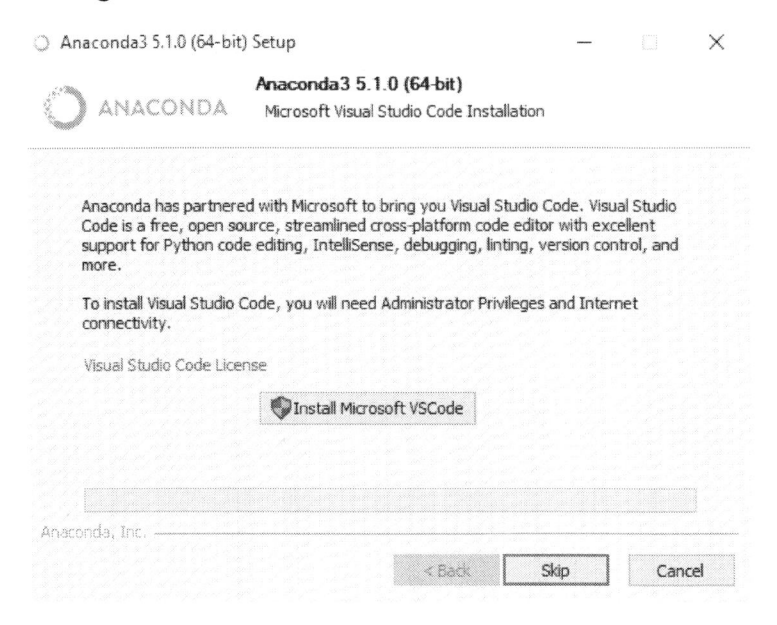

10. You have successfully installed Anaconda on your Windows. Excellent job. The next step is to uncheck both checkboxes on the dialog box. Now, click on the **Finish** button.

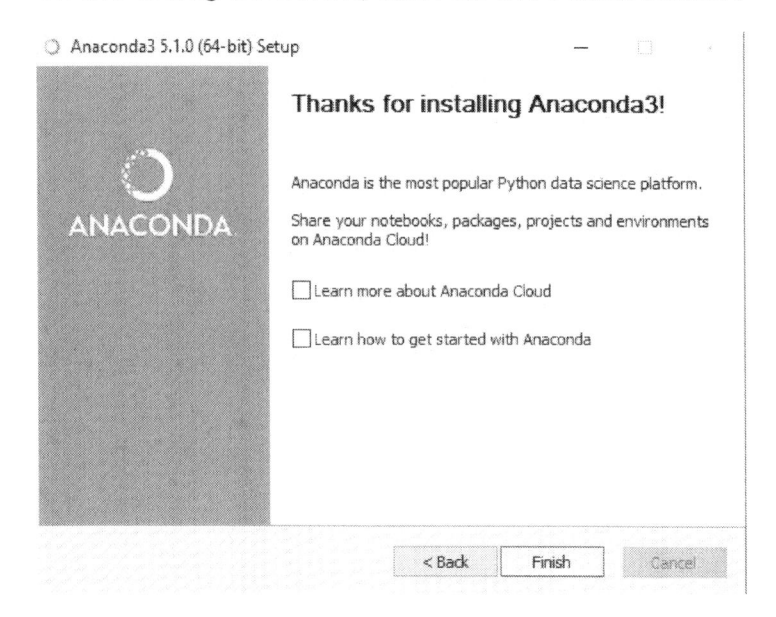

2.1.2 Mac Setup

Anaconda's installation process is almost the same for Mac. It may differ graphically, but you will follow the same steps you followed for Windows.

The only difference is that you have to download the executable file, which is compatible with Mac operating system.

This section explains how you can download and install Anaconda on Mac.

Follow these steps to download and install Anaconda.

1. Open the following URL in your browser.

   https://www.anaconda.com/distribution/

2. The browser will take you to the following webpage. Select the latest version of Python for Mac. (3.7 at the time of writing this book). Now, click the **Download** button to download the executable file. Depending upon the speed of your internet, the file will download within 2–3 minutes.

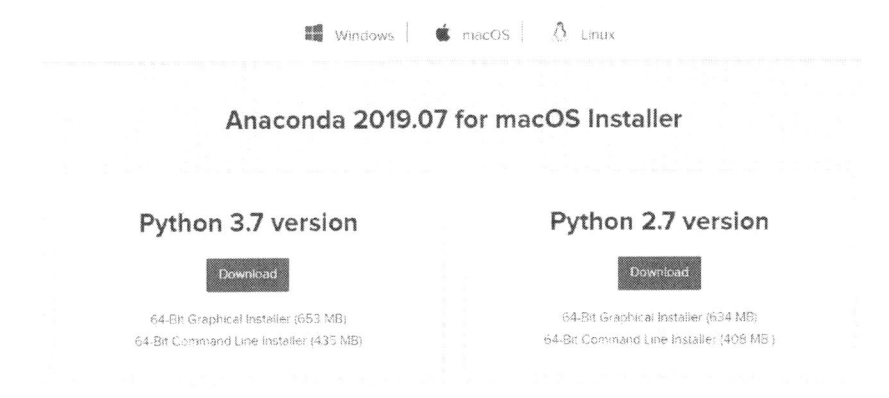

   Anaconda 2019.07 for macOS Installer

   Python 3.7 version

   Python 2.7 version

   64-Bit Graphical Installer (653 MB)
   64-Bit Command Line Installer (435 MB)

   64-Bit Graphical Installer (634 MB)
   64-Bit Command Line Installer (409 MB)

3. Run the executable file after the download is complete. You will most likely find the downloaded file in your download folder. The name of the file should be similar to "Anaconda3-5.1.0-Windows-x86_64." The installation

wizard will open when you run the file, as shown in the following figure. Click the **Continue** button.

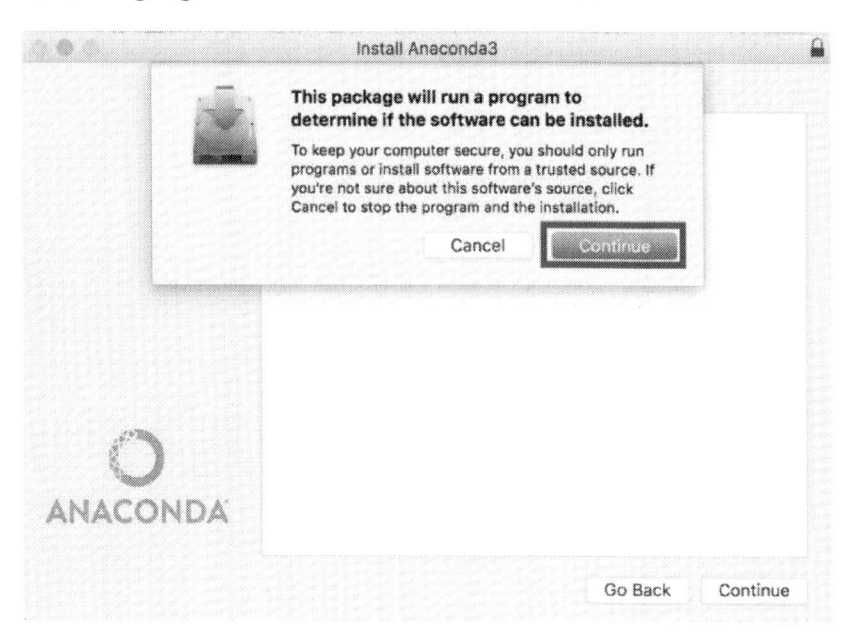

4. Now click **Continue** on the *Welcome to Anaconda 3 Installer* window, as shown in the following screenshot.

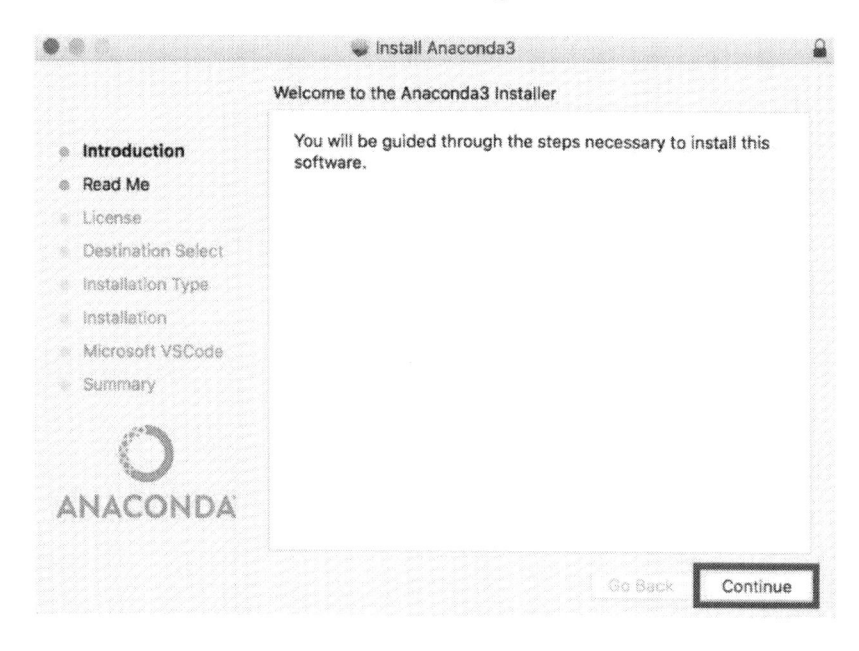

5. The *Important Information* dialog will pop up. Simply click **Continue** to go with the default version that is Anaconda 3.

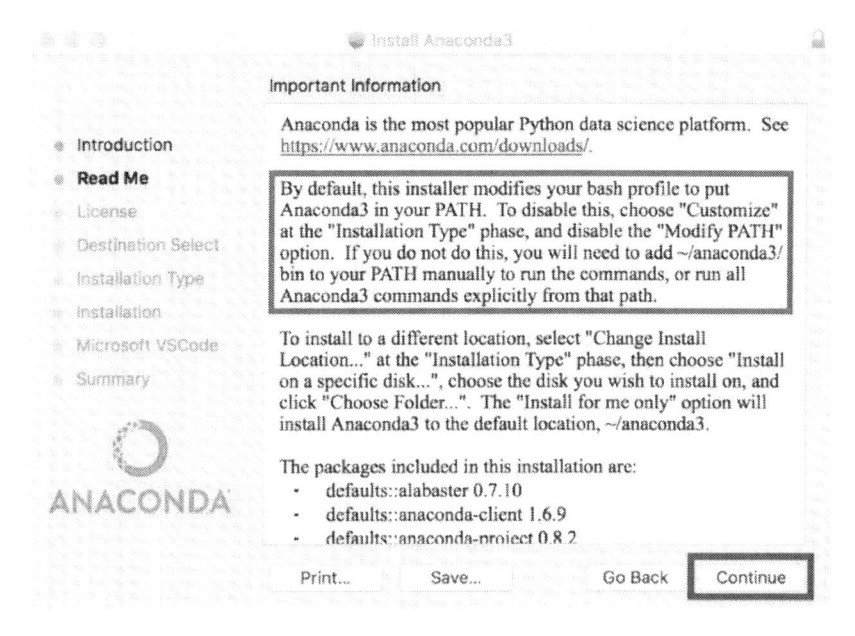

6. Click **Continue** on the *Software License Agreement Dialog*.

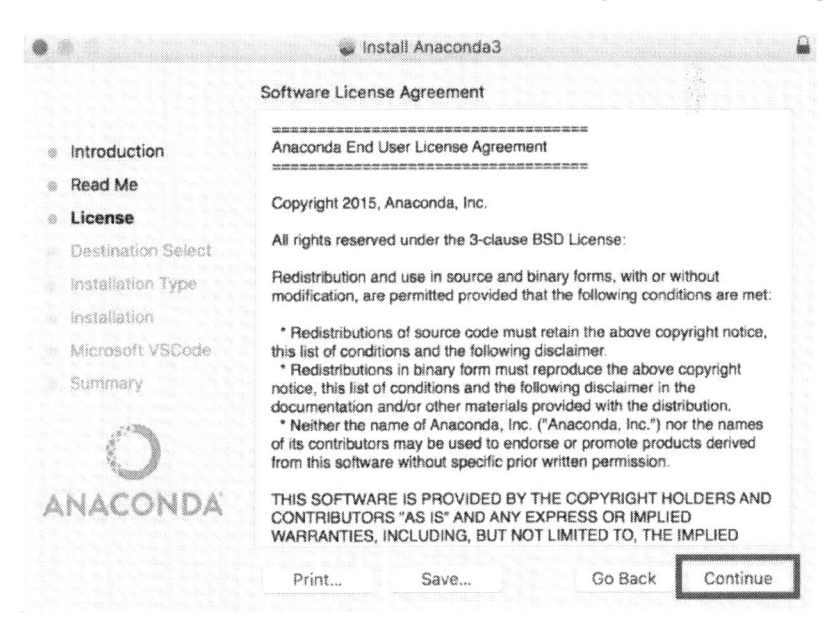

7. It is mandatory to read the license agreement and click the **Agree** button before you can click the *Continue button again.*

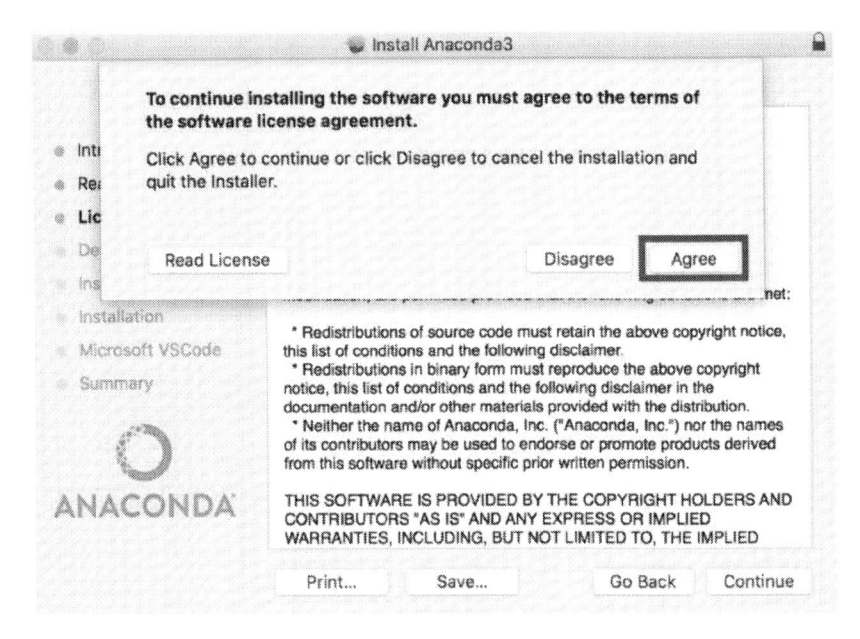

8. Simply click **Install** on the next window that appears.

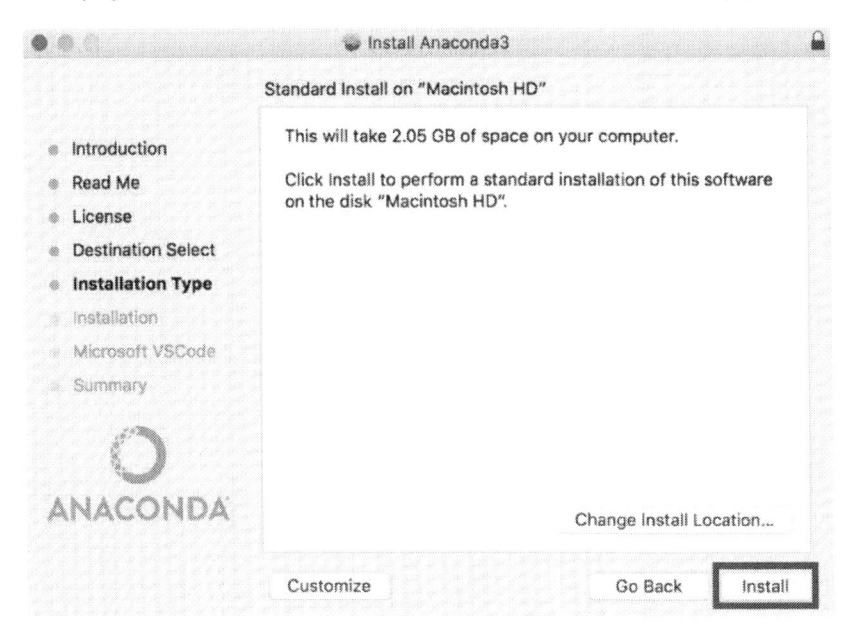

The system will prompt you to give your password. Use the same password you use to login to your Mac computer. Now, click on **Install Software**.

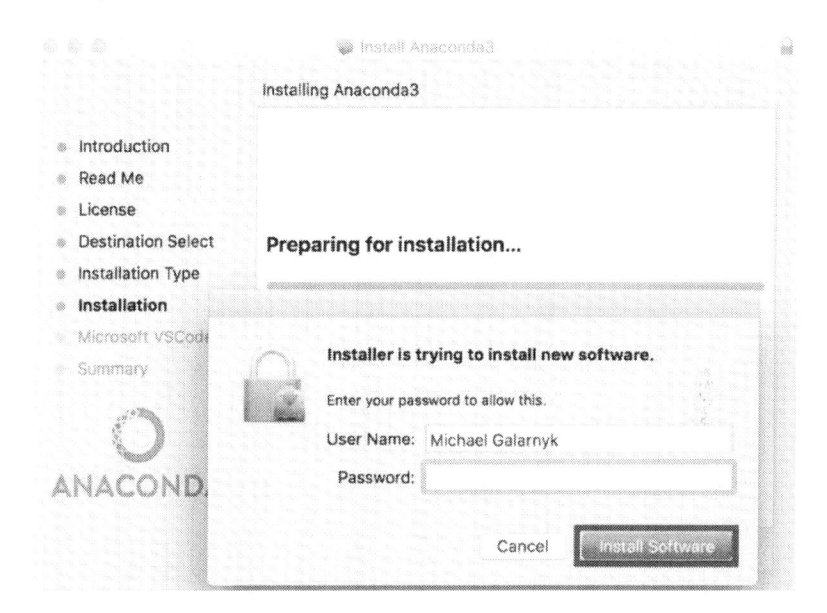

9. Click *Continue* on the next window. You also have the option to install Microsoft VSCode at this point.

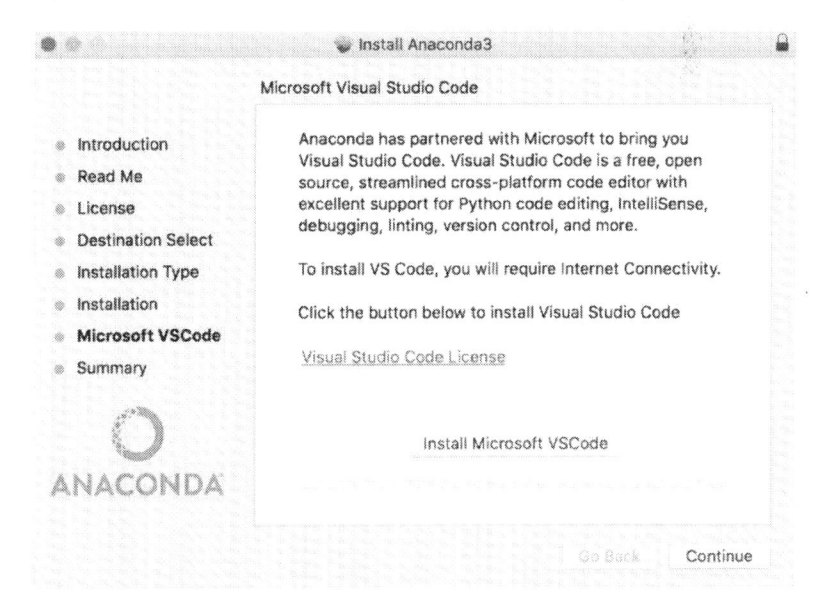

The next screen will display the message that the installation has been completed successfully. Click on the **Close** button to close the installer.

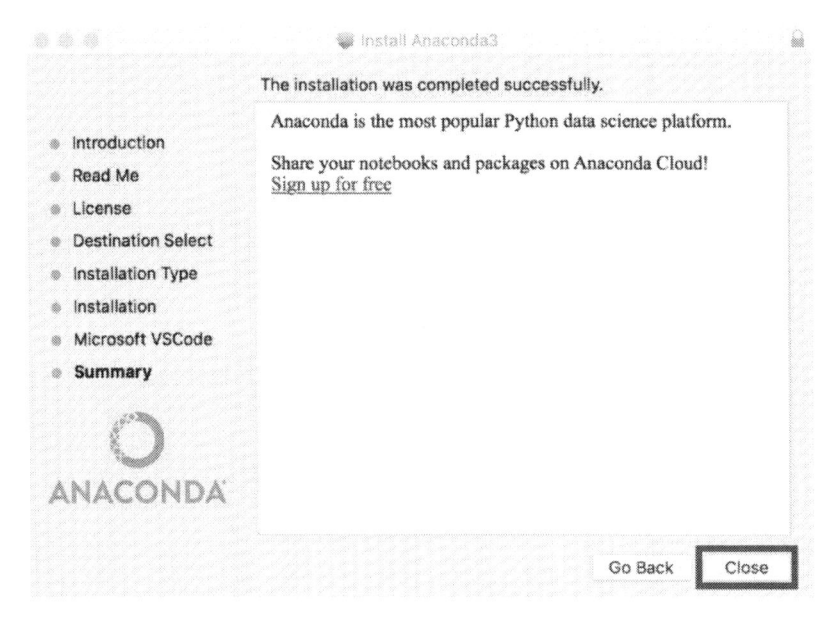

There you have it. You have successfully installed Anaconda on your Mac computer. Now, you can write Python code in Jupyter and Spyder the same way you wrote it in Windows.

2.1.3 Linux Setup

We have used Python's graphical installers for installation on Windows and Mac. However, we will use the command line to install Python on Ubuntu or Linux. Linux is also more resource-friendly, and the installation of software is particularly easy as well.

Follow these steps to install Anaconda on Linux (Ubuntu distribution).

1. Go to the following link to copy the installer bash script from the latest available version.

https://www.anaconda.com/distribution/

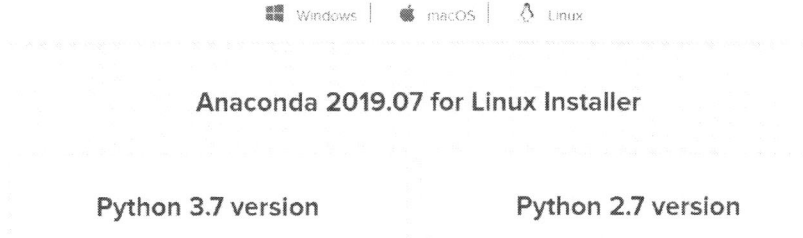

■ Windows ● macOS ⚬ Linux

Anaconda 2019.07 for Linux Installer

Python 3.7 version

Download

64-Bit (x86) Installer (517 MB)
64-Bit (PowerP8 and Power9) Installer (326 MB)

Python 2.7 version

Download

64-Bit (x86) Installer (476 MB)
64-Bit (Power8 and Power9) Installer (298 MB)

2. The second step is to download the installer bash script. Log into your Linux computer and open your terminal. Now, go to /temp directory and download the bash you downloaded from Anaconda's home page using curl.

```
$ cd / tmp

$ curl -o https://repo.anaconda.com.archive/Anaconda3-
5.2.0-Linux-x86_64.sh
```

3. You should also use the cryptographic hash verification through SHA-256 checksum to verify the integrity of the installer.

```
$ sha256sum Anaconda3-5.2.0-Linux-x86_64.sh
```

You will get the following output.

```
09f53738b0cd3bb96f5b1bac488e5528df9906be248
0fe61df40e0e0d19e3d48 Anaconda3-5.2.0-Linux- x86_64.sh
```

4. The fourth step is to run the Anaconda Script, as shown in the following figure.

```
$ bash Anaconda3-5.2.0-Linux-x86_64.sh
```

The command line will produce the following output. You will be asked to review the license agreement. Keep on pressing **Enter** until you reach the end.

```
Output

Welcome to Anaconda3 5.2.0

In order to continue the installation process, please
review the license agreement.
Please, press Enter to continue
>>>
...
Do you approve the license terms? [yes|No]
```

Type **Yes** when you get to the bottom of the License Agreement.

5. The installer will ask you to choose the installation location after you agree to the license agreement.

   Simply press **Enter** to choose the default location. You can also specify a different location if you want.

```
Output

Anaconda3 will now be installed on this location:
/home/tola/anaconda3

-   Press ENTER to confirm the location
-   Press CTRL-C to abort the installation
-   Or specify a different location below

[/home/tola/anaconda3] >>>
```

The installation will proceed once you press **Enter**. Once again, you have to be patient as the installation process takes some time to complete.

6. You will receive the following result when the installation is complete. If you wish to use the conda command, type *Yes*.

```
Output
...
Installation finished.
Do you wish the installer to prepend Anaconda3 install
location to path in your /home/tola/.bashrc? [yes|no]
[no]>>>
```

At this point, you will also have the option to download the Visual Studio Code. Type *yes* or *no* to install or decline, respectively.

7. Use the following command to activate your brand-new installation of Anaconda3.

```
$ source `/.bashrc
```

8. You can also test the installation using the conda command.

```
$ conda list
```

Congratulations. You have successfully installed Anaconda on your Linux system.

2.1.4 Using Google Colab Cloud Environment

In addition to local Python environments such as Anaconda, you can run deep learning applications on Google Colab, as well, which is Google's platform for deep learning with GPU support. All the codes in this book have been run using Google Colab. Therefore, I would suggest that you use Google Colab, too.

To run deep learning applications via Google Colab, all you need is a Google/Gmail account. Once you have a Google/Gmail account, you can simply go to:

https://colab.research.google.com/

Next, click on File -> New notebook, as shown in the following screenshot.

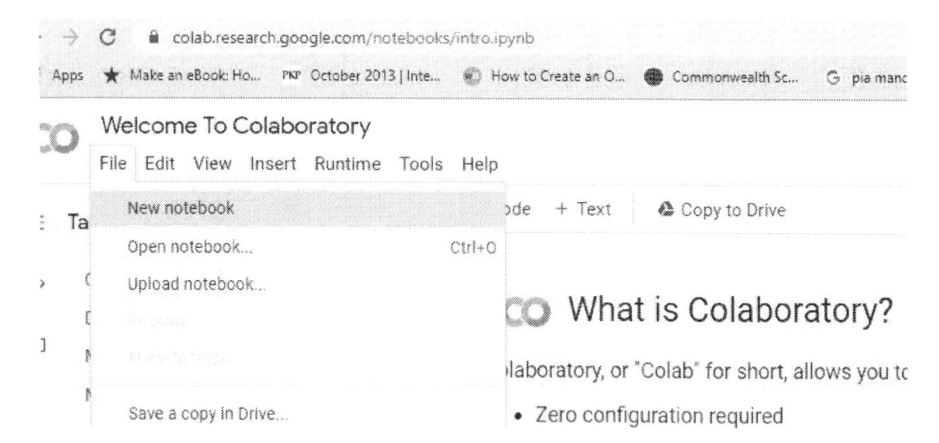

Next, to run your code using GPU, from the top menu, select Runtime -> Change runtime type, as shown in the following screenshot:

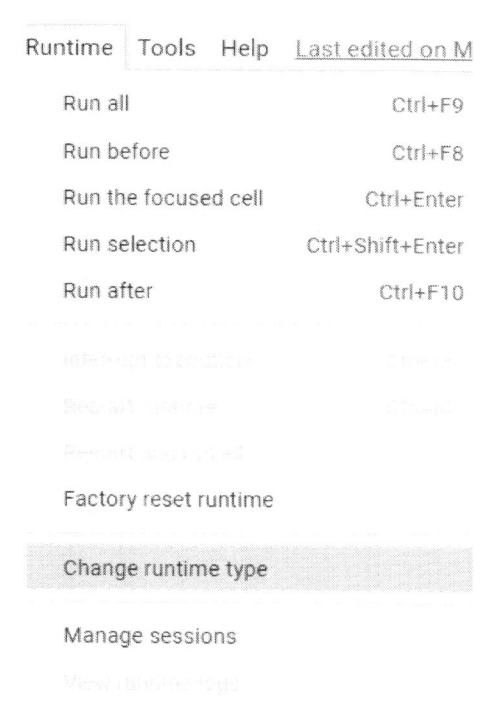

You should see the following window. Here, from the dropdown list, select GPU and click the **Save** button.

Notebook settings

Runtime type
Python 3

Hardware accelerator
GPU

To get the most out of Colab, avoid using
a GPU unless you need one. Learn more

☐ Omit code cell output when saving this notebook

CANCEL   SAVE

To make sure you are running the latest version of TensorFlow, execute the following script in the Google Colab notebook cell. The following script will update your TensorFlow version.

```
pip install --upgrade tensorflow
```

To check if you are really running TensorFlow version > 2.0, execute the following script.

```
1.    import tensorflow as tf
2.    print(tf.__version__)
```

With Google Cloud, you can import the datasets from your Google drive. Execute the following script. And click on the link that appears, as shown below:

```
from google.colab import drive
drive.mount('/gdrive')

Go to this URL in a browser: https://accounts.google.com/o/oauth2/auth

Enter your authorization code:
```

You will be prompted to allow Google Colab to access your Google drive. Click the **Allow** button, as shown below:

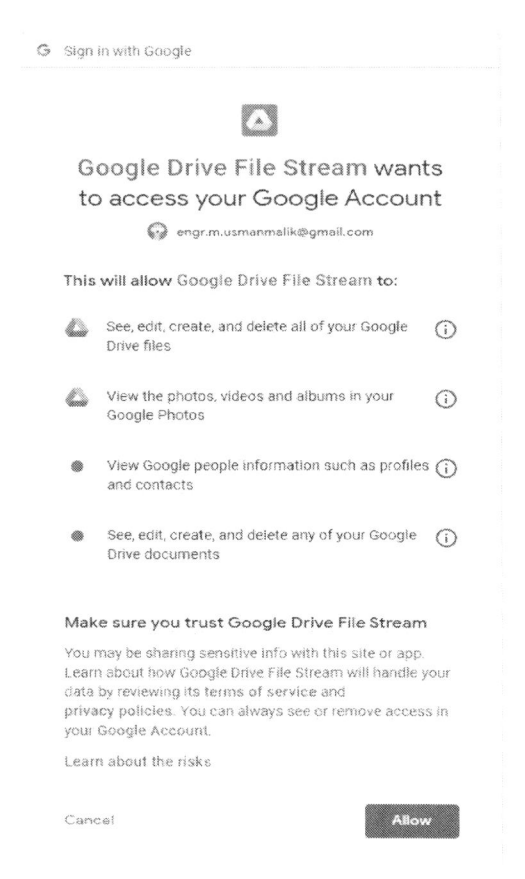

You will see a link appear, as shown in the following image (the link has been blinded here).

Copy the link, and paste it in the empty field in the Google Colab cell, as shown below:

```
from google.colab import drive
drive.mount('/gdrive')

Go to this URL in a browser: https://accounts.google.com/o/oauth2/auth

Enter your authorization code:
```

This way, you can import datasets from your Google drive to your Google Colab environment.

2.2 Python Crash Course

If you are familiar with the basic concepts of the Python programming language, you can skip this section. For those who are absolute beginners to Python, this section provides a very brief overview of some of the most basic concepts of Python. Python is a very vast programming language, and this section is by no means a substitute for a complete Python book. However, if you want to see how various operations and commands are executed in Python, you are welcome to follow along with the rest of this section.

2.2.1 Writing Your First Program

You have already installed Python on your computer and established a unique environment in the form of Anaconda. Now, it is time to write your first program, that is the *Hello World!*

In order to write a program in Anaconda, you have to launch Anaconda Navigator. Search *Anaconda Navigator* in your Windows Search Box. Now, click on the Anaconda Navigator application icon, as shown in the following figure.

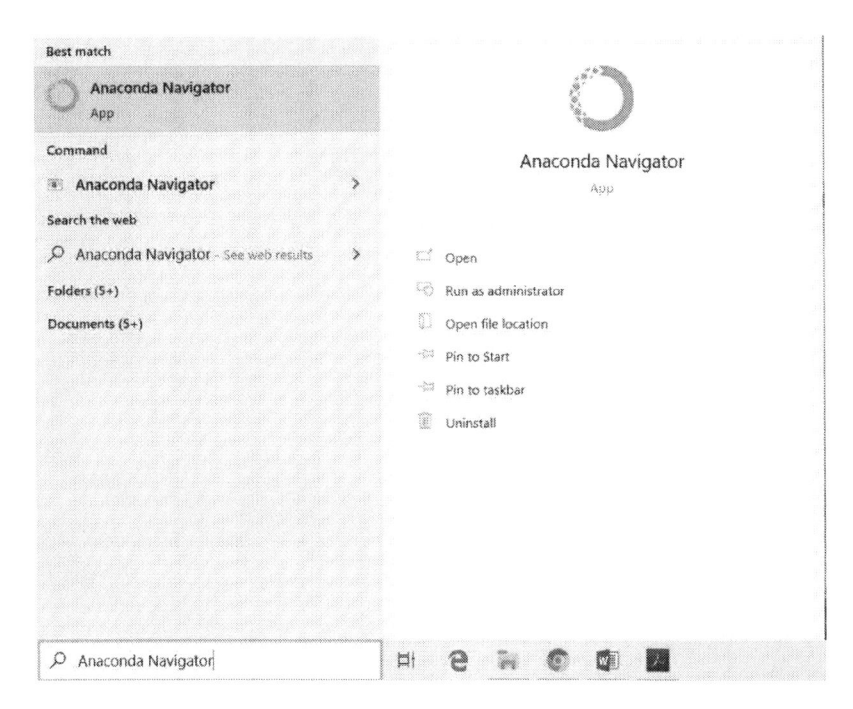

Once you click on the application, Anaconda's Dashboard will open. The dashboard offers you myriad tools to write your code. We will use the *Jupyter Notebook*, the most popular of these tools, to write and explain the code throughout this book.

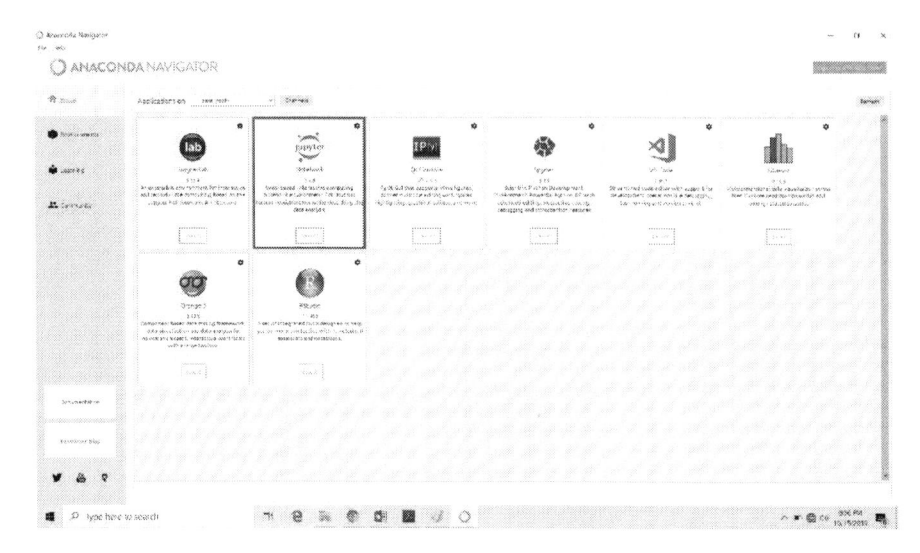

The Jupyter Notebook is available at the second position from the top of the dashboard. You can use Jupyter Notebook even if you don't have access to the internet, as it runs right in your default browser. Another method to open Jupyter Notebook is to type Jupyter Notebook in the Window's search bar. Subsequently, click on the Jupyter Notebook application. The application will open in a new tab on your browser.

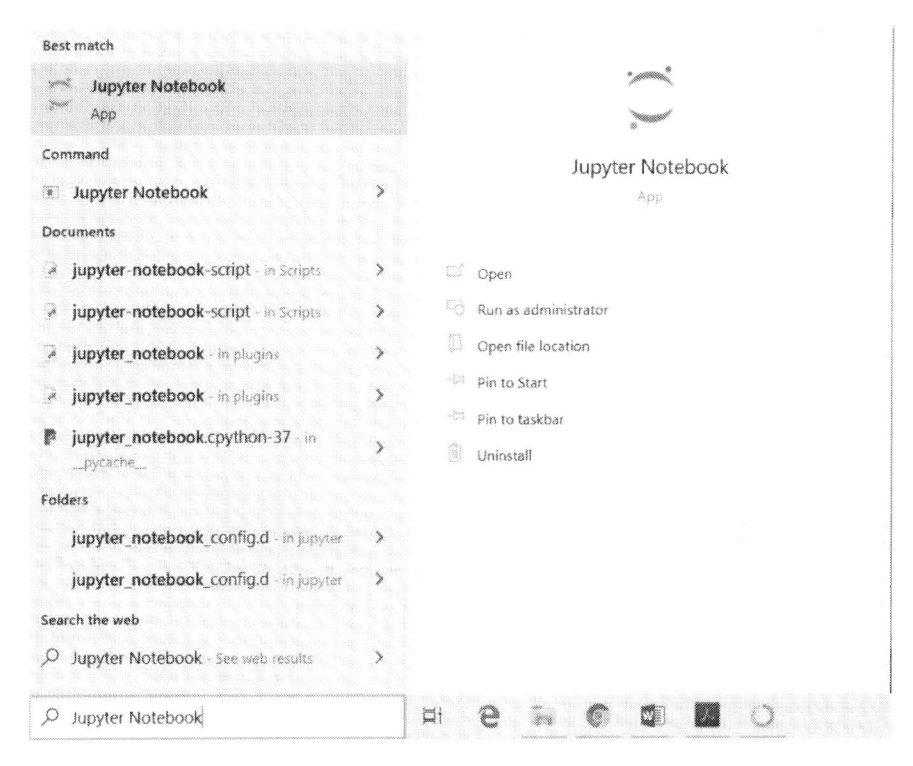

The top right corner of Jupyter Notebook's own dashboard houses a *New* button, which you have to click to open a new document. A dropdown containing several options will appear. Click on *Python 3*.

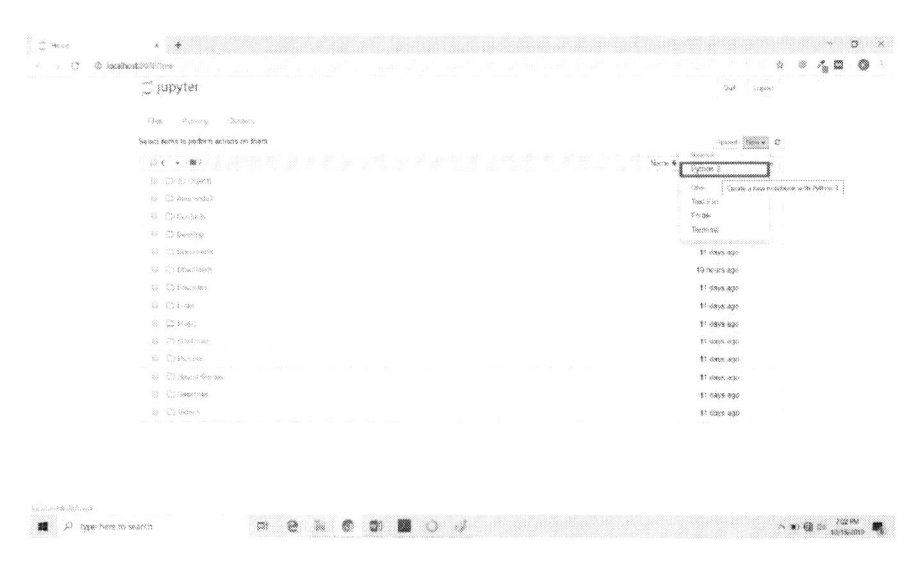

34 | ENVIRONMENT SETUP AND PYTHON CRASH COURSE

A new Python notebook will appear for you to write your programs. It looks as follows.

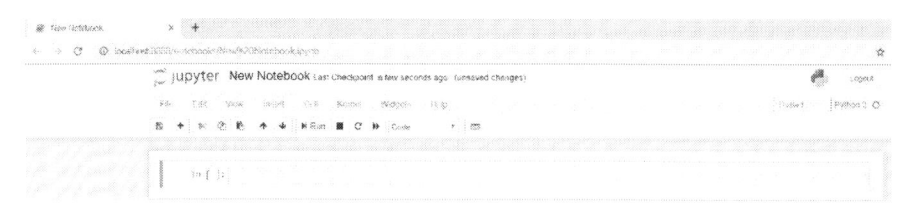

Jupyter Notebook consists of cells, as evident from the above image, making its layout very simple and straightforward. You will write your code inside these cells. Let us write our first ever Python program in Jupyter Notebook.

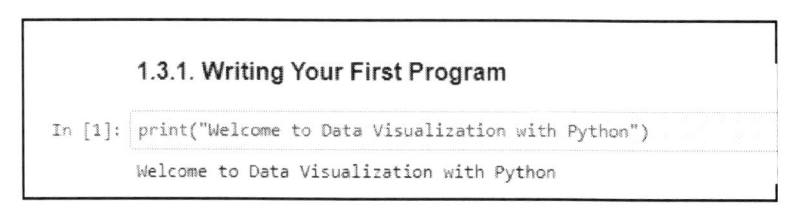

1.3.1. Writing Your First Program

```
In [1]: print("Welcome to Data Visualization with Python")
Welcome to Data Visualization with Python
```

The above script basically prints a string value in the output using the **print()** method. The **print()** method is used to print on the console any string passed to it. If you see the following output, you have successfully run your first Python program.

Output:

```
Welcome to Data Visualization with Python
```

Let's now explore some of the other important Python concepts starting with Variables and Data Types.

Requirements – Anaconda, Jupyter, and Matplotlib

- All the scripts in this book have been executed via Jupyter notebook. Therefore, you should have Jupyter notebook installed.

Hands-on Time – Source Codes

All IPython notebooks for the source code of all the scripts in this chapter can be found in theCodes folder in the booj resources. I would suggest that you write all the code in this chapter yourself and see if you can get the same output as mentioned in this Chapter.

2.2.2 Python Variables and Data Types

Data types in a programming language refer to the type of data that the language is capable of processing. The following are the major data types supported by Python:

a. Strings
b. Integers
c. Floating Point Numbers
d. Booleans
e. Lists
f. Tuples
g. Dictionaries

A variable is an alias for the memory address where actual data is stored. The data or the values stored at a memory address can be accessed and updated via the variable name. Unlike other programming languages like C++, Java, and C#, Python is loosely typed, which means that you don't have to specify the data type while creating a variable. Rather, the type of data is evaluated at runtime.

The following example demonstrates how to create different data types and how to store them in their corresponding variables. The script also prints the type of the variables via the **type()** function.

Script 2:

```
1.  # A string Variable
2.  first_name = "Joseph"
3.  print(type(first_name))
4.
5.  # An Integer Variable
6.  age = 20
7.  print(type(age))
8.
9.  # A floating point variable
10. weight = 70.35
11. print(type(weight))
12.
13. # A Boolean Variable
14. married = False
15. print(type(married))
16.
17. #List
18. cars = ["Honda", "Toyota", "Suzuki"]
19. print(type(cars))
20.
21. #Tuples
22. days = ("Sunday", "Monday", "Tuesday", "Wednesday", "Thursday", "Friday", "Saturday")
23. print(type(days))
24.
25. #Dictionaries
26. days2 = {1:"Sunday", 2:"Monday", 3:"Tuesday", 4:"Wednesday", 5:"Thursday", 6:"Friday", 7:"Saturday"}
27. print(type(days2))
```

Output:

```
<class 'str'>
<class 'int'>
<class 'float'>
<class 'bool'>
<class 'list'>
<class 'tuple'>
<class 'dict'>
```

2.2.3 Python Operators

Python programming language contains the following types of operators:

a. Arithmetic Operators
b. Logical Operators
c. Comparison Operators
d. Assignment Operators
e. Membership Operators

Let's briefly review each of these types of operators.

§ Arithmetic Operators

Arithmetic operators are used to perform arithmetic operations in Python. The following table summarizes the arithmetic operators supported by Python. Suppose X = 20, and Y = 10.

Operator Name	Symbol	Functionality	Example
Addition	+	Adds the operands on either side	X+ Y= 30
Subtraction	-	Subtracts the operands on the right from the operand on the left	X - Y= 10
Multiplication	*	Multiplies the operands on either side	X * Y= 200
Division	/	Divides the operand on the left by the one on Right	X / Y= 2.0
Modulus	%	Divides the operand on left by the one on the right and returns remainder	X % Y= 0

| Exponent | ** | Takes exponent of the operand on the left to the power of Right | X ** Y = 1024 x e^{10} |

Here is an example of arithmetic operators with output:

Script 3:

```
1. X = 20
2. Y = 10
3. print(X + Y)
4. print(X - Y)
5. print(X * Y)
6. print(X / Y)
7. print(X ** Y)
```

Output:

```
30
10
200
2.0
10240000000000
```

§ Logical Operators

Logical operators are used to perform logical **AND, OR**, and **NOT** operations in Python. The following table summarizes the logical operators. Here, **X** is **True,** and **Y** is **False**.

Operator	Symbol	Functionality	Example
Logical AND	And	If both the operands are true, then the condition becomes true.	(X and Y) = False
Logical OR	Or	If any of the two operands are true, then condition becomes true.	(X or Y) = True
Logical NOT	Not	Used to reverse the logical state of its operand.	not(X and Y) =True

Here is an example that explains the usage of the Python logical operators.

Script 4:

```
1.  X = True
2.  Y = False
3.  print(X and Y)
4.  print(X or Y)
5.  print(not(X and Y))
```

Output:

```
1.  False
2.  True
3.  True
```

§ Comparison Operators

Comparison operators, as the name suggests, are used to compare two or more than two operands. Depending upon the relation between the operands, comparison operators return Boolean values. The following table summarizes comparison operators in Python. Here, X is 20, and Y is 35.

Operator	Symbol	Description	Example
Equality	==	Returns true if values of both the operands are equal	(X == Y) = false
Inequality	!=	Returns true if values of both the operands are not equal	(X = Y) = true
Greater than	>	Returns true if value of the left operand is greater than the right one	(X > Y) = False
Smaller than	<	Returns true if value of the left operand is smaller than the right one	(X < Y) = True

| Greater than or equal to | >= | Returns true if value of the left operand is greater than or equal to the right one | (X > =Y) = False |
| Smaller than or equal to | <= | Returns true if value of the left operand is smaller than or equal to the right one | (X <= Y) = True |

The comparison operators have been demonstrated in action in the following example:

Script 5

```
1. X = 20
2. Y = 35
3.
4. print(X == Y)
5. print(X != Y)
6. print(X > Y)
7. print(X < Y)
8. print(X >= Y)
9. print(X <= Y)
```

Output:

```
False
True
False
True
False
True
```

§ Assignment Operators

Assignment operators are used to assign values to variables. The following table summarizes the assignment operators. Here, X is 20, and Y is equal to 10.

Operator	Symbol	Description	Example
Assignment	=	Used to assign value of the sum of the operands on the right to the operand on the left side of the assignment operator.	R = X+ Y assigns 30 to R
Add and assign	+=	Adds the operands on either side and assigns the result to the left operand	X += Y assigns 30 to X
Subtract and assign	-=	Subtracts the operands on either side and assigns the result to the left operand	X -= Y assigns 10 to X
Multiply and Assign	*=	Multiplies the operands on either side and assigns the result to the left operand	X *= Y assigns 200 to X
Divide and Assign	/=	Divides the operands on the left by the right and assigns the result to the left operand	X /= Y assigns 2 to X
Take modulus and assign	%=	Divides the operands on the left by the right and assigns the remainder to the left operand	X %= Y assigns 0 to X
Take exponent and assign	**=	Takes exponent of the operand on the left to the power of right and assign the remainder to the left operand	X **= Y assigns 1024 x e^{10} to X

Take a look at script 6 to see Python assignment operators in action.

Script 6:

```
1.  X = 20; Y = 10
2.  R = X + Y
3.  print(R)
4.
5.  X = 20;
6.  Y = 10
7.  X += Y
8.  print(X)
9.
10. X = 20;
11. Y = 10
12. X -= Y
13. print(X)
14.
15. X = 20;
16. Y = 10
17. X *= Y
18. print(X)
19.
20. X = 20;
21. Y = 10
22. X /= Y
23. print(X)
24.
25. X = 20;
26. Y = 10
27. X %= Y
28. print(X)
29.
30. X = 20;
31. Y = 10
32. X **= Y
33. print(X)
```

Output:

```
30
30
10
200
2.0
0
10240000000000
```

§ Membership Operators

Membership operators are used to find if an item is a member of a collection of items or not. There are two types of membership operators: the **in** operator and the **not in** operator. The following script shows the **in** operator in action.

Script 7:

```
1. days = ("Sunday", "Monday", "Tuesday", "Wednesday", "Thursday", "Friday", "Saturday")
2. print('Sunday' in days)
```

Output:

```
True
```

And here is an example of the **not in** operator.

Script 8:

```
1. days = ("Sunday", "Monday", "Tuesday", "Wednesday", "Thursday", "Friday", "Saturday")
2. print('Xunday' not in days)
```

Output:

```
True
```

2.2.4 Conditional Statements

Conditional statements in Python are used to implement conditional logic in Python. Conditional statements help you decide whether to execute a certain code block or not. There are three main types of conditional statements in Python:

  a. If statement
  b. If-else statement
  c. If-elif statement

§ IF Statement

If you have to check for a single condition and you are not concerned about the alternate condition, you can use the **if** statement. For instance, if you want to check if 10 is greater than 5, and based on that, you want to print a statement, you can use the **if** statement. The condition evaluated by the **if** statement returns a Boolean value.

If the condition evaluated by the **if** statement is true, the code block that follows the **if** statement executes. It is important to mention that in Python, a new code block starts at a new line with an on tab indented from the left when compared with the outer block.

Here, in the following example, the condition 10 > 5 is evaluated, which returns true. Hence, the code block that follows the **if** statement executes, and a message is printed on the console.

Script 9:

```
1.  # The if statement
2.
3.  if 10 > 5:
4.      print("Ten is greater than 10")
```

Output:

```
Ten is greater than 10
```

§ IF-Else Statement

The **If-else** statement comes in handy when you want to execute an alternate piece of code in case the condition for the **if** statement returns false. For instance, in the following example, the condition 5 > 10 will return false. Hence, the code block that follows the **else** statement will execute.

Script 10:

```
1.  # if-else statement
2.
3.  if  5 > 10:
4.      print("5 is greater than 10")
5.  else:
6.      print("10 is greater than 5")
```

Output:

```
10 is greater than 5
```

§ IF-Elif Statement

The **if-elif** statement comes handy when you have to evaluate multiple conditions. For instance, in the following example, we first check if 5 > 10, which evaluates to false. Next, an **elif** statement evaluates the condition 8 < 4, which also returns false. Hence, the code block that follows the last **else** statement executes.

Script 11:

```
1.  #if-elif and else
2.
3.  if  5 > 10:
4.  print("5 is greater than 10")
5.  elif 8 < 4:
6.  print("8 is smaller than 4")
7.  else:
8.  print("5 is not greater than 10 and 8 is not smaller than 4")
```

Output:

```
5 is not greater than 10 and 8 is not smaller than 4
```

2.2.5 Iteration Statements

Iteration statements, also known as loops, are used to iteratively execute a certain piece of code. There are two main types of iteration statements in Python:

  a. For loop
  b. While Loop

§ For Loop

The **for loop** is used to iteratively execute a piece of code a certain number of times. You should use **for loop** when you know the exact number of iterations or repetitions for which you want to run your code. A **for loop** iterates over a collection of items. In the following example, we create a collection of five integers using the **range()** method. Next, a **for loop** iterates five times and prints each integer in the collection.

Script 12:

```
1.  items = range(5)
2.  for item in items:
3.      print(item)
```

Output:

```
0
1
2
3
4
```

§ While Loop

The **while loop** keeps executing a certain piece of code unless the evaluation condition becomes false. For instance, the **while loop** in the following script keeps executing unless the variable c becomes greater than 10.

Script 13:

```
1.  c = 0
2.  while c < 10:
3.      print(c)
4.      c = c +1
```

Output:

```
0
1
2
3
4
5
6
7
8
9
```

2.2.6 Functions

Functions in any programming language are used to implement the piece of code that is required to be executed multiple times at different locations in the code. In such cases, instead of writing long pieces of code, again and again, you can simply define a function that contains the piece of code, and then you can call the function wherever you want in the code.

To create a function in Python, the def keyword is used, followed by the name of the function and opening and closing parenthesis.

Once a function is defined, you have to call it in order to execute the code inside a function body. To call a function, you simply have to specify the name of the function followed by the opening and closing parenthesis. In the following script, we create a function named **myfunc,** which prints a simple statement on the console using the **print()** method.

Script 14:
```
1.  def myfunc():
2.  print("This is a simple function")
3.
4.  ### function call
5.  myfunc()
```

Output:
```
This is a simple function
```

You can also pass values to a function. The values are passed inside the parenthesis of the function call. However, you must specify the parameter name in the function definition, too. In the following script, we define a function named **myfuncparam()**. The function accepts one parameter, i.e., **num**. The value passed in the parenthesis of the function call will be stored in this **num** variable and will be printed by the **print()** method inside the **myfuncparam()** method.

Script 15:
```
1.  def myfuncparam(num):
2.  print("This is a function with parameter valu e: "+num)
3.
4.  ### function call
5.  myfuncparam("Parameter 1")
```

Output:
```
This is a function with parameter value: Parameter 1
```

Finally, a function can also return values to the function call. To do so, you simply have to use the return keyword followed by the value that you want to return. In the following script, the `myreturnfunc()` function returns a string value to the calling function.

Script 16:

```
1.  def myreturnfunc():
2.    return "This function returns a value"
3.
4.  val = myreturnfunc()
5.  print(val)
```

Output:

```
This function returns a value
```

2.2.7 Objects and Classes

Python supports object-oriented programming (OOP). In OOP, any entity that can perform some function and have some attributes is implemented in the form of an object.

For instance, a car can be implemented as an object since a car has some attributes, such as price, color, model, and it can perform some functions, such as drive car, change gear, stop car, etc.

Similarly, a fruit can also be implemented as an object since a fruit has a price, name and you can eat a fruit, grow a fruit and perform functions with a fruit.

To create an object, you have to first define a class. For instance, in the following example, a class **Fruit** has been defined. The class has two attributes, **name** and **price,** and one method **eat_fruit()**. Next, we create an object **f** of class Fruit, and then call the **eat_fruit()** method from the **f** object. We also access the **name** and **price** attributes of the **f** object and print them on the console.

Script 17:

```
1.  class Fruit:
2.
3.      name = "apple"
4.      price = 10
5.
6.      def eat_fruit(self):
7.          print("Fruit has been eaten")
8.
9.
10. f = Fruit()
11. f.eat_fruit()
12. print(f.name)
13. print(f.price)
```

Output:

```
Fruit has been eaten apple
10
```

A class in Python can have a special method called a constructor. The name of the constructor method in Python is **_init_()**. The constructor is called whenever an object of a class is created. Look at the following example to see a constructor in action.

Script 18:

```
1.  class Fruit:
2.
3.      name = "apple"
4.      price = 10
5.
6.      def __init__(self, fruit_name, fruit_price):
7.          Fruit.name = fruit_name
```

```
8.      Fruit.price = fruit_price
9.
10.     def eat_fruit(self):
11.     print("Fruit has been eaten")
12.
13.
14. f = Fruit("Orange", 15)
15. f.eat_fruit()
16. print(f.name)
17. print(f.price)
```

Output:

```
Fruit has been eaten Orange
15
```

Further Readings – Python [1]

To study more about Python, please check Python 3 Official Documentation. (https://bit.ly/3rfaLke). Get used to searching and reading this documentation. It is a great resource of knowledge.

Hands-on Time – Exercise

Now, it is your turn. Follow the instructions in **the exercises below** to check your understanding of the basic Python programming language concepts. The answers to these questions are given at the end of the book.

Exercise 2.1

Question 1

Which iteration should be used when you want to repeatedly execute a code specific number of times?

    A. For Loop

    B. While Loop

    C. Both A & B

    D. None of the above

Question 2

What is the maximum number of values that a function can return in Python?

    A. Single Value

    B. Double Value

    C. More than two values

    D. None

Question 3

Which of the following membership operators are supported by Python?

    A. In

    B. Out

    C. Not In

    D. Both A and C

Exercise 2.2.

Print the table of integer 9 using a while loop.

3

Data Preprocessing with Scikit-Learn

With the huge amount of data at disposal, more and more researchers and industry professionals are finding ways to use this data for research and commercial benefits. However, most of the data available by default is too raw. It is important to preprocess it before it can be used to identify important patterns or can be used to train statistical models that can be used to make predictions.

Data preprocessing involves cleaning and engineering data in a way that it can be used as input to several important data science tasks, such as data visualization, machine learning, deep learning, and data analytics. Some of the most common data preparation tasks include feature scaling, handling missing values, categorical variable encoding, data discretization, etc.

Scikit-learn library contains various modules and libraries that you can employ to perform different types of data processing tasks, as you will in this chapter. So, let's begin without much ado.

3.1 Feature Scaling

A dataset can have different attributes. The attributes can have different magnitudes, variances, standard deviations, mean values, etc. For instance, salary can be in thousands, whereas age is normally a two-digit number.

The difference in the scale or magnitude of attributes can actually affect statistical models. For instance, variables with bigger ranges dominate those with smaller ranges for linear models. In this section, you will see different feature scaling techniques.

3.1.1 Standardization

Standardization is the process of centering a variable at zero and standardizing the data variance to 1. To standardize a dataset, you simply have to subtract each data point from the mean of all the data points and divide the result by the standard deviation of the data.

Feature scaling is applied on numeric columns only. The following script imports the Titanic dataset and then filters the age, fare, and places columns. We will be applying feature scaling techniques on these three columns only.

Script 1:

```
1.  import pandas as pd
2.  import matplotlib.pyplot as plt
3.  import numpy as np
4.  import seaborn as sns
5.
6.
7.  plt.rcParams["figure.figsize"] = [8,6]
8.  sns.set_style("darkgrid")
9.
10. titanic_data = sns.load_dataset('titanic')
11.
12. titanic_data  = titanic_data[["age","fare","pclas s"]]
13. titanic_data.head()
```

Output:

	age	fare	pclass
0	22.0	7.2500	3
1	38.0	71.2833	1
2	26.0	7.9250	3
3	35.0	53.1000	1
4	35.0	8.0500	3

Let's see the mean, std, min and max values for the age, fare, and pclass columns.

Script 2:

```
1.  titanic_data.describe()
```

Output:

	age	fare	pclass
count	714.000000	891.000000	891.000000
mean	29.699118	32.204208	2.308642
std	14.526497	49.693429	0.836071
min	0.420000	0.000000	1.000000
25%	20.125000	7.910400	2.000000
50%	28.000000	14.454200	3.000000
75%	38.000000	31.000000	3.000000
max	80.000000	512.329200	3.000000

You can see that the mean, min and max values for the three columns are very different.

To standardize the data, you can use the **StandardScaler** class from the **sklearn.preprocessing** module. You have to pass the Pandas dataframe containing the dataset to the **fit()** method of the class and then to the **transorm()** method of the class. The following script applies standard scaling on the age, fare, and pclass columns of the Titanic dataset.

Script 3:
```
1.  from sklearn.preprocessing import StandardScaler
2.
3.  scaler = StandardScaler()
4.  scaler.fit(titanic_data)
5.
6.  titanic_data_scaled = scaler.transform(titanic_data)
```

The following script creates a dataframe of the scaled columns and displays the first five rows of the scaled dataset.

Script 4:

```
1. titanic_data_scaled = pd.DataFrame(titanic_data_s caled,
   columns = titanic_data.columns)
2. titanic_data_scaled.head()
```

You can see from the output that values have been scaled.

Output:

	age	fare	pclass
0	-0.530377	-0.502445	0.827377
1	0.571831	0.786845	-1.566107
2	-0.254825	-0.488854	0.827377
3	0.365167	0.420730	-1.566107
4	0.365167	-0.486337	0.827377

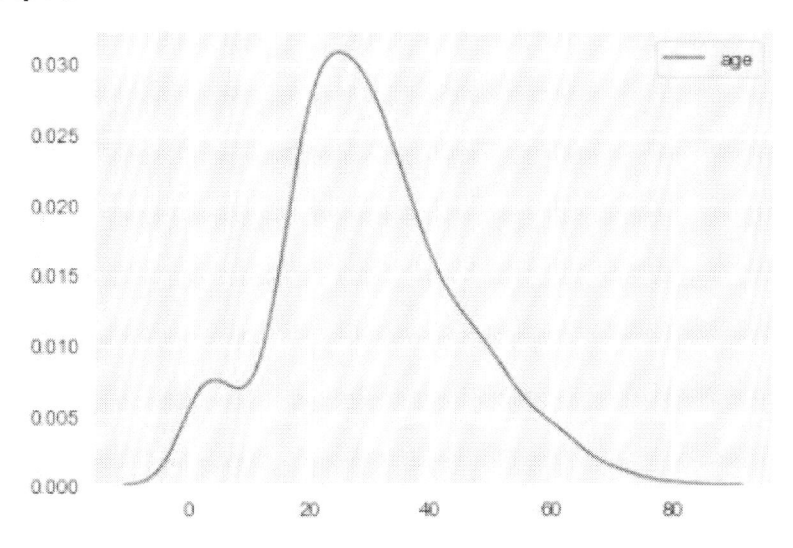

The following script plots a kernel density plot for the unscaled columns.

Script 5:

```
1. sns.kdeplot(titanic_data['age'])
```

Output:

The following script plots a kernel density plot for the scaled columns.

Script 6:
```
1.  sns.kdeplot(titanic_data_scaled['age'])
```
Output:

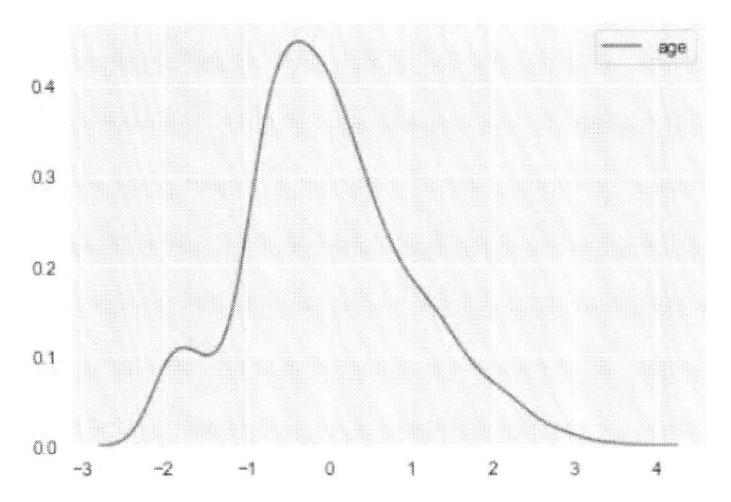

The output from scripts 5 and 6 shows that the standard scaling doesn't actually affect the default data distribution.

3.1.2 Min/Max Scaling

In min/max scaling, you subtract each value by the minimum value and then divide the result by the difference of minimum and maximum value in the dataset.

To implement the min/max scaling, you can use the **MinMaxScaler** class from the **sklearn.preprocessing** module.

You have to pass the Pandas dataframe containing the dataset to the **fit()** method of the class and then to the **transorm()** method of the **MinMaxScaler** class. The following script implements min/max scaling on the age, fare, and pclass columns of the Titanic dataset.

Script 7:

```
1. from sklearn.preprocessing import MinMaxScaler
2.
3. scaler = MinMaxScaler()
4. scaler.fit(titanic_data)
5.
6. titanic_data_scaled = scaler.transform(titanic_data)
```

The following script creates a dataframe of the scaled columns and displays the first five rows of the scaled dataset.

Script 8:

```
1. titanic_data_scaled = pd.DataFrame(titanic_data_s caled,
   columns = titanic_data.columns)
2. titanic_data_scaled.head()
```

Output:

	age	fare	pclass
0	0.271174	0.014151	1.0
1	0.472229	0.139136	0.0
2	0.321438	0.015469	1.0
3	0.434531	0.103644	0.0
4	0.434531	0.015713	1.0

Let's plot the kernel density plot to see if the data distribution has changed or not.

Script 9:

```
1. sns.kdeplot(titanic_data_scaled['age'])
```

Output:

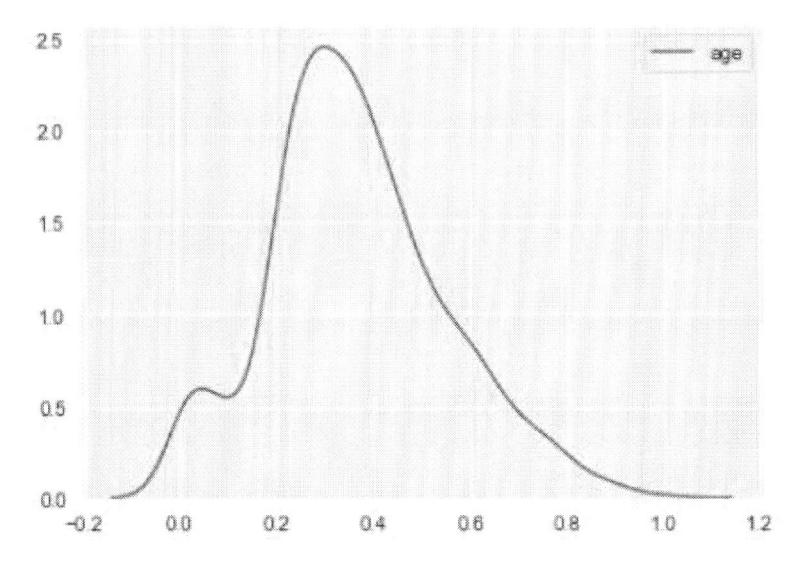

The output shows that the min/max scaling doesn't change the data distribution of the dataset.

3.1.3 Mean Normalization

Mean normalization is very similar to min/max scaling, except in mean normalization the mean of the dataset is subtracted from each value and the result is divided by the range, i.e., the difference between the minimum and maximum values.

The following script calculates the mean values for all the columns.

Script 10:

```
1. mean_vals = titanic_data.mean(axis=0)
2. mean_vals
```

Output:

```
age       29.699118
fare      32.204208
pclass     2.308642
dtype: float64
```

The following script finds the range or the difference between the minimum and maximum values for all the columns.

Script 11:

```
1.  range_vals = titanic_data.max(axis=0) - titanic_data.
    min(axis=0)
2.  range_vals
```

Output:

```
age        79.5800
fare      512.3292
pclass      2.0000
dtype:   float64
```

Finally, the following script applies mean normalization to the complete dataset.

Script 12:

```
1.  titanic_data_scaled = (titanic_data - mean_vals) / range_
    vals
```

Let's plot the kernel density plot to see if the data distribution has been affected or not. Execute the following script:

Script 13:

```
1.  sns.kdeplot(titanic_data_scaled['age'])
```

Output:

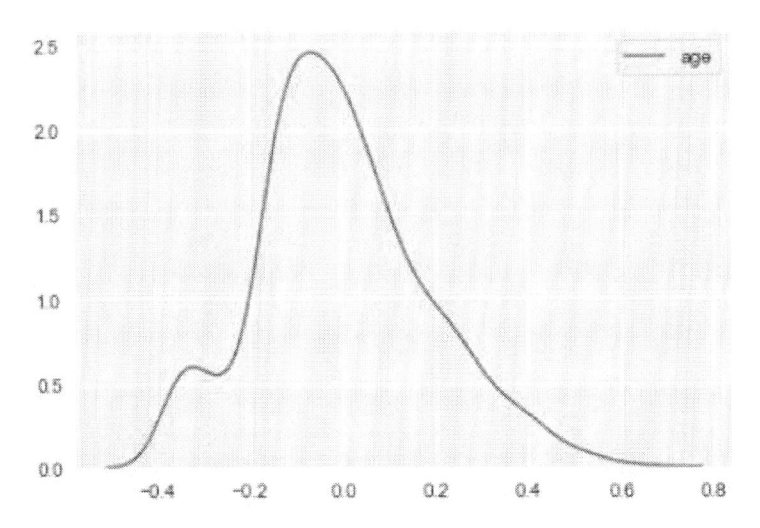

The output shows that the data distribution has not been affected.

3.2 Handling Missing Data

Missing values, as the name suggests, are those observations in the dataset that do not contain any value. Missing values can totally change data patterns, and, therefore, it is extremely important to understand why missing values occur in the dataset and how to handle them. In this section, you will see examples of how you can use the Scikit-learn library to handle missing values.

Data can be missed cause of two reasons:

1. Missing Data Randomly: When the missing observations do not relate to any other column in the dataset, we can say that data has been missed randomly. For instance, if you cannot find a person's city in a dataset, it is missed

randomly, and you cannot logically find the reason behind the missing value.

2. Missing data not Randomly: In this case, you can attribute the missing data to a logical reason. For instance, the research shows that depressed patients are more likely to leave empty fields in forms compared to the patients that are not depressed. Therefore, the missing data is not random; there has been an established reason for missing data.

3.2.1 Handling Missing Numerical Data

One of the most commonly occurring data types is numeric data, which consists of numbers. To handle missing numerical data, we can use statistical techniques. The use of statistical techniques or algorithms to replace missing values with statistically generated values is called *imputation*.

Complete case analysis (CCA), also known as list wise deletion is the most basic technique for handling missing data. In CCA, you simply move all the rows or records where any column or field contain a missing value. Only those records are processed where an actual value is present for all the columns in the dataset.

§ Mean or Median Imputation

In mean or median imputation, missing values in a column are replaced by the mean or median of all the remaining values in that particular column.

For instance, if you have a column with the following data:

Age
15
NA
20
25
40

In the above Age column, the second value is missing. Therefore, with mean and median imputation, you can replace the second value with either the mean or median of all the other values in the column. For instance, the following column contains the mean of all the remaining values, i.e., 25 in the second row. You could also replace this value with median if you want.

Age
15
25
20
25
40

Let's see a practical example of mean and median imputation. We will import the Titanic dataset and find the columns that contain missing values. Then, we will apply mean and median imputation to the columns containing missing values, and, finally, we will see the effect of applying mean and median imputation to the missing values.

You do not need to download the Titanic dataset. If you import the Seaborn library, the Titanic data will be downloaded with it. The following script imports the Titanic dataset and displays its first five rows.

Script 14:

```
1.  import matplotlib.pyplot as plt
2.  import seaborn as sns
3.
4.  plt.rcParams["figure.figsize"] = [8,6]
5.  sns.set_style("darkgrid")
6.
7.  titanic_data = sns.load_dataset('titanic')
8.
9.  titanic_data.head()
```

Output:

	survived	pclass	sex	age	sibsp	parch	fare	embarked	class	who	adult_male	deck	embark_town	alive	alone
0	0	3	male	22.0	1	0	7.2500	S	Third	man	True	NaN	Southampton	no	False
1	1	1	female	38.0	1	0	71.2833	C	First	woman	False	C	Cherbourg	yes	False
2	1	3	female	26.0	0	0	7.9250	S	Third	woman	False	NaN	Southampton	yes	True
3	1	1	female	35.0	1	0	53.1000	S	First	woman	False	C	Southampton	yes	False
4	0	3	male	35.0	0	0	8.0500	S	Third	man	True	NaN	Southampton	no	True

Let's filter some of the numeric columns from the dataset and see if they contain any missing values.

Script 15:

```
1.  titanic_data = titanic_data[["survived", "pclass", "age",
    "fare"]]
2.  titanic_data.head()
```

Output:

	survived	pclass	age	fare
0	0	3	22.0	7.2500
1	1	1	38.0	71.2833
2	1	3	26.0	7.9250
3	1	1	35.0	53.1000
4	0	3	35.0	8.0500

To find the missing values from the aforementioned columns, you need to first call the **isnull()** method on the **titanic_data** dataframe, and then, you need to call the **mean()** method, as shown below:

Script 16:

```
1. titanic_data.isnull().mean()
```

Output:

```
survived    0.000000
pclass      0.000000
age         0.198653
fare        0.000000
dtype:      float64
```

The output shows that only the *age* column contains missing values. And the ratio of missing values is around 19.86 percent.

Let's now find out the median and mean values for all the non-missing values in the *age* column.

Script 17:

```
1. median = titanic_data.age.median()
2. print(median)
3.
4. mean = titanic_data.age.mean()
5. print(mean)
```

Output:

```
28.0
29.69911764705882
```

The *age* column has a median value of 28 and a mean value of 29.6991.

To plot the kernel density plots for the actual age and median and mean age, we will add columns to the Pandas dataframe.

Script 18:

```
1.  import numpy as np
2.
3.  titanic_data['Median_Age'] = titanic_data.age.
    fillna(median)
4.
5.  titanic_data['Mean_Age'] = titanic_data.age.fillna(mean)
6.
7.  titanic_data['Mean_Age']  = np.round(titanic_data['Mean_
    Age'], 1)
8.
9.  titanic_data.head(20)
```

The above script adds **Median_Age** and **Mean_Age** columns to the **titanic_data** dataframe and prints the first 20 records. Here is the output of the above script:

Output:

	survived	pclass	age	fare	Median_Age	Mean_Age
0	0	3	22.0	7.2500	22.0	22.0
1	1	1	38.0	71.2833	38.0	38.0
2	1	3	26.0	7.9250	26.0	26.0
3	1	1	35.0	53.1000	35.0	35.0
4	0	3	35.0	8.0500	35.0	35.0
5	0	3	NaN	8.4583	28.0	29.7
6	0	1	54.0	51.8625	54.0	54.0
7	0	3	2.0	21.0750	2.0	2.0
8	1	3	27.0	11.1333	27.0	27.0
9	1	2	14.0	30.0708	14.0	14.0
10	1	3	4.0	16.7000	4.0	4.0
11	1	1	58.0	26.5500	58.0	58.0
12	0	3	20.0	8.0500	20.0	20.0
13	0	3	39.0	31.2750	39.0	39.0
14	0	3	14.0	7.8542	14.0	14.0
15	1	2	55.0	16.0000	55.0	55.0
16	0	3	2.0	29.1250	2.0	2.0
17	1	2	NaN	13.0000	28.0	29.7
18	0	3	31.0	18.0000	31.0	31.0
19	1	3	NaN	7.2250	28.0	29.7

The highlighted rows in the above output show that NaN, i.e., null values in the **age** column have been replaced by the median values in the `Median_Age` column and by mean values in the `Mean_Age` columns.

The mean and median imputation can affect the data distribution for the columns containing the missing values. Especially, the variance of the column is decreased by mean and median imputation since now more values are added to the center of the distribution. The following script plots the distribution of data for the **age, Median_Age,** and **Mean_Age** columns.

Script 19:

```
1.  plt.rcParams["figure.figsize"] = [8,6]
2.
3.  fig = plt.figure()
4.  ax = fig.add_subplot(111)
5.
6.  titanic_data['age'].plot(kind='kde', ax=ax)
7.
8.  titanic_data['Median_Age'].plot(kind='kde', ax=ax, color='red')
9.
10. titanic_data['Mean_Age'].plot(kind='kde', ax=ax, color='green')
11.
12. lines, labels = ax.get_legend_handles_labels()
13. ax.legend(lines, labels, loc='best')
```

Here is the output of the script above:

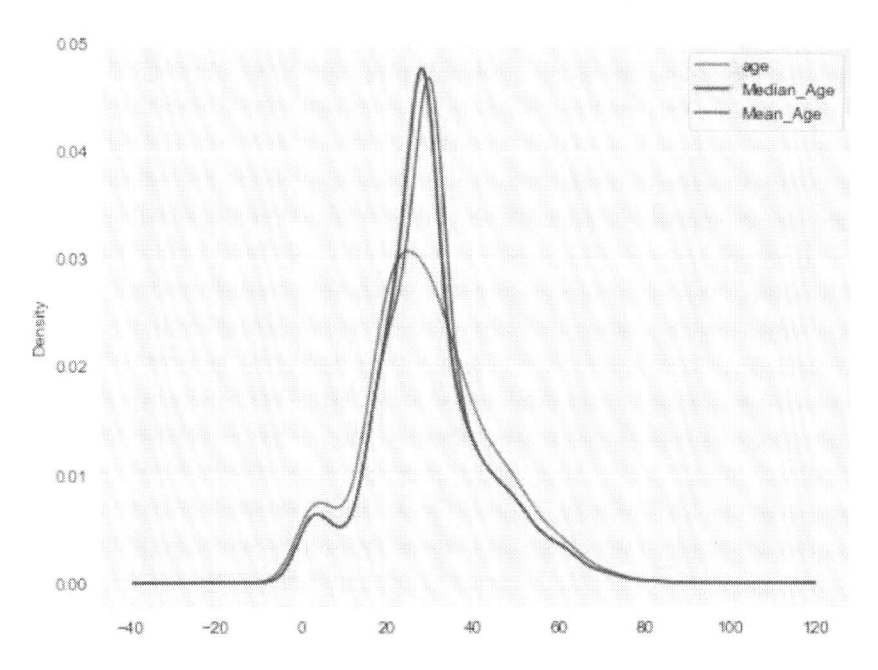

You can clearly see that the default values in the *age* columns have been distorted by mean and median imputation, and the overall variance of the dataset has also been decreased.

§ End of Distribution Imputation

The mean and median imputation and the CCA are not good techniques for missing value imputations in case the data is not randomly missing. For randomly missing data, the most commonly used techniques are end of distribution/ end of tail imputation.

In the end of tail imputation, a value is chosen from the tail end of the data. This value signifies that the actual data for the record was missing. Hence, data that is not randomly missing can be taken to account while training statistical models on the data.

In case the data is normally distributed, the end of the distribution value can be calculated by multiplying the mean with three standard deviations. In the case of skewed data distributions, the Inter Quartile Rule can be used to find the tail values.

IQR = 75th Quantile – 25th Quantile

Upper IQR Limit = 75th Quantile + IQR x 1.5 Lower IQR Limit = 25th Quantile – IQR x 1.5

Let's perform the end of tail imputation on the *age* column of the Titanic dataset.

The following script imports the Titanic dataset, filters the numeric columns, and then finds the percentage of missing values in each column.

Script 20:
```
1.  import matplotlib.pyplot as plt
2.  import seaborn as sns
3.
4.  plt.rcParams["figure.figsize"] = [8,6]
5.  sns.set_style("darkgrid")
6.
7.  titanic_data = sns.load_dataset('titanic')
8.
9.
10.
11. titanic_data = titanic_data[["survived", "pclass", "age",
    "fare"]]
12.
13.
14. titanic_data.isnull().mean()
```

Output:

```
survived       0.000000
pclass         0.000000
age            0.198653
fare           0.000000
dtype:     float64
```

The above output shows that only the age column has missing values, which are around 20 percent of the whole dataset.

The next step is plotting the data distribution for the *age* column. A histogram can reveal the data distribution of a column.

Script 21:
```
titanic_data.age.hist(bins=50)
```

Output:

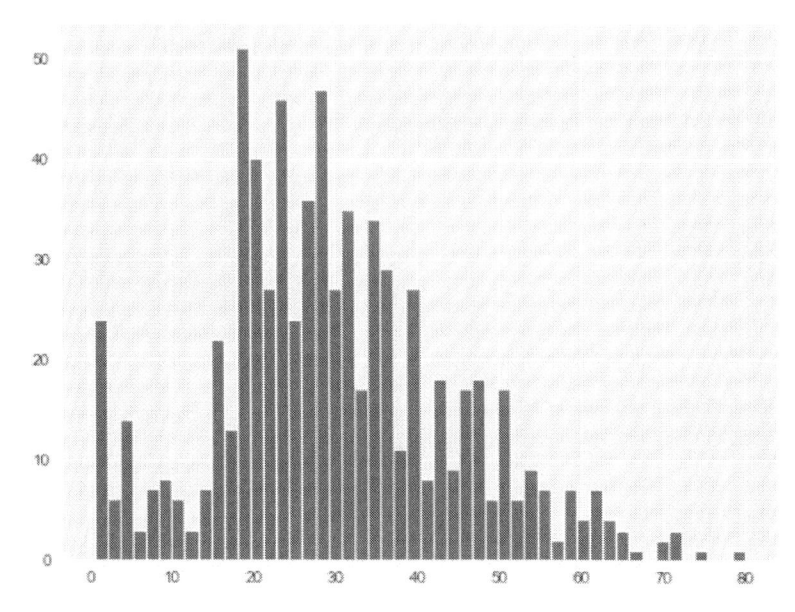

The output shows that the *age* column has an almost normal distribution. Hence, the end of distribution value can be calculated by multiplying the mean value of the *age* column by three standard deviations, as shown in the following script:

Script 22:

```
eod_value = titanic_data.age.mean() + 3 *titanic_data.age.std()
print(eod_value)
```

Output:

```
73.278
```

Finally, the missing values in the *age* column can be replaced by the end of tail value calculated in script 22.

Script 23:

```
1. import numpy as np
2.
3. titanic_data['age_eod'] = titanic_data.age.fillna(eod_
   value)
4. titanic_data.head(20)
```

Output:

	survived	pclass	age	fare	age_eod
0	0	3	22.0	7.2500	22.00000
1	1	1	38.0	71.2833	38.00000
2	1	3	26.0	7.9250	26.00000
3	1	1	35.0	53.1000	35.00000
4	0	3	35.0	8.0500	35.00000
5	0	3	NaN	8.4583	73.27861
6	0	1	54.0	51.8625	54.00000
7	0	3	2.0	21.0750	2.00000
8	1	3	27.0	11.1333	27.00000
9	1	2	14.0	30.0708	14.00000
10	1	3	4.0	16.7000	4.00000
11	1	1	58.0	26.5500	58.00000
12	0	3	20.0	8.0500	20.00000
13	0	3	39.0	31.2750	39.00000
14	0	3	14.0	7.8542	14.00000
15	1	2	55.0	16.0000	55.00000
16	0	3	2.0	29.1250	2.00000
17	1	2	NaN	13.0000	73.27861
18	0	3	31.0	18.0000	31.00000
19	1	3	NaN	7.2250	73.27861

The above output shows that the end of distribution value i.e., ~73 has replaced the NaN values in the *age* column.

Finally, you can plot the kernel density estimation plot for the original *age* column and the *age* column with the end of distribution imputation.

Script 24:

```
1.  plt.rcParams["figure.figsize"] = [8,6]
2.
3.  fig = plt.figure()
4.  ax = fig.add_subplot(111)
5.
6.  titanic_data['age'] .plot(kind='kde', ax=ax)
7.  titanic_data['age_eod'] .plot(kind='kde', ax=ax)
8.  lines, labels = ax.get_legend_handles_labels()
9.  ax.legend(lines, labels, loc='best')
```

Output:

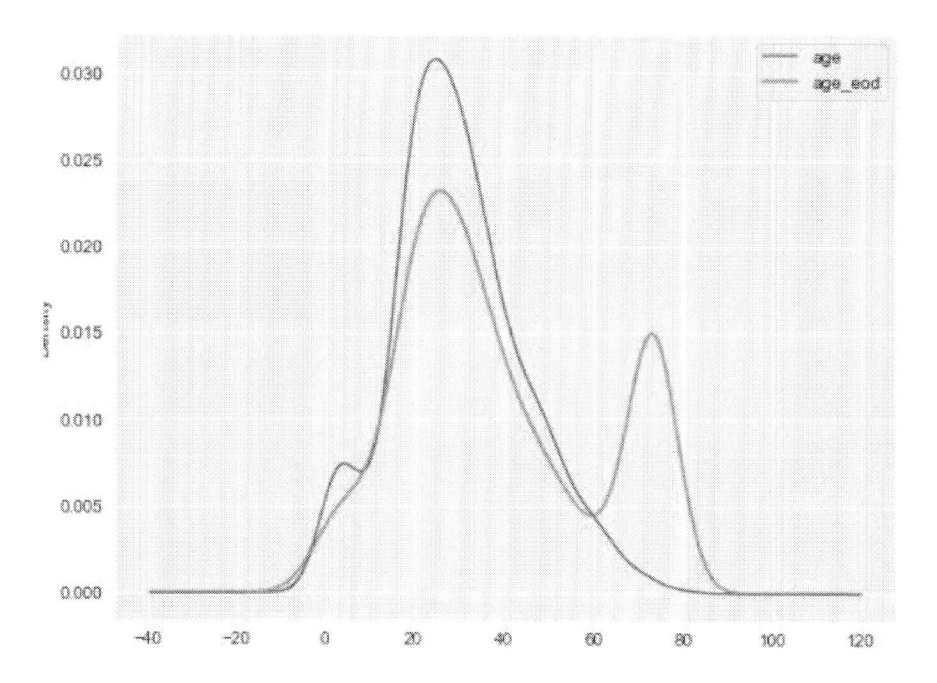

3.2.2 Handling Missing Categorical Data

§ Frequent Category Imputation

One of the most common ways of handling missing values in a categorical column is to replace the missing values with the most frequently occurring values, i.e., the mode of the column. Let's see a real-world example of the frequent category imputation.

We will again use the Titanic dataset. We will first try to find the percentage of missing values in the *age*, *fare,* and *embarked_town* columns.

Script 25:

```
1.  import matplotlib.pyplot as plt
2.  import seaborn as sns
3.
4.  plt.rcParams["figure.figsize"] = [8,6]
5.  sns.set_style("darkgrid")
6.
7.  titanic_data = sns.load_dataset('titanic')
8.
9.  titanic_data  = titanic_data[["embark_town", "age", "fare"]]
10. titanic_data.head()
11. titanic_data.isnull().mean()
```

Output:

embark_town	0.002245
age	0.198653
fare	0.000000
dtype: float64	

The output shows that *embark_town* and age columns have missing values. The ratio of missing values for the *embark_town* column is very less. Let's plot the bar plot that shows each category in the *embark_town* column against the number of passengers.

Script 26:

```
1. titanic_data.embark_town.value_counts().sort_
   values(ascending=False).plot.bar()
2. plt.xlabel('Embark Town')
3. plt.ylabel('Number of Passengers')
```

The output clearly shows that most of the passengers embarked from Southampton.

Output:

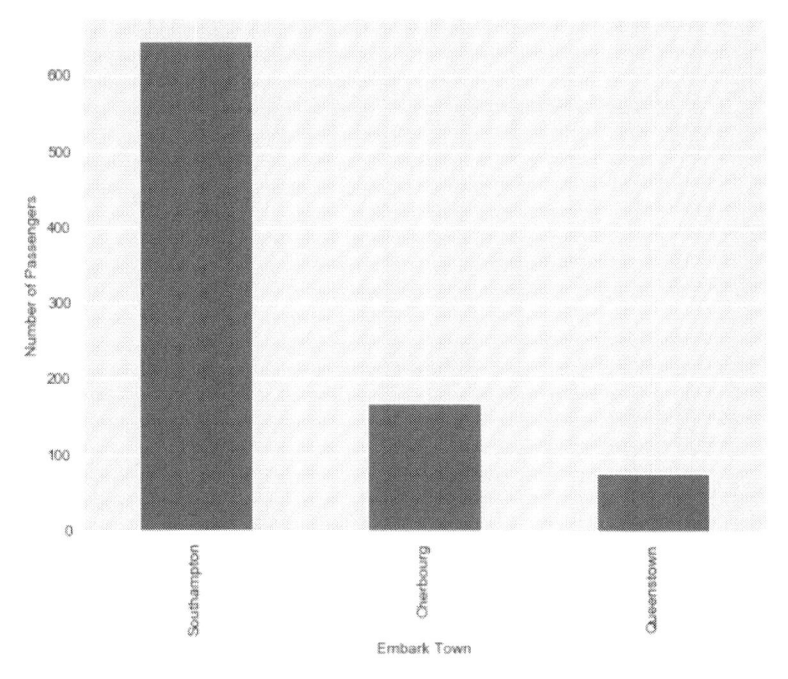

Let's make sure if *Southampton* is actually the mode value for the *embark_town* column.

Script 27:

```
1. titanic_data.embark_town.mode()
```

Output:

```
0       Southampton
dtype: object
```

Next, we can simply replace the missing values in the embark town column by *Southampton*.

Script 28:

```
1. titanic_data.embark_town.fillna('Southampton', inplace=True)
```

Let's now find the mode of the *age* column and use it to replace the missing values in the *age* column.

Script 29:

```
1. titanic_data.age.mode()
```

Output:

```
24.0
```

The output shows that the mod of the *age* column is 24. Therefore, we can use this value to replace the missing values in the *age* column.

Script 30:

```
1. import numpy as np
2.
3. titanic_data['age_mode'] = titanic_data.age.fillna(24)
4. titanic_data.head(20)
```

Output:

	embark_town	age	fare	age_mode
0	Southampton	22.0	7.2500	22.0
1	Cherbourg	38.0	71.2833	38.0
2	Southampton	26.0	7.9250	26.0
3	Southampton	35.0	53.1000	35.0
4	Southampton	35.0	8.0500	35.0
5	Queenstown	NaN	8.4583	24.0
6	Southampton	54.0	51.8625	54.0
7	Southampton	2.0	21.0750	2.0
8	Southampton	27.0	11.1333	27.0
9	Cherbourg	14.0	30.0708	14.0
10	Southampton	4.0	16.7000	4.0
11	Southampton	58.0	26.5500	58.0
12	Southampton	20.0	8.0500	20.0
13	Southampton	39.0	31.2750	39.0
14	Southampton	14.0	7.8542	14.0
15	Southampton	55.0	16.0000	55.0
16	Queenstown	2.0	29.1250	2.0
17	Southampton	NaN	13.0000	24.0
18	Southampton	31.0	18.0000	31.0
19	Cherbourg	NaN	7.2250	24.0

Finally, let's plot the kernel density estimation plot for the original *age* column and the *age* column that contains the mode of the values in place of the missing values.

Script 31:

```
1.  plt.rcParams["figure.figsize"] = [8,6]
2.
3.  fig = plt.figure()
4.  ax = fig.add_subplot(111)
5.
6.  titanic_data['age'].plot(kind='kde', ax=ax)
7.
8.  titanic_data['age_mode'].plot(kind='kde', ax=ax,
    color='red')
9.
10.
11. lines, labels = ax.get_legend_handles_labels()
12. ax.legend(lines, labels, loc='best')
```

Output:

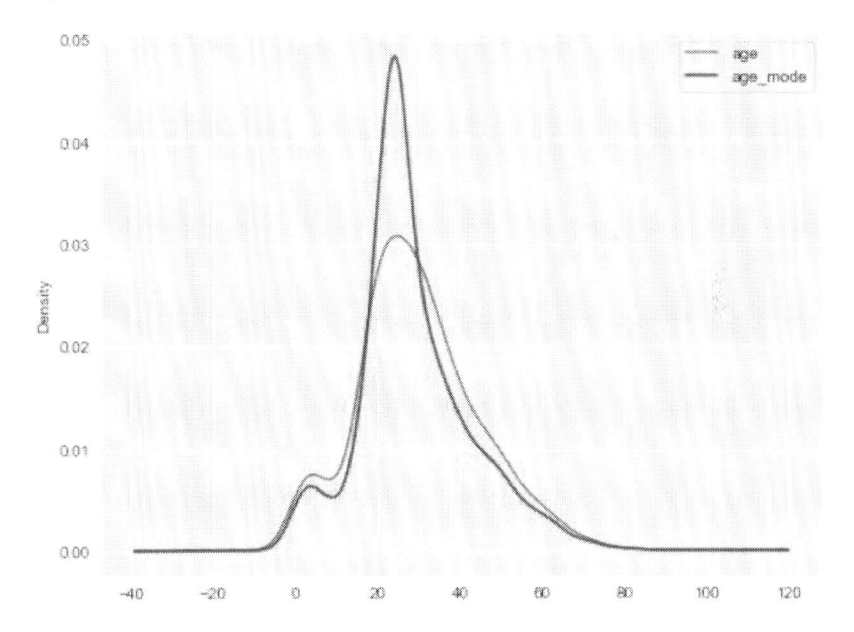

§ Missing Category Imputation

Missing category imputation is similar to arbitrary value imputation. In the case of categorical value, missing value imputation adds an arbitrary category, e.g., *missing* in place of the missing values.

82 | Data Preprocessing with Scikit-Learn

Let's load the Titanic dataset and see if any categorical value contains missing values.

Script 32:

```
1.  import matplotlib.pyplot as plt
2.  import seaborn as sns
3.
4.  plt.rcParams["figure.figsize"] = [8,6]
5.  sns.set_style("darkgrid")
6.
7.  titanic_data = sns.load_dataset('titanic')
8.
9.  titanic_data  = titanic_data[["embark_town", "age", "fare"]]
10. titanic_data.head()
11. titanic_data.isnull().mean()
```

Output:

```
embark_town    0.002245
age            0.198653
fare           0.000000
dtype: float64
```

The output shows that the *embark_town* is a categorical column that contains some missing values, too. We will apply missing value imputation to this column.

Script 33:

```
1.  titanic_data.embark_town.fillna('Missing', inplace=True)
```

After applying the missing value imputation, if you plot the bar plot for the *embark_town* column, you can see that we have a very small, almost negligible plot for the *missing* column.

Script 34:

```
1.  titanic_data.embark_town.value_counts().sort_
    values(ascending=False).plot.bar()
2.  plt.xlabel('Embark Town')
3.  plt.ylabel('Number of Passengers')
```

Output:

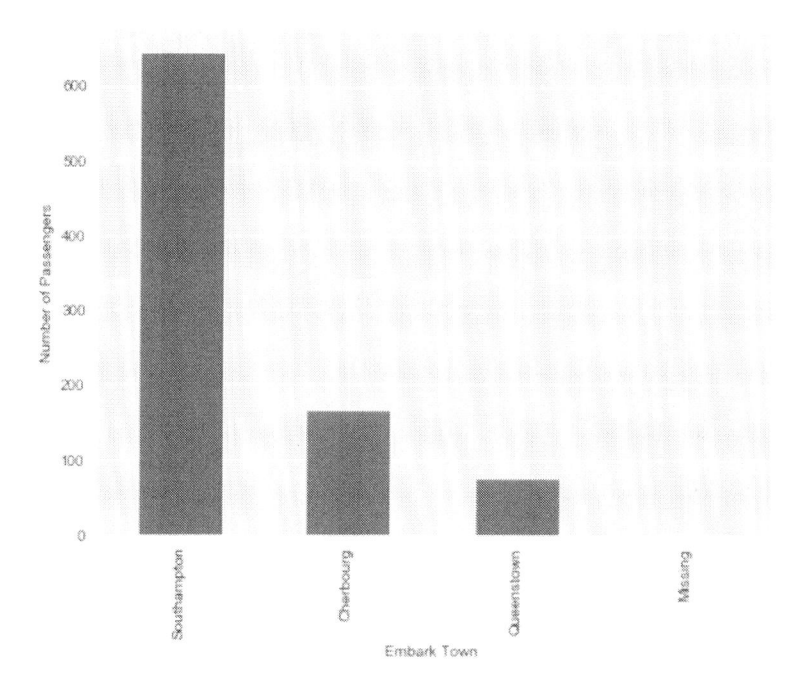

3.3 Categorical Data Encoding

Models based on statistical algorithms, such as machine learning and deep learning, work with numbers. However, datasets can contain numerical, categorical, date time, and mixed variables. A mechanism is needed to convert categorical data to its numeric counterpart so that the data can be used to build statistical models. The techniques used to convert numeric data into categorical data are called categorical data encoding schemes. In this section, you will see some of the most commonly used categorical data encoding schemes.

3.3.1 One Hot Encoding

One hot encoding is one of the most commonly used categorical encoding schemes. In one hot encoding, for each unique value in the categorical column, a new column is added. Integer 1 is added to the column that corresponds to original label, and all the remaining columns are filled with zeros. Let's take a look at a very simple example of one hot encoding.

In the following table, we have a categorical column, *Country*. The column contains three unique values: USA, UK, and France.

Country	Target
USA	1
UK	0
USA	1
FRANCE	1
USA	0
UK	0

The following table contains the one hot encoded version of the above table. In the following table, you can see that three columns have been added, i.e., USA, UK, and FRANCE. In the original column, we had USA as the label in the first row of the *Country* column. In the newly added one hot encoded table, we have 1 in the USA column. Similarly, the original table contained UK as the label in the second row. In the one hot encoded table, we have 1 in the second row for UK column.

USA	UK	France	Target
1	0	0	1
0	1	0	0
1	0	0	1
0	0	1	1
1	0	0	0
0	1	0	0

As a matter of fact, you only need N-1 columns in the one hot encoded dataset for a column that originally contained N unique labels. Look at the following table:

UK	France	Target
0	0	1
1	0	0
0	0	1
0	1	1
0	0	0
1	0	0

In the table above, the USA column has been removed. However, we can still capture the information that the first column contained. For instance, the row where both UK and France columns contain zero actually represent that this record corresponds to USA.

Let's see one hot encoding with the help of an example. Execute the following script to download the Titanic dataset, as we did in the previous chapters.

Script 35:

```
1.  import matplotlib.pyplot as plt
2.  import seaborn as sns
3.
4.  plt.rcParams["figure.figsize"] = [8,6]
5.  sns.set_style("darkgrid")
6.
7.  titanic_data = sns.load_dataset('titanic')
8.
9.  titanic_data.head()
```

Output:

	survived	pclass	sex	age	sibsp	parch	fare	embarked	class	who	adult_male	deck	embark_town	alive	alone
0	0	3	male	22.0	1	0	7.2500	S	Third	man	True	NaN	Southampton	no	False
1	1	1	female	38.0	1	0	71.2833	C	First	woman	False	C	Cherbourg	yes	False
2	1	3	female	26.0	0	0	7.9250	S	Third	woman	False	NaN	Southampton	yes	True
3	1	1	female	35.0	1	0	53.1000	S	First	woman	False	C	Southampton	yes	False
4	0	3	male	35.0	0	0	8.0500	S	Third	man	True	NaN	Southampton	no	True

Let's filter the **titanic_data** dataframe by removing all the columns except **sex, class,** and **embark_town** columns. These are categorical columns.

Script 36:

```
1. titanic_data = titanic_data[["sex", "class", "embark_
   town"]]
2. titanic_data.head()
```

Output:

	sex	class	embark_town
0	male	Third	Southampton
1	female	First	Cherbourg
2	female	Third	Southampton
3	female	First	Southampton
4	male	Third	Southampton

Let's print the unique values in the three columns in the **titanic_data** dataframe.

Script 37:

```
1. print(titanic_data['sex'].unique())
2. print(titanic_data['class'].unique())
3. print(titanic_data['embark_town'].unique())
```

Output:

```
['male' 'female'] [Third, First, Second]
Categories (3, object): [Third, First, Second]
['Southampton' 'Cherbourg' 'Queenstown' nan]
```

The easiest way to convert a column into one hot-encoded column is by using the **get_dummies()** method of the Pandas dataframe, as shown below:

Script 38:

```
1.  import pandas as pd
2.  temp = pd.get_dummies(titanic_data['sex'])
3.
4.  temp.head()
```

In the output, you will see two columns, one for males and one for females.

Output:

	female	male
0	0	1
1	1	0
2	1	0
3	1	0
4	0	1

Let's display the actual sex name and the one hot encoded version for the sex column in the same dataframe.

Script 39:

```
1.  pd.concat([titanic_data['sex'], pd.get_dummies(titanic_data['sex'])], axis=1).head()
```

Output:

	sex	female	male
0	male	0	1
1	female	1	0
2	female	1	0
3	female	1	0
4	male	0	1

88 | Data Preprocessing with Scikit-Learn

From the above output, you can see that in the first row, 1 has been added in the male column because the actual value in the sex column is male. Similarly, in the second row, 1 is added to the female column since the actual value in the sex column is female.

In the same way, we can convert the *embark_town* column into a one hot encoded vector, as shown below:

Script 40:

```
1.  import pandas as pd
2.  temp = pd.get_dummies(titanic_data['embark_town'])
3.
4.  temp.head()
```

Output:

	Cherbourg	Queenstown	Southampton
0	0	0	1
1	1	0	0
2	0	0	1
3	0	0	1
4	0	0	1

As you saw earlier, you can have N-1 one hot encoded columns for the categorical column that contains N unique labels. You can remove the first column created by the **get_dummies()** method by passing **True** as the value for the **drop_first** parameter, as shown below:

Script 41:

```
1.  import pandas as pd
2.  temp = pd.get_dummies(titanic_data['embark_town'], drop_
    first = True)
3.
4.  temp.head()
```

Output:

	Queenstown	Southampton
0	0	1
1	0	0
2	0	1
3	0	1
4	0	1

Also, you can create one hot encoded columns for null values in the actual column by passing **True** as a value for the **dummy_na** parameter.

Script 42:

```
1. import pandas as pd
2. temp = pd.get_dummies(titanic_data['embark_town'], dummy_
   na = True ,drop_first = True)
3.
4. temp.head()
```

Output:

	Queenstown	Southampton	NaN
0	0	1	0
1	0	0	0
2	0	1	0
3	0	1	0
4	0	1	0

The main advantage of one hot encoding is that it makes no assumption about the dataset, and all the categorical values can be successfully encoded. A major drawback of this approach is that the feature space can become very large since a categorical column can have a lot of unique values.

3.3.2 Label Encoding

In label encoding, labels are replaced by integers. This is why label encoding is also called integer encoding.

Consider the following table:

Country	Target
USA	1
UK	0
USA	1
FRANCE	1
USA	0
UK	0

The above table has been label encoded as follows. You can see that USA has been labeled as 1, UK is labeled as 2, and France has been labeled as 3.

Country	Target
1	1
2	0
1	1
3	1
1	0
2	0

To implement label encoding, you can use the **LabelEncoder** class from the **sklearn.preprocessing** module, as shown below. You have to create an object of the `label_encoder` class. Next, you need to call the `fit()` method of the `label_encoder` object and pass it your categorical column. Finally, to convert the categorical column to numerical, call the `transform()` method of the `label_encoder` object and pass it the categorical column.

The following script performs label encoding on the *class* column of the Titanic dataset.

Script 43:

```
1.  # for integer encoding using sklearn
2.  from sklearn.preprocessing import LabelEncoder
3.
4.  le = LabelEncoder()
5.
6.  le.fit(titanic_data['class'])
7.
8.  titanic_data['le_class'] = le.transform(titanic_
    data['class'])
9.
10. titanic_data.head()
```

Output:

	sex	class	embark_town	le_class
0	male	Third	Southampton	2
1	female	First	Cherbourg	0
2	female	Third	Southampton	2
3	female	First	Southampton	0
4	male	Third	Southampton	2

From the above output, you can see that class *Third* has been labeled as 2, the class *First* is labeled as 0, and so on. It is important to mention that label encoding starts from 0.

3.4 Data Discretization

In the previous section, you studied how to perform numerical encoding of the categorical values. In this section, you will see how to convert continuous numeric values into discrete intervals.

The process of converting continuous numeric values, such as price, age, and weight, into discrete intervals is called discretization or binning.

Discretization is particularly helpful in cases where you have a skewed distribution of data.

There are various ways to perform discretization. In this section, you will study equal width discretization and equal frequency discretization.

3.4.1 Equal Width Discretization

The most common type of discretization approach used is fixed width discretization. In fixed width discretization, the width or the size of all the intervals remain the same. An interval is also called a bin. Equal width discretization is a type of unsupervised discretization technique.

Let's see a practical example of equal width discretization. We will perform equal width discretization on the price column of the *Diamonds* dataset. The diamonds dataset comes preloaded with Python's Seaborn library, and, therefore, you do not have to download it separately. You only have to have the Seaborn library installed. Execute the following script to load the *Diamonds* dataset and to display its first five rows.

Script 44:

```
1.  import matplotlib.pyplot as plt
2.  import seaborn as sns
3.  import pandas as pd
4.  import numpy as np
5.  plt.rcParams["figure.figsize"] = [8,6]
6.  sns.set_style("darkgrid")
7.
8.  diamond_data = sns.load_dataset('diamonds')
9.
10. diamond_data.head()
```

Output:

	carat	cut	color	clarity	depth	table	price	x	y	z
0	0.23	Ideal	E	SI2	61.5	55.0	326	3.95	3.98	2.43
1	0.21	Premium	E	SI1	59.8	61.0	326	3.89	3.84	2.31
2	0.23	Good	E	VS1	56.9	65.0	327	4.05	4.07	2.31
3	0.29	Premium	I	VS2	62.4	58.0	334	4.20	4.23	2.63
4	0.31	Good	J	SI2	63.3	58.0	335	4.34	4.35	2.75

The output shows that the dataset contains 10 columns. We will only perform discretization on the *price* column. Let's first plot a histogram for the *price* column.

Script 45:

```
sns.distplot(diamond_data['price'])
```

Output:

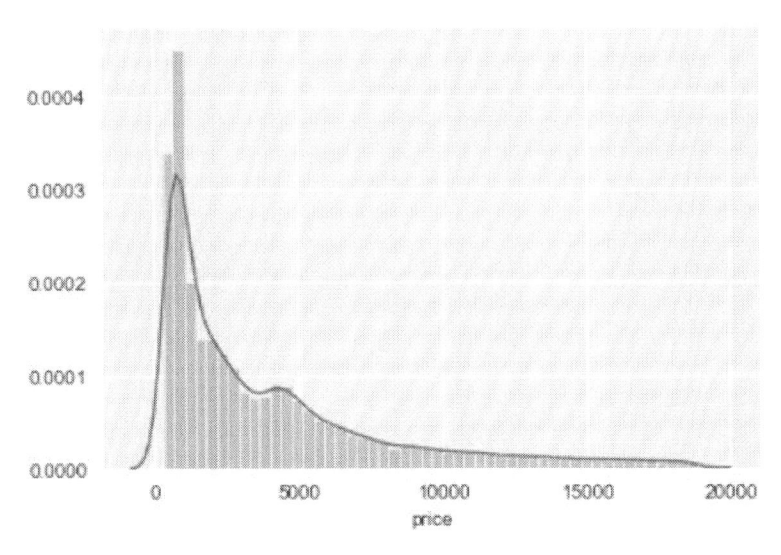

The histogram for the *price* column shows that our dataset is positively skewed. We can use discretization on this type of data distribution.

Let's now find the total price range by subtracting the minimum price from the maximum price.

Script 46:

```
1. price_range = diamond_data['price'].max() - diamond_
   data['price'].min()
2. print(price_range )
```

Output:

```
18497
```

The price range is 18497. We will create 10 equal width intervals. To find the length or width of each interval, we simply need to divide the price by the number of intervals.

Script 47:

```
1. price_range  / 10
```

Output:

```
1849.7
```

The output shows the interval length for each of the 10 intervals.

The minimum price will be rounded off to the floor, while the maximum price will be rounded off to the ceiling. The price will be rounded off to the nearest integer value. The following script does that:

Script 48:
```
1. lower_interval = int(np.floor( diamond_data['price'].min()))
2. upper_interval = int(np.ceil( diamond_data['price'].max()))
3.
4.
5. interval_length = int(np.round(price_range / 10))
6.
7. print(lower_interval)
8. print(upper_interval)
9. print(interval_length)
```

Output:

```
326
18823
1850
```

Next, let's create the 10 bins for our dataset. To create bins, we will start with the minimum value and add the bin interval or length to it. To get the second interval, the interval length will be added to the upper boundary of the first interval and so on. The following script creates 10 equal width bins.

Script 49:

```
1.  total_bins = [i for i in range(lower_interval, upper_
    interval+interval_length, interval_length)]
2.  print(total_bins)
```

The following output shows the boundary for each bin.

Output:

```
[326, 2176, 4026, 5876, 7726, 9576, 11426, 13276, 15126,
16976, 18826]
```

Next, we will create string labels for each bin. You can give any name to the bin labels.

Script 50:

```
1.  bin_labels = ['Bin_no_' + str(i) for i in range(1,
    len(total_bins))]
2.  print(bin_labels)
```

Output:

```
['Bin_no_1', 'Bin_no_2', 'Bin_no_3', 'Bin_no_4', 'Bin_no_5',
'Bin_no_6', 'Bin_no_7', 'Bin_no_8', 'Bin_no_9', 'Bin_no_10']
```

The output shows the bin labels for our dataset.

You can create Pandas libraries "**cut()**" method to convert continuous column values to numeric bin values. You need to pass the data column that you want to be discretized, along with the bin intervals and the bin labels, as shown below.

Script 51:

```
1.  diamond_data['price_bins'] = pd.cut(x=diamond_dat
    a['price'], bins=total_bins, labels=bin_labels, include_
    lowest=True)
2.  diamond_data.head(10)
```

Output:

	carat	cut	color	clarity	depth	table	price	x	y	z	price_bins
0	0.23	Ideal	E	SI2	61.5	55.0	326	3.95	3.98	2.43	Bin_no_1
1	0.21	Premium	E	SI1	59.8	61.0	326	3.89	3.84	2.31	Bin_no_1
2	0.23	Good	E	VS1	56.9	65.0	327	4.05	4.07	2.31	Bin_no_1
3	0.29	Premium	I	VS2	62.4	58.0	334	4.20	4.23	2.63	Bin_no_1
4	0.31	Good	J	SI2	63.3	58.0	335	4.34	4.35	2.75	Bin_no_1
5	0.24	Very Good	J	VVS2	62.8	57.0	336	3.94	3.96	2.48	Bin_no_1
6	0.24	Very Good	I	VVS1	62.3	57.0	336	3.95	3.98	2.47	Bin_no_1
7	0.26	Very Good	H	SI1	61.9	55.0	337	4.07	4.11	2.53	Bin_no_1
8	0.22	Fair	E	VS2	65.1	61.0	337	3.87	3.78	2.49	Bin_no_1
9	0.23	Very Good	H	VS1	59.4	61.0	338	4.00	4.05	2.39	Bin_no_1

In the above output, you can see that a column *price_bins* has been added that shows the bin value for the price.

Next, let's plot a bar plot that shows the frequency of prices in each bin.

Script 52:

```
1. diamond_data.groupby('price_bins')['price'].count().plot.
   bar()
2. plt.xticks(rotation=45)
```

Output:

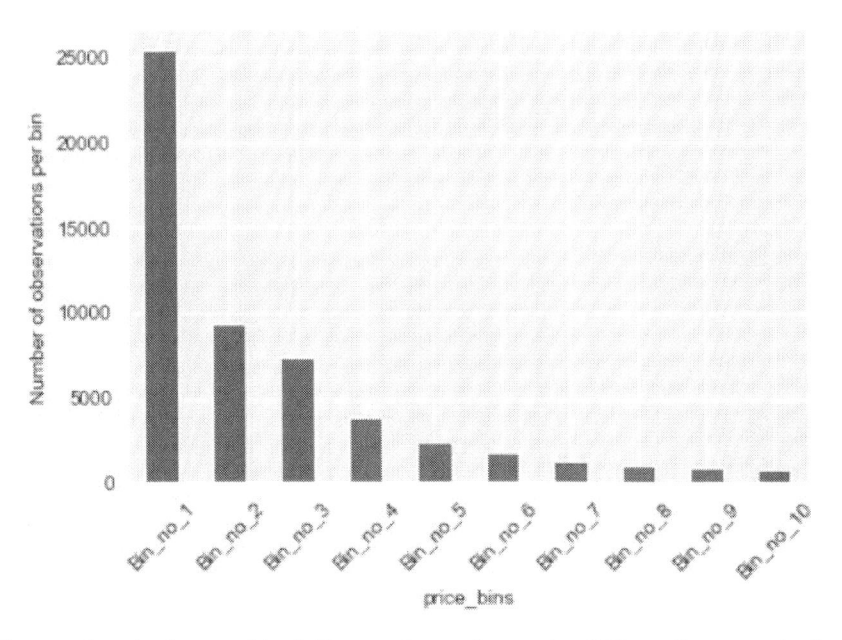

[Bar chart showing number of observations per bin across price_bins Bin_no_1 through Bin_no_10, with Bin_no_1 having ~25000 observations and decreasing counts in subsequent bins.]

The output shows that the price of most of the diamonds lies in the first bin or the first interval.

3.4.2 Equal Frequency Discretization

In equal frequency discretization, the bin width is adjusted automatically in such a way that each bin contains exactly the same number of records or has the same frequency. Hence, the name equal frequency discretization. In equal frequency discretization, the bin interval may not be the same. Equal frequency discretization, like equal width discretization, is a supervised discretization technique.

Let's apply equal frequency discretization on the *price* column of the *Diamonds* dataset, as we did previously, and see what bins do we get.

The following script downloads the *Diamonds* dataset.

Script 53:

```
1.  import matplotlib.pyplot as plt
2.  import seaborn as sns
3.  import pandas as pd
4.  import numpy as np
5.  plt.rcParams["figure.figsize"] = [8,6]
6.  sns.set_style("darkgrid")
7.
8.  diamond_data = sns.load_dataset('diamonds')
9.
10. diamond_data.head()
```

Output:

	carat	cut	color	clarity	depth	table	price	x	y	z
0	0.23	Ideal	E	SI2	61.5	55.0	326	3.95	3.98	2.43
1	0.21	Premium	E	SI1	59.8	61.0	326	3.89	3.84	2.31
2	0.23	Good	E	VS1	56.9	65.0	327	4.05	4.07	2.31
3	0.29	Premium	I	VS2	62.4	58.0	334	4.20	4.23	2.63
4	0.31	Good	J	SI2	63.3	58.0	335	4.34	4.35	2.75

To convert a continuous column into equal frequency discretized bins, you can use the **"qcut()"** function. The function returns quartiles equal to the number of specified intervals along with the bins. You have to pass the dataset column, the number of intervals and the labels as mandatory parameters for the **"qcut()"** function. The following script returns equal frequency 10 bins for the *price* column of the *Diamond* dataset. Next, we create a dataframe that shows the actual price and the quartile information.

Script 54:

```
1. discretised_price, bins = pd.qcut(diamond_data['p
   rice'], 10, labels=None, retbins=True, precision=3,
   duplicates='raise')
2.
3. pd.concat([discretised_price, diamond_data['price']],
   axis=1).head(10)
```

Output:

	price	price
0	(325.999, 646.0]	326
1	(325.999, 646.0]	326
2	(325.999, 646.0]	327
3	(325.999, 646.0]	334
4	(325.999, 646.0]	335
5	(325.999, 646.0]	336
6	(325.999, 646.0]	336
7	(325.999, 646.0]	337
8	(325.999, 646.0]	337
9	(325.999, 646.0]	338

To see the bin intervals, simply print the *bins* returned by the "qcut()" function, as shown below:

Script 55:

```
1. print(bins)
2. print(type(bins))
```

Output:

```
[  326.   646.   837.  1087.  1698.  2 401.  3465.  4662.
 6301.2  9821.  18823. ]
<class 'numpy.ndarray'>
```

Next, let's find the number of records per bin. Execute the following script:

Script 56:

```
1. discretised_price.value_counts()
```

Output:

```
(325.999, 646.0]      5411
(1698.0, 2401.0]      5405
(837.0, 1087.0]       5396
(6301.2, 9821.0]      5395
(3465.0, 4662.0]      5394
(9821.0, 18823.0]     5393
(4662.0, 6301.2]      5389
(1087.0, 1698.0]      5388
(646.0, 837.0]        5385
(2401.0, 3465.0]      5384
Name: price, dtype: int64
```

From the output, you can see that all the bins have more or less the same number of records. This is what equal frequency discretization does, i.e., create bins with an equal number of records.

Next, to create a Pandas dataframe containing the bins, we first create 10 labels since we created 10 bins.

Script 57:

```
1. bin_labels = ['Bin_no_' +str(i) for i in range(1,11)]
2. print(bin_labels)
```

Output:

```
['Bin_no_1', 'Bin_no_2', 'Bin_no_3', 'Bin_no_4', 'Bin_no_5',
'Bin_no_6', 'Bin_no_7', 'Bin_no_8', 'Bin_no_9', 'Bin_no_10']
```

To perform binning, we can again use the Pandas library's "**cut()**" method, as shown below:

Script 58:

```
1. diamond_data['price_bins'] = pd.cut(x=diamond_dat
   a['price'], bins=bins, labels=bin_labels, include_
   lowest=True)
2. diamond_data.head(10)
```

Output:

	carat	cut	color	clarity	depth	table	price	x	y	z	price_bins
0	0.23	Ideal	E	SI2	61.5	55.0	326	3.95	3.98	2.43	Bin_no_1
1	0.21	Premium	E	SI1	59.8	61.0	326	3.89	3.84	2.31	Bin_no_1
2	0.23	Good	E	VS1	56.9	65.0	327	4.05	4.07	2.31	Bin_no_1
3	0.29	Premium	I	VS2	62.4	58.0	334	4.20	4.23	2.63	Bin_no_1
4	0.31	Good	J	SI2	63.3	58.0	335	4.34	4.35	2.75	Bin_no_1
5	0.24	Very Good	J	VVS2	62.8	57.0	336	3.94	3.96	2.48	Bin_no_1
6	0.24	Very Good	I	VVS1	62.3	57.0	336	3.95	3.98	2.47	Bin_no_1
7	0.26	Very Good	H	SI1	61.9	55.0	337	4.07	4.11	2.53	Bin_no_1
8	0.22	Fair	E	VS2	65.1	61.0	337	3.87	3.78	2.49	Bin_no_1
9	0.23	Very Good	H	VS1	59.4	61.0	338	4.00	4.05	2.39	Bin_no_1

In the output above, you can see a new column, i.e., *price_bins*. This column contains equal frequency discrete bin labels.

Finally, we can plot a bar plot that displays the frequency of records per bin.

Script 59:

```
1. diamond_data.groupby('price_bins')['price'].count().plot.
   bar()
2. plt.xticks(rotation=45)
```

Output:

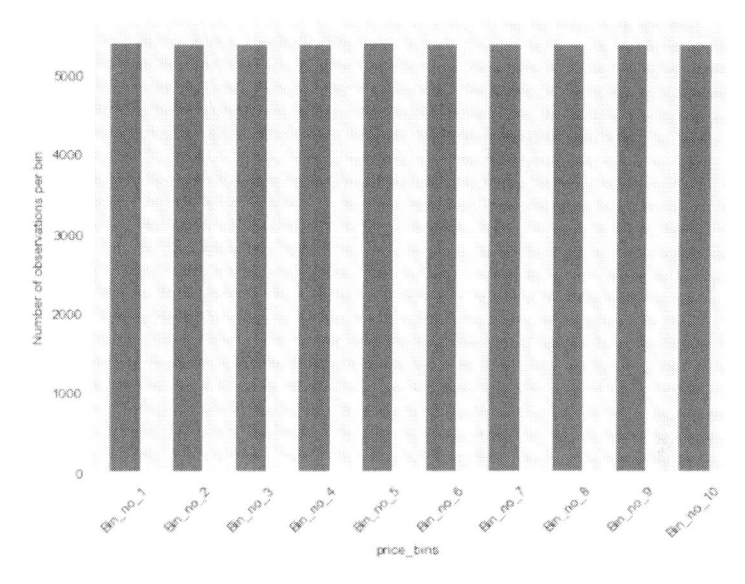

You can see that the number of records is almost the same for all the bins.

3.5 Handling Outliers

Outliers are the values that are too far from the rest of the observations in the columns. For instance, if the weight of most of the people in the sample varies between 50–100 kgs, an observation of 500kg will be considered as an outlier since such an observation occurs rarely.

Outliers can occur due to various reasons. For instance, if you access your online bank account from a particular city 95 percent of the time, an online check-in to your account from another city will be considered as an outlier. Such an outlier can be helpful as it can identify online frauds. However, outliers can also occur due to technical faults, human errors, machine readability, etc. In such cases, the outliers should be removed from the dataset.

There are four main techniques to handle outliers:

1. You can either totally remove the outliers from the dataset.
2. You can treat outliers as missing values and then apply any data imputation technique that you studied in chapter 3.
3. You can apply discretization techniques to a dataset that will include outliers along with other data points at the tail.
4. You can cap or censor the outliers and replace them with maximum and minimum values that can be found via several techniques.

You have already studied discretization and missing value imputation in the previous sections. In this section, you will study trimming and capping.

3.5.1 Outlier Trimming

Outlier trimming, as the name suggests, refers to simply removing the outliers beyond a certain threshold value. One of the main advantages of outlier trimming is that it is extremely quick and doesn't distort the data. A downside to outlier trimming is that it can reduce the data size.

There are several ways to find the thresholds for outlier trimming.

Let's remove the outliers from the *age* column of the Titanic dataset. The Titanic dataset contains records of the passengers who traveled on the unfortunate *Titanic* ship that sank in 1912. The following script imports the Titanic dataset from the Seaborn library.

Script 60:

```
1.  import matplotlib.pyplot as plt
2.  import seaborn as sns
3.  import pandas as pd
4.  import numpy as np
5.
6.  plt.rcParams["figure.figsize"] = [8,6]
7.  sns.set_style("darkgrid")
8.
9.  titanic_data = sns.load_dataset('titanic')
10.
11. titanic_data.head()
```

The first five rows of the Titanic dataset look like this.

Output:

	survived	pclass	sex	age	sibsp	parch	fare	embarked	class	who	adult_male	deck	embark_town	alive	alone
0	0	3	male	22.0	1	0	7.2500	S	Third	man	True	NaN	Southampton	no	False
1	1	1	female	38.0	1	0	71.2833	C	First	woman	False	C	Cherbourg	yes	False
2	1	3	female	26.0	0	0	7.9250	S	Third	woman	False	NaN	Southampton	yes	True
3	1	1	female	35.0	1	0	53.1000	S	First	woman	False	C	Southampton	yes	False
4	0	3	male	35.0	0	0	8.0500	S	Third	man	True	NaN	Southampton	no	True

To visualize the outliers, you can simply plot the box plot for the *age* column, as shown below:

Script 61:

```
1.  sns.boxplot( y='age', data=titanic_data)
```

Output:

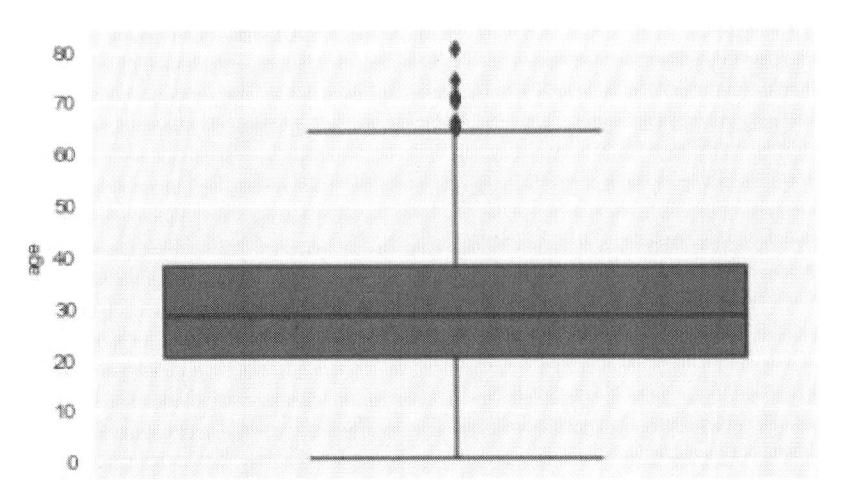

You can see that there are few outliers in the form of black dots at the upper end of the age distribution in the box plot.

To remove outliers, we first need to define the values that will be considered outliers. There are various ways to do so. One of the most common ways to do so is to find the Inter Quartile Range (IQR), multiply it by 1.5, and then subtract it from the first quartile value (0.25 quantile) to find the lower limit. To find the upper limit, add the product of IQR and 1.5 to the 3rd quartile value (0.75 quantile). IQR can be calculated by subtracting the first quartile value from the 4th quartile.

The following script finds the lower and upper limits for the outliers for the *age* column.

Script 62:

```
1.  IQR = titanic_data["age"].quantile(0.75) - titanic_
    data["age"].quantile(0.25)
2.
3.  lower_age_limit = titanic_data["age"].quantile(0.25) -
    (IQR * 1.5)
4.  upper_age_limit = titanic_data["age"].quantile(0.75) +
    (IQR * 1.5)
5.
6.  print(lower_age_limit)
7.  print(upper_age_limit)
```

Output:

```
-6.6875
64.8125
```

The output shows that any age value larger than 64.81 and smaller than −6.68 will be considered an outlier. The following script finds the rows containing the outlier values:

Script 63:

```
1.  age_outliers = np.where(titanic_data["age"] > upper_age_
    limit, True,
2.  np.where(titanic_data["age"] < lower_age_limit, True,
    False))
```

Finally, the following script removes the rows containing the outlier values from the actual Titanic dataset.

Script 64:

```
1.  titanic_without_age_outliers = titanic_data.loc[~(age_
    outliers), ]
2.
3.  titanic_data.shape, titanic_without_age_outliers.shape
```

The output shows the number of records before and after removing the outliers.

Output:

```
((891, 15), (880, 15))
```

Finally, you can plot a box plot to see if outliers have actually been removed.

Script 65:

```
1.  sns.boxplot( y='age', data = titanic_without_age_outliers)
```

Output:

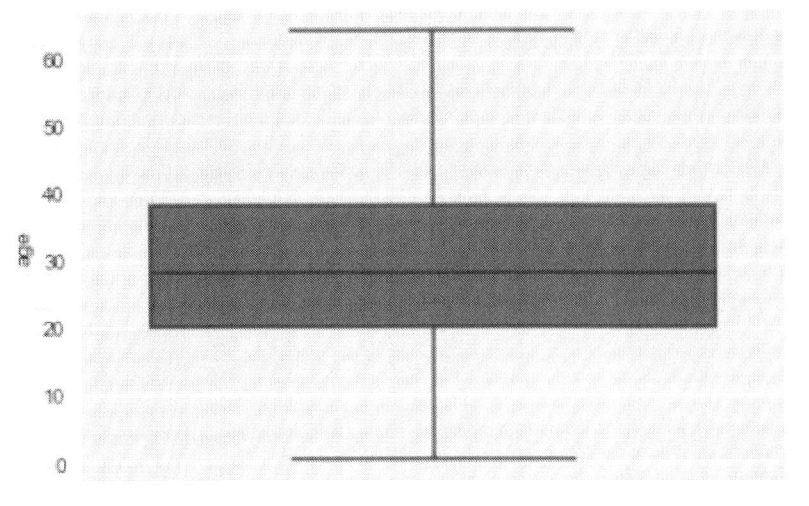

You can see from the above output that the dataset doesn't contain any outliers now.

3.5.2 Outlier Capping Using Mean and Std

Instead of using the IQR method, the upper and lower thresholds for outliers can be calculated via the mean and standard deviation method. To find the upper threshold, the mean of the data is added to three times the standard deviation value. Similarly, to find the lower threshold, you have to multiply the standard deviation by 3 and then remove the result from the mean.

The following script imports the Titanic dataset.

Script 66:

```
1.  import matplotlib.pyplot as plt
2.  import seaborn as sns
3.  import pandas as pd
4.  import numpy as np
5.
6.  plt.rcParams["figure.figsize"] = [8,6]
7.  sns.set_style("darkgrid")
8.
9.  titanic_data = sns.load_dataset('titanic')
```

Let's plot a box plot that displays the distribution of data in the Age column of the Titanic dataset.

Script 67:

```
1.  sns.boxplot( y='age', data=titanic_data)
```

Output:

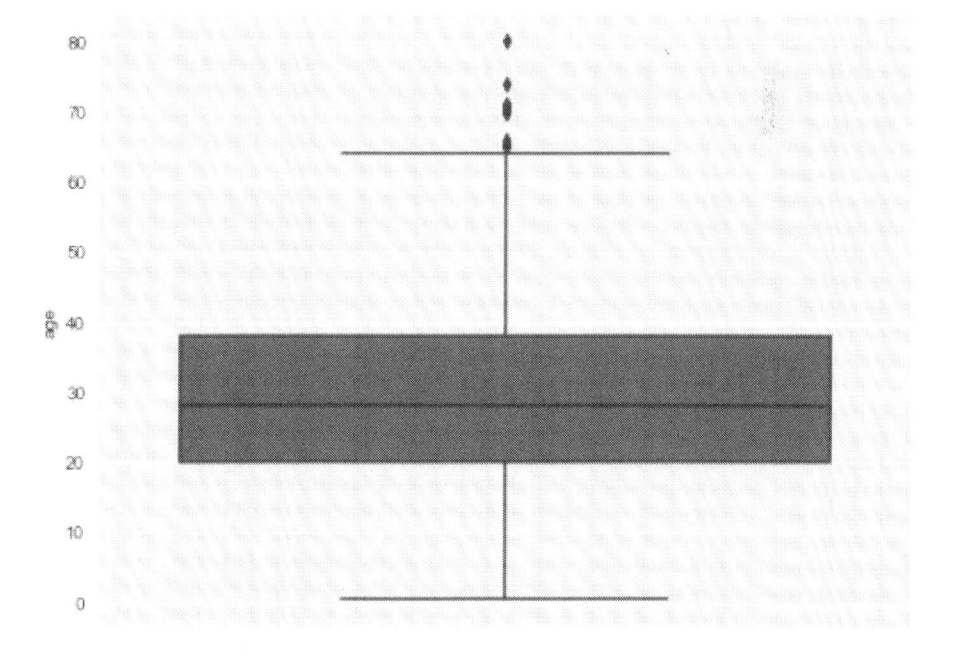

The following script finds the upper and lower threshold for the *age* column of the Titanic dataset, using the mean and standard deviation capping.

Script 68:

```
1.  lower_age_limit = titanic_data["age"].mean() - (3*
    titanic_data["age"].std())
2.  upper_age_limit = titanic_data["age"].mean() + (3*
    titanic_data["age"].std())
3.
4.  print(lower_age_limit)
5.  print(upper_age_limit)
```

Output:

```
-13.88037434994331
73.27860964406095
```

The output shows that the upper threshold value obtained via mean and standard deviation capping is 73.27 and the lower limit or threshold is −13.88.

The following script replaces the outlier values with the upper and lower limits.

Script 69:

```
1.  titanic_data["age"]= np.where(titanic_data["age"]> upper_
    age_limit, upper_age_limit,
2.  np.where(titanic_data["age"] < lower_age_limit, lower_age_
    limit, titanic_data["age"]))
```

Script 70:

```
1.  sns.boxplot( y='age', data=titanic_data)
```

The box plot shows that we still have some outlier values after applying mean and standard deviation capping on the *age* column of the Titanic dataset.

Output:

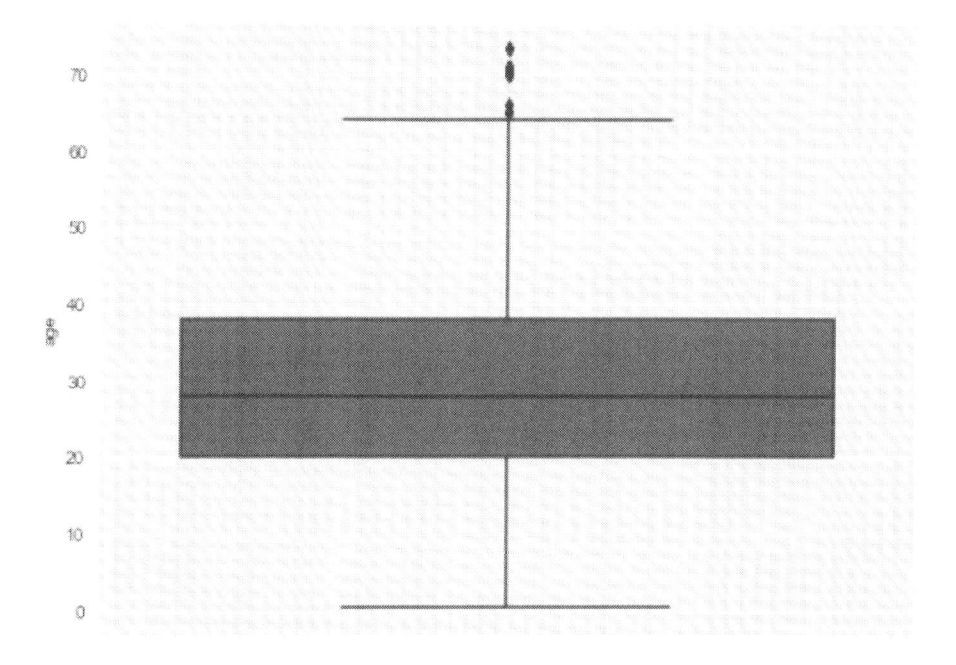

Exercise 3.1

Question 1

Which of the following techniques can be used to remove outliers from a dataset?

   A. Trimming

   B. Censoring

   C. Discretization

   D. All of the above

Question 2

Which attribute is set to True to remove the first column from the one-hot encoded columns generated via the get_dummies() method?

    A. drop_first

    B. remove_first

    C. delete_first

    D. None of the above

Question 3

After standardization, the mean value of the dataset becomes:

    A. 1

    B. 0

    C. −1

    D. None of the above

Exercise 3.2

Replace the missing values in the *deck* column of the Titanic dataset with the most frequently occurring categories in that column. Plot a bar plot for the updated *deck* column.

4

Feature Selection with Python Scikit- Learn Library

Machine learning algorithms learn from datasets. A dataset consists of features. A feature refers to a single characteristic or dimension of data. Features are also known as attributes. For instance, a dataset of cars has features like car models, car color, seating capacity, etc. Selecting the right set of features can not only improve the performance of your machine learning model but also speed up the training time of your algorithm.

In this chapter, you will study some of the most common feature selection approaches. You will use Python's Scikit-learn library to see various feature selection approaches in action.

4.1 Feature Selection Based on Variance

Features having constant or very similar values do not really play any significant role in machine learning tasks, such as classification and regression. Therefore, features that are very similar should be removed from the dataset. There are various ways to remove very similar features from the dataset. One of the ways is to find the variance for a particular feature and remove features having variance less than a certain threshold. A feature with low variance has a higher degree of similarity among its data points and vice versa.

Let's see an example of feature selection based on variance.

The following script reads the winequalit-red.csv dataset from the data repository and prints the header of the dataset.

Script 1:

```
1.  import pandas as pd
2.  import numpy as np
3.
4.  # importing the dataset
5.  wine_data = pd.read_csv("E:/Datasets/winequality-red.csv",
    sep =";" )
6.
7.  #printing dataset header
8.  wine_data.head()
```

Output:

	fixed acidity	volatile acidity	citric acid	residual sugar	chlorides	free sulfur dioxide	total sulfur dioxide	density	pH	sulphates	alcohol	quality
0	7.4	0.70	0.00	1.9	0.076	11.0	34.0	0.9978	3.51	0.56	9.4	5
1	7.8	0.88	0.00	2.6	0.098	25.0	67.0	0.9968	3.20	0.68	9.8	5
2	7.8	0.76	0.04	2.3	0.092	15.0	54.0	0.9970	3.26	0.65	9.8	5
3	11.2	0.28	0.56	1.9	0.075	17.0	60.0	0.9980	3.16	0.58	9.8	6
4	7.4	0.70	0.00	1.9	0.076	11.0	34.0	0.9978	3.51	0.56	9.4	5

The output shows that the dataset has 12 columns. Next, we divide the data into the feature and label set.

Script 2:

```
1.  # dividing data into features and labels
2.  features = wine_data.drop(["quality"], axis = 1)
3.  labels = wine_data.filter(["quality"], axis = 1)
```

Feature selection based on variance doesn't depend upon the output label. Variance shows how far a set of data is spread out. You can find the variance of all the features in a Pandas dataframe using the `var()` function, as shown below.

Script 3:

```
1.  #printing variance
2.  features.var()
```

Output:

```
fixed acidity              3.031416
volatile acidity           0.032062
citric acid                0.037947
residual sugar             1.987897
chlorides                  0.002215
free sulfur dioxide      109.414884
total sulfur dioxide    1082.102373
density                    0.000004
pH                         0.023835
sulphates                  0.028733
alcohol                    1.135647
dtype: float64
```

Scikit-learn library contains `VarianceThreshold` class, which you can use to filter features based on variance. The threshold value is passed to the threshold parameter of the constructor. The feature set is passed to the fit() method of the `VarianceThreshold` class object, as shown in the script below. The following script will filter all the features with a variance value of 0.1.

Script 4:

```
1.  # filtering features based on threshold
2.
3.  from sklearn.feature_selection import VarianceThreshold
4.
5.  var_sel = VarianceThreshold(threshold=(0.1))
6.  var_sel.fit(features)
```

Output:

```
VarianceThreshold(threshold=0.1)
```

To get the selected features, you need to call the `get_support()` method of the `VarianceThreshold` class. The value returned by the method is passed to the columns list of the feature set, which returns the columns with variance greater than the threshold. Look at the following script for reference.

Script 5:

```
1.  attributes_to_retain = features.columns[var_sel.get_
    support()]
2.  attributes_to_retain
```

Output:

```
Index(['fixed acidity', 'residual sugar', 'free sulfur
dioxide', 'total sulfur dioxide', 'alcohol'],dtype='object')
```

You can also get the attribute names that are not selected using the following script.

Script 6:

```
1.  attributes_to_filter = [attr for attr in features.columns
    if attr not in features.columns[var_sel.get_support()]]
2.  attributes_to_filter
```

Output:

```
1.  ['volatile acidity', 'citric acid', 'chlorides', 'density',
    'pH', 'sulphates']
```

To get the final dataset with the selected features, you can simply remove the features that are not selected based on the variance threshold. Execute the following script to get the final dataset containing the selected features only.

Script 7:
```
1. filtered_dataset = features.drop(attributes_to_filter, axis = 1)
2. filtered_dataset.head()
```

Output:

	fixed acidity	residual sugar	free sulfur dioxide	total sulfur dioxide	alcohol
0	7.4	1.9	11.0	34.0	9.4
1	7.8	2.6	25.0	67.0	9.8
2	7.8	2.3	15.0	54.0	9.8
3	11.2	1.9	17.0	60.0	9.8
4	7.4	1.9	11.0	34.0	9.4

One of the main issues with variance-based feature selection is that it doesn't take the relationship between mutual features into account while feature selection. Hence, with variance-based feature selection, redundant features may be selected. To avoid selecting redundant features, you can use the feature selection method based on correlation.

4.2 Feature Selection Based on Correlation

In feature selection based on correlation, the features are selected using the following steps:

1. Mutual correlation between all the features is calculated.
2. The correlation threshold is set.
3. Features having mutual correlation greater than the correlation threshold with any other feature are removed from the dataset.

To find the correlation between all the columns of a Pandas dataframe, you can use the `corr()` function, which returns a correlation matrix containing mutual correlation between all the features. Execute the following script to do so.

Script 8:

```
1. #printing correlation
2. correlation_matrix = features.corr()
3. correlation_matrix
```

Output:

	fixed acidity	volatile acidity	citric acid	residual sugar	chlorides	free sulfur dioxide	total sulfur dioxide	density	pH	sulphates	alcohol
fixed acidity	1.000000	-0.256131	0.671703	0.114777	0.093705	-0.153794	-0.113181	0.668047	-0.682978	0.183006	-0.061668
volatile acidity	-0.256131	1.000000	-0.552496	0.001918	0.061298	-0.010504	0.076470	0.022026	0.234937	-0.260987	-0.202288
citric acid	0.671703	-0.552496	1.000000	0.143577	0.203823	-0.060978	0.035533	0.364947	-0.541904	0.312770	0.109903
residual sugar	0.114777	0.001918	0.143577	1.000000	0.055610	0.187049	0.203028	0.355283	-0.085652	0.005527	0.042075
chlorides	0.093705	0.061298	0.203823	0.055610	1.000000	0.005562	0.047400	0.200632	-0.265026	0.371260	-0.221141
free sulfur dioxide	-0.153794	-0.010504	-0.060978	0.187049	0.005562	1.000000	0.667666	-0.021946	0.070377	0.051658	-0.069408
total sulfur dioxide	-0.113181	0.076470	0.035533	0.203028	0.047400	0.667666	1.000000	0.071269	-0.066495	0.042947	-0.205654
density	0.668047	0.022026	0.364947	0.355283	0.200632	-0.021946	0.071269	1.000000	-0.341699	0.148506	-0.496180
pH	-0.682978	0.234937	-0.541904	-0.085652	-0.265026	0.070377	-0.066495	-0.341699	1.000000	-0.196648	0.205633
sulphates	0.183006	-0.260987	0.312770	0.005527	0.371260	0.051658	0.042947	0.148506	-0.196648	1.000000	0.093595
alcohol	-0.061668	-0.202288	0.109903	0.042075	-0.221141	-0.069408	-0.205654	-0.496180	0.205633	0.093595	1.000000

You can also plot the correlation matrix using the `heatmap()` plot from the seaborn library, as shown below:

Script 9:

```
1. #displaying seaborn heatmap for correlation
2. import seaborn as sns
3. sns.heatmap(correlation_matrix)
```

Output:

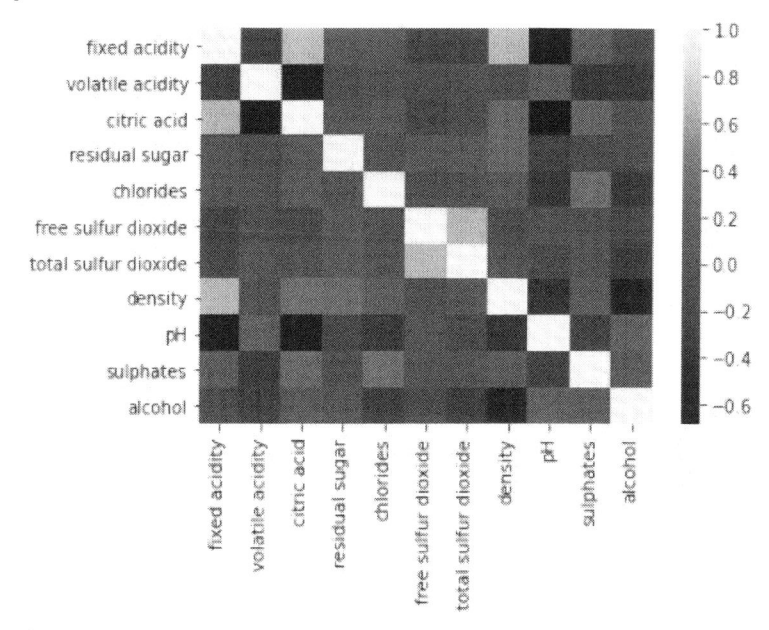

In the above script, the correlation between features is represented in the form of black to white boxes. You can see that the correlation varies between -0.6 to 1.0, where darker boxes represent high negative correlation while a lighter box represents high positive correlation.

To find all the correlated features, you can iterate through the rows in the feature correlation matrix and then select the features that have a correlation higher than a certain threshold. For example, in the following script, all the features with an absolute correlation higher than 0.6 are selected and added to the correlated feature matrix set.

Script 10:

```
1.  #creating a correlation matrix for features
2.
3.  correlated_features_matrix = set()
4.  for i in range(len(correlation_matrix.columns)):
5.      for j in range(i):
6.          if abs(correlation_matrix.iloc[i, j]) > 0.6:
7.              corr_col = correlation_matrix.columns[i]
8.              correlated_features_matrix.add(corr_col)
```

Let's see how many features have a correlation higher than 0.6 with the other features.

Script 11:

```
1.  len(correlated_features_matrix)
```

Output:

```
4
```

Let's print the set containing the correlated features.

Script 12:

```
1.  print(correlated_features_matrix)
```

The following four features have correlations higher than 0.6 with at least one of the other features in the dataset.

Output:

```
{'pH', 'total sulfur dioxide', 'density', 'citric acid'}
```

Finally, you can create the final feature set by removing the correlated features, as shown in the following script.

Script 13:

```
1.  filtered_dataset = features.drop(correlated_features_
    matrix, axis = 1)
2.  filtered_dataset.head()
```

Output:

	fixed acidity	volatile acidity	residual sugar	chlorides	free sulfur dioxide	sulphates	alcohol
0	7.4	0.70	1.9	0.076	11.0	0.56	9.4
1	7.8	0.88	2.6	0.098	25.0	0.68	9.8
2	7.8	0.76	2.3	0.092	15.0	0.65	9.8
3	11.2	0.28	1.9	0.075	17.0	0.58	9.8
4	7.4	0.70	1.9	0.076	11.0	0.56	9.4

4.3 Feature Selection Based on Recursive Elimination

Feature selection based on variance and correlation does not depend upon the output label. There are feature selection methods where features are selected based on their predictive power. One such method is feature selection based on recursive elimination.

In recursive feature elimination (RFE), a machine learning model is trained to make predictions. The predictions are compared with actual labels, and the predictive power of each feature is calculated. The feature with the least predictive power is eliminated.

The model is again trained, and in the second iteration, again, one feature with the least predictive power is eliminated. The process continues until a minimum number of features is achieved.

You can use `RFE` class from the `feature_selection` module of the Scikit-learn library to implement recursive feature selection.

To implement feature selection using RFE, you need to pass the model, the number of features to select, and the recursive elimination step to the RFE class constructor. To finally select the features, you need to call the fit() method of the RFE class and pass it both the features and labels. For instance, the following script selects four features using the linear regression model while eliminating one feature at a time.

Script 14:

```
1.  from sklearn.linear_model import LinearRegression
2.  from sklearn.feature_selection import RFE
3.
4.  # feature selection using RFE
5.  lr = LinearRegression()
6.  rfe = RFE(estimator=lr, n_features_to_select=4, step=1)
7.  rfe.fit(features, labels)
```

Output:

```
RFE(estimator=LinearRegression(), n_features_to_select=4)
```

To find the feature names, you can first retrieve the index value of the selected features using the ranking attribute of the RFE class, as shown below.

Script 15:

```
1.  rfe.ranking_
```

The features with index values of 1 are the selected features.

Output:

```
array([5, 1, 4, 6, 1, 7, 8, 1, 2, 1, 3])
```

The following script returns the indexes of the selected features.

Script 16:

```
1.  attributes_to_retain = rfe.get_support(1)
2.  attributes_to_retain
```

Output:

```
array([1, 4, 7, 9], dtype=int64)
In [36]:
```

Finally, you can create a dataset of the selected features using the following script.

Script 17:

```
1.  filtered_dataset = features[features.columns[attributes_to_retain]]
2.  filtered_dataset.head()
```

Output:

	volatile acidity	chlorides	density	sulphates
0	0.70	0.076	0.9978	0.56
1	0.88	0.098	0.9968	0.68
2	0.76	0.092	0.9970	0.65
3	0.28	0.075	0.9980	0.58
4	0.70	0.076	0.9978	0.56

4.4. Feature Selection Based on Model Performance

Finally, you can also select features based on feature importance, such as the one calculated by feature importance attribute or regression coefficient in the case of linear regression. To do so, you can use the `SelectFromModel` class from the Sklearn model. To select the features, you first need to train your machine learning model using features and labels. The trained model is then passed to the `SelectFromModelClass` constructor along with the threshold value, which can be mean, median, etc., of the feature importance.

The following scripts 18 and 19 train `RandomForestRegressor` on the dataset and then use the `SelectFromModel` class to select the features with feature importance value greater than the mean feature importance value.

Script 18:

```
1. from sklearn.feature_selection import SelectFromModel
2. from sklearn.ensemble import RandomForestRegressor
3.
4. # selecting features based on the performance of
   RandomForest
5. rfr = RandomForestRegressor()
6. rfr.fit(features, labels)
```

Script 19:

```
1. model = SelectFromModel(rfr, prefit=True, threshold='mean')
2. X_transformed = model.transform(features)
```

To get the selected features, you can use the `get_support()` method of the `SelectFromModel` class, as shown in the following script.

Script 20:

```
1. #retrieving selected features
2. cols = model.get_support(indices=True)
```

Finally, the following script creates the final dataset with the selected features.

Script 21:

```
1. #printing dataset with selected features
2. filtered_dataset = features[features.columns[cols]]
3. filtered_dataset.head()
```

Output:

	volatile acidity	sulphates	alcohol
0	0.70	0.56	9.4
1	0.88	0.68	9.8
2	0.76	0.65	9.8
3	0.28	0.58	9.8
4	0.70	0.56	9.4

In this chapter, you saw some of the most commonly used feature selection methods. In the next chapter, you will see how to solve regression problems in machine learning using the Python Scikit-learn library.

> **Hands-on Time – Exercise**
>
> Now, it is your turn. Follow the instructions in **the exercises below** to check your understanding of the feature selection algorithms in machine learning. The answers to these questions are given at the end of the book.

Exercise 4.1

Question 1

Which of the following feature types should you retain in the dataset?

    A. Features with low Variance

    B. Features with high Variance

    C. Features with high standard deviation

    D. Both B and C

Question 2

Which of the following features should you remove from the dataset?

    A. Features with high mutual correlation

    B. Features with low mutual correlation

    C. Features with high correlation with output label

    D. None of the above

Question 3

Which of the following feature selection method does not depend upon the output label?

    A. Feature selection based on Model performance

    B. Feature selection based on recursive elimination

    C. Feature selection based on mutual feature variance

    D. All of the above

Exercise 4.2

Using the `winequalit-white` dataset from the `Dataset and Source Codes` folder, apply the recursive elimination technique for feature selection.

5

Solving Regression Problems in Machine Learning Using Sklearn Library

Machine learning is a branch of artificial intelligence that enables computer programs to automatically learn and improve from experience. Machine learning algorithms learn from datasets and then, based on the patterns identified from the datasets, make predictions on unseen data.

Machine learning algorithms can be broadly categorized into two types: Supervised learning and unsupervised learning algorithms.

Supervised machine learning algorithms are those algorithms where the input dataset and the corresponding output or true prediction is available, and the algorithms try to find the relationship between inputs and outputs.

On the other hand, in unsupervised machine learning algorithms, the true labels for the outputs are not known. Rather, the algorithms try to find similar patterns in the data. Clustering algorithms are a typical example of unsupervised learning.

Supervised learning algorithms are further divided into two types: regression algorithms and classification algorithms.

Regression algorithms predict a continuous value, for example, the price of a house, the blood pressure of a person, and a student's score in a particular exam. Classification algorithms, on the flip side, predict a discrete value, such as whether or not a tumor is malignant, whether a student is going to pass or fail an exam, etc.

In this chapter, you will study how machine learning algorithms can be used to solve regression problems, i.e., predict a continuous value using the Sklearn library (https://bit.ly/2Zvy2Sm). In chapter 6, you will see how to solve classification problems via Sklearn.

5.1 Preparing Data for Regression Problems

Machine learning algorithms require data to be in a certain format before the algorithms can be trained on the data. In this section, you will see various data preprocessing steps that you need to perform before you can train machine learning algorithms using the Sklearn library.

You can read data from CSV files. However, the datasets we are going to use in this section are available by default in the Seaborn library. To view all the datasets, you can use the `get_dataset_names()` function, as shown in the following script:

Script 1:

```
1.  # importing required libraries
2.  import pandas as pd
3.  import numpy as np
4.  import seaborn as sns
5.
6.  #get dataset names from the seaborn library
7.  sns.get_dataset_names()
```

Output:

```
['anagrams',
 'anscombe',
 'attention',
 'brain_networks',
 'car_crashes',
 'diamonds',
 'dots',
 'exercise',
 'flights',
 'fmri',
 'gammas',
 'geyser',
 'iris',
 'mpg',
 'penguins',
 'planets',
 'tips',
 'titanic']
```

To read a particular dataset into the Pandas dataframe, pass the dataset name to the `load_dataset()` method of the Seaborn library.

The following script loads the Tips dataset and displays its first five rows.

Script 2:

```
1.  # importing the tips dataset
2.  tips_df = sns.load_dataset("tips")
3.
4.  #printing dataset header
5.  tips_df.head()
```

Output:

	total_bill	tip	sex	smoker	day	time	size
0	16.99	1.01	Female	No	Sun	Dinner	2
1	10.34	1.66	Male	No	Sun	Dinner	3
2	21.01	3.50	Male	No	Sun	Dinner	3
3	23.68	3.31	Male	No	Sun	Dinner	2
4	24.59	3.61	Female	No	Sun	Dinner	4

Similarly, the following script loads the Diamonds dataset and displays its first five rows.

Script 3:

```
1.  # importing the diamonds dataset
2.  diamond_df = sns.load_dataset("diamonds")
3.
4.  #printing dataset header
5.  diamond_df.head()
```

	carat	cut	color	clarity	depth	table	price	x	y	z
0	0.23	Ideal	E	SI2	61.5	55.0	326	3.95	3.98	2.43
1	0.21	Premium	E	SI1	59.8	61.0	326	3.89	3.84	2.31
2	0.23	Good	E	VS1	56.9	65.0	327	4.05	4.07	2.31
3	0.29	Premium	I	VS2	62.4	58.0	334	4.20	4.23	2.63
4	0.31	Good	J	SI2	63.3	58.0	335	4.34	4.35	2.75

In this section, we will be working with the Tips dataset. We will be using machine learning algorithms to predict the *tip* for a particular record based on the remaining features, such as *total_bill*, *sex*, *day*, *time*, etc.

5.1.1 Dividing Data into Features and Labels

As a first step, we divide the data into features and labels set. Our labels set consists of values from the *tip* column, while the feature set consists of values from the remaining columns. The following script divides data into features and labels set.

Script 4:

```
1.  #extracting features
2.  X = tips_df.drop(['tip'], axis=1)
3.
4.  #extracting labels
5.  y = tips_df["tip"]
```

Let's print the features set.

Script 5:

```
1.  #printing features
2.  X.head()
```

Output:

	total_bill	sex	smoker	day	time	size
0	16.99	Female	No	Sun	Dinner	2
1	10.34	Male	No	Sun	Dinner	3
2	21.01	Male	No	Sun	Dinner	3
3	23.68	Male	No	Sun	Dinner	2
4	24.59	Female	No	Sun	Dinner	4

And the following script prints the labels set.

Script 6:

```
1.  #printing labels header
2.  y.head()
```

Output:

```
0    1.01
1    1.66
2    3.50
3    3.31
4    3.61
Name: tip, dtype: float64
```

5.1.2 Converting Categorical Data to Numbers

Machine learning algorithms can only work with numbers. Therefore, it is important to convert categorical data into a numeric format.

In this regard, the first step is to create a dataset of all numeric values. To do so, drop the categorical columns from the dataset, as shown below.

Script 7:

```
1.  #removing categorical features
2.  numerical = X.drop(['sex', 'smoker', 'day', 'time'], axis
    = 1)
```

The output below shows that the dataframe *numerical* contains numeric columns only.

Script 8:

```
1.  #printint numeric features only
2.  numerical.head()
```

Output:

	total_bill	size
0	16.99	2
1	10.34	3
2	21.01	3
3	23.68	2
4	24.59	4

Next, you need to create a dataframe that contains only categorical columns.

Script 9:

```
1.  #filtering categorical features
2.  categorical = X.filter(['sex', 'smoker', 'day', 'time'])
3.
4.  #printing categorical features header
5.  categorical.head()
```

Output:

	sex	smoker	day	time
0	Female	No	Sun	Dinner
1	Male	No	Sun	Dinner
2	Male	No	Sun	Dinner
3	Male	No	Sun	Dinner
4	Female	No	Sun	Dinner

One of the most common approaches to convert a categorical column to a numeric one is via one-hot encoding. In one-hot encoding, for every unique value in the original columns, a new column is created. For instance, for sex, two columns: Female and Male, are created. If the original sex column contained male, a 1 is added in the newly created Male column, while 0 is added in the Female column.

However, it can be noted that we do not really need two columns. A single column, i.e., Female is enough since when a customer is female, we can add 1 in the Female column, else 1 can be added in that column. Hence, we need N-1 one-hot encoded columns for all the N values in the original column.

The following script converts categorical columns into one-hot encoded columns using the pd.get_dummies() method.

Script 10:

```
1.  #performing one hot encoding
2.  import pandas as pd
3.  cat_numerical = pd.get_dummies(categorical,drop_first=True)
4.  cat_numerical.head()
```

The output shows the newly created one-hot encoded columns.

Output:

	sex_Female	smoker_No	day_Fri	day_Sat	day_Sun	time_Dinner
0	1	1	0	0	1	1
1	0	1	0	0	1	1
2	0	1	0	0	1	1
3	0	1	0	0	1	1
4	1	1	0	0	1	1

The final step is to join the numerical columns with the one-hot encoded columns. To do so, you can use the concat() function from the Pandas library, as shown below:

Script 11:

```
1.  #concating numeric and one hot encoded features
2.
3.  X = pd.concat([numerical, cat_numerical], axis =1)
4.  X.head()
```

The final dataset looks like this. You can see that it doesn't contain any categorical value.

Output:

	total_bill	size	sex_Female	smoker_No	day_Fri	day_Sat	day_Sun	time_Dinner
0	16.99	2	1	1	0	0	1	1
1	10.34	3	0	1	0	0	1	1
2	21.01	3	0	1	0	0	1	1
3	23.68	2	0	1	0	0	1	1
4	24.59	4	1	1	0	0	1	1

5.1.3 Divide Data into Training and Test Sets

After a machine learning algorithm has been trained, it needs to be evaluated to see how well it performs on unseen data. Therefore, we divide the dataset into two sets, i.e., train set and test set. The dataset is trained via the train set and evaluated on the test set. To split the data into training and test sets, you can use the `train_test_split()` function from the Sklearn library, as shown below. The following script divides the data into 80 percent train set and 20 percent test set.

Script 12:

```
1.  #dividing data into training and test sets
2.  from sklearn.model_selection import train_test_split
3.
4.  X_train, X_test, y_train, y_test = train_test_split(X, y,
    test_size=0.20, random_state=0)
```

5.1.4 Data Scaling/Normalization

The final step (optional) before data is passed to machine learning algorithms is to scale the data. You can see that some columns of the dataset contain small values, while the others contain very large values.

It is better to convert all values to a uniform scale. To do so, you can use the `StandardScaler()` function from the `sklearn.preprocessing` module, as shown below:

Script 13:

```
1.  # feature scaling using standard scaler
2.  from sklearn.preprocessing import StandardScaler
3.  sc = StandardScaler()
4.  X_train = sc.fit_transform(X_train)
5.  X_test = sc.transform (X_test)
```

We have converted data into a format that can be used to train machine learning algorithms for regression from the Sklearn library. Details, including functionalities and usage of all the machine learning algorithms, are available at this link. You can check all the regression algorithms by going to that link.

In the following section, we will review some of the most commonly used regression algorithms.

5.2 Single Output Regression Problems

In this section, you will solve regression problems with one possible output. In a regression problem with a single output, you have to predict a single continuous value, such as the price of a house, the blood pressure of a patient, or the marks of a student. In multi-output regression problems, there is more than one continuous value in the output. For instance, if you have to predict the x and y coordinates for the four vertices of a square, you have to predict eight values.

Let's first see examples of solving regression problems containing one output. To do so, you will be using the Scikit-learn library. A complete list of regression algorithms provided by the Scikit-learn library can be found at this link (http://bit.ly/38gXKOb).

In this section, you will only be using three of the most commonly used regression algorithms: linear regression, KNN regression, and random forest regression. In the next section, you will see how we can perform multi-output regression.

5.2.1 Linear Regression

Linear regression is a linear model that assumes a linear relationship between inputs and outputs and minimizes the cost of error between the predicted and actual output using functions like mean absolute error.

Why Use Linear Regression Algorithm?

Linear regression algorithm is particularly useful because:

1. Linear regression is a simple to implement and easily interpretable algorithm.
2. Takes less training time to train, even for huge datasets.
3. Linear regression coefficients are easy to interpret.

Disadvantages of Linear Regression Algorithm

Following are the disadvantages of the linear regression algorithm:

1. Performance is easily affected by outlier presence.
2. Assumes a linear relationship between dependent and independent variables, which can result in an increased error.

Implementing Linear Regression with Sklearn

To implement linear regression with Sklearn, you can use the `LinearRegression` class from the `sklearn.linear_model` module. To train the algorithm, the training and test sets, i.e., `X_train` and `X_test` in our case, are passed to the fit()

method of the object of the `LinearRegression` class. To make predictions, the test set is passed to the `predict()` method of the class. The process of training and making predictions with the linear regression algorithm is as follows:

Script 14:

```
1.  #importing linear regression model from sklearn
2.  from sklearn.linear_model import LinearRegression
3.
4.  lin_reg = LinearRegression()
5.
6.  #training the model
7.  regressor = lin_reg.fit(X_train, y_train)
8.
9.  #making predictions on the test set
10. y_pred = regressor.predict(X_test)
```

Once you have trained a model and have made predictions on the test set, the next step is to know how well your model has performed for making predictions on the unknown test set. There are various metrics to check that. However, mean absolute error, mean squared error, and root mean squared error are three of the most common metrics.

§ Mean Absolute Error

Mean absolute error (MAE) is calculated by taking the average of absolute error obtained by subtracting real values from predicted values. The equation for calculating MAE is given below:

$$MAE = \frac{\sum_{i=1}^{n}|y_i - \hat{y}_1|}{n}$$

§ Mean Squared Error

Mean squared error (MSE) is similar to MAE. However, the error for each record is squared in the case of MSE in order to punish data records with a huge difference between predicted and actual values. The equation to calculate mean squared error is as follows:

$$\text{MSE} = \frac{1}{n} \sum_{i=1}^{n} (y_i - \hat{y})^2$$

§ Root Mean Squared Error

Root Mean Squared Error is simply the under the root of mean squared error and can be calculated as follows:

$$\text{RMSE} = \sqrt{\frac{1}{n} \sum_{i=1}^{n} (y_i - \hat{y})^2}$$

The methods used to find the value for these metrics are available in `sklearn.metrics` class. The predicted and actual values have to be passed to these methods, as shown in the output.

Script 15:

```
1.  #evaluating model performance
2.  from sklearn import metrics
3.
4.  print('Mean Absolute Error:', metrics.mean_absolute_
    error(y_test, y_pred))
5.  print('Mean Squared Error:', metrics.mean_squared_error(y_
    test, y_pred))
6.  print('Root Mean Squared Error:', np.sqrt(metrics.mean_
    squared_error(y_test, y_pred)))
```

Here is the output. By looking at the mean absolute error, it can be concluded that, on average, there is an error of 0.70 for predictions, which means that on average, the predicted tip values are 0.70$ more or less than the actual tip values.

Output:

```
Mean Absolute Error: 0.7080218832979829
Mean Squared Error: 0.893919522160961
Root Mean Squared Error: 0.9454731736865732
```

> **Further Readings – Linear Regression**
> To study more about linear regression, please check these links:
> 1. https://bit.ly/2ZyCa49
> 2. https://bit.ly/2RmLhAp

5.2.2 KNN Regression

KNN stands for K-nearest neighbors. KNN is a lazy learning algorithm, which is based on finding the Euclidean distance between different data points.

Why Use KNN Algorithm?

KNN algorithm is particularly useful because:

1. KNN Algorithm doesn't assume any relationship between the features.
2. Useful for a dataset where data localization is important.
3. Only have to tune the parameter K, which is the number of nearest neighbors.
4. No training is needed, as it is a lazy learning algorithm.
5. Recommender systems and finding semantic similarity between the documents are major applications of the KNN algorithm.

Disadvantages of KNN Algorithm

Following are the disadvantages of the KNN algorithm:

1. You have to find the optimal value for K, which is not easy.
2. Not suitable for very high dimensional data.

Implementing KNN Algorithm with SKlearn

With Sklearn, it is extremely easy to implement KNN regression. To do so, you can use the `KNeighborsRegressor` class.

The process of training and testing is the same as linear regression. For training, you need to call the `fit()` method, and for testing, you need to call the `predict()` method.

The following script shows the process of training, testing, and evaluating the KNN regression algorithm for predicting the values for the *tip* column from the Tips dataset.

Script 16:

```
1.  #importing the KNN model from Sklearn
2.  from sklearn.neighbors import KNeighborsRegressor
3.  knn_reg = KNeighborsRegressor(n_neighbors=5)
4.
5.  #training the model
6.  regressor = knn_reg.fit(X_train, y_train)
7.
8.  #making predictions
9.  y_pred = regressor.predict(X_test)
10.
11. #evaluating model performance
12. from sklearn import metrics
13.
14. print('Mean Absolute Error:', metrics.mean_absolute_
    error(y_test, y_pred))
15. print('Mean Squared Error:', metrics.mean_squared_error(y_
    test, y_pred))
16. print('Root Mean Squared Error:', np.sqrt(metrics.mean_
    squared_error(y_test, y_pred)))
```

Output:

```
Mean Absolute Error: 0.7513877551020406
Mean Squared Error: 0.9462902040816326
Root Mean Squared Error: 0.9727744877830794
```

> To study more about KNN regression, please check these links:
> 1. https://bit.ly/33r2Zbq

5.2.3 Random Forest Regression

Random forest is a tree-based algorithm that converts features into tree nodes and then uses entropy loss to make predictions.

Why Use Random Forest Algorithm?

Random forest algorithm is particularly useful when:

1. You have lots of missing data or an imbalanced dataset.
2. With a large number of trees, you can avoid overfitting while training. Overfitting occurs when machine learning models perform better on the training set but worse on the test set.
3. Random forest algorithms can be used when you have very higher-dimensional data.
4. Through cross-validation, the random forest can return higher accuracy.
5. The random forest algorithm can solve both classification and regression tasks and finds its application in a variety of tasks ranging from credit card fraud detection, stock market prediction, and finding fraudulent online transactions.

Disadvantages of Random Forest Algorithm

There are two major disadvantages of Random forest algorithms:

1. Using a large number of trees can slow down the algorithm.
2. Random forest algorithm is a predictive algorithm, which can only predict the future but cannot explain what happened in the past using the dataset.

Implementing Random Forest Regressor using Sklearn

RandomForestRegressor class from the Sklearn.ensemble module can be used to implement a random forest regressor algorithm, as shown below.

Script 17:

```
1.  #importing the random forest algorithm from Sklearn
2.  from sklearn.ensemble import RandomForestRegressor
3.  rf_reg = RandomForestRegressor(random_state=42, n_
    estimators=500)
4.
5.  #training the model
6.  regressor = rf_reg.fit(X_train, y_train)
7.
8.  #making predictions on the test set
9.  y_pred = regressor.predict(X_test)
10.
11.
12. #evaluating the model performance
13. from sklearn import metrics
14.
15. print('Mean Absolute Error:', metrics.mean_absolute_
    error(y_test, y_pred))
16. print('Mean Squared Error:', metrics.mean_squared_error(y_
    test, y_pred))
17. print('Root Mean Squared Error:', np.sqrt(metrics.mean_
    squared_error(y_test, y_pred)))
```

The mean absolute error value of 0.70 shows that random forest performs better than both linear regression and KNN for predicting a *tip* in the Tips dataset.

Output:

```
Mean Absolute Error: 0.7054065306122449
Mean Squared Error: 0.8045782841306138
Root Mean Squared Error: 0.8969828783932354
```

Further Readings – Random Forest Regression
To study more about Random Forest Regression in Sklearn, please check these links: 1. https://bit.ly/35u3BzH

Which Model to Use?

From the results obtained from sections 6.2 to 6.5, we can see that Random Forest Regressor algorithm results in the minimum MAE, MSE, and RMSE values. The choice of algorithm to use depends totally upon your dataset and evaluation metrics. Some algorithms perform better on one dataset, while the other algorithms perform better on the other dataset. It is better that you use all the algorithms to see which gives the best results. However, as a rule of thumb, if you only have limited options, try starting with ensemble learning algorithms such as Random Forest. They yield the best result. You will study more about model selection strategies in chapter 9.

5.2.4 Making Prediction on a Single Record

In the previous sections, you saw how to make predictions on a complete test set. In this section, you will see how to make a prediction using a single record as an input.

Let's pick the 101st record from our dataset, which is located at the 100th index.

Script 18:

```
1.  #printing information about the 101st record in the dataset
2.  tips_df.loc[100]
```

The output shows that the value of the tip in the 100th record in our dataset is 2.5.

Output:

```
total_bill         11.35
tip                 2.5
sex              Female
smoker              Yes
day                 Fri
time             Dinner
size                2
Name: 100, dtype: object
```

We will try to predict the value of the tip of the 100th record using the random forest regressor algorithm and see what output we get. Look at the script below:

Note: You have to scale your single record before it can be used as input to your machine learning algorithm.

Script 19:

```
1.  # importing random forest regressor from sklearn
2.  from sklearn.ensemble import RandomForestRegressor
3.  rf_reg = RandomForestRegressor(random_state=42, n_
    estimators=500)
4.
5.  #training the algorithm on training set
6.  regressor = rf_reg.fit(X_train, y_train)
7.
8.  #making predictions on the 101st record from thedataset
9.  single_record = sc.transform (X.values[100].reshape(1,
    -1))
10. predicted_tip = regressor.predict(single_record)
11.
12. #printing the predicted value
13. print(predicted_tip)
```

Output:

```
[2.2609]
```

The predicted value of the tip is 2.26, which is pretty close to 2.5, i.e., the actual value.

5.3 Multi-output Regression Problems

As explained earlier, multi-output regression is a type of regression where you have to predict more than one continuous value in the output.

Let's create a dummy dataset of 2,000 records with eight features and three values in the output. To do so, you can execute the following script. The script also prints the shape of the features (X) and labels (y) in the dataset.

Script 20:

```
1.  # example of multi-output regression problem
2.  from sklearn.datasets import make_regression
3.
4.  # create dummy dataset
5.  X, y = make_regression(n_samples=2000, n_features=8, n_
    informative=4, n_targets=3, random_state=42, noise=0.3)
6.
7.  # print dataset shape
8.  print(X.shape, y.shape)
```

Output:

```
(2000, 8) (2000, 3)
```

The output shows that you have 2,000 records with eight features and three outputs. Thus, this is a multi-output regression problem.

Let's divide the dummy dataset into training and test sets, and apply feature scaling on it.

Script 21:

```
1.  #dividing data into training and test sets
2.  from sklearn.model_selection import train_test_split
3.
4.  X_train, X_test, y_train, y_test = train_test_split(X, y,
    test_size=0.20, random_state=0)
5.
6.  # feature scaling using standard scaler
7.  from sklearn.preprocessing import StandardScaler
8.  sc = StandardScaler()
9.  X_train = sc.fit_transform(X_train)
10. X_test = sc.transform (X_test)
```

Some of the algorithms in the Scikit-learn library support multi-output regression by default. For example, you can use Linear Regression and Random Forest Regression without any modification to predict multi-output regression values.

5.3.1 Linear Regression for Multi-output Regression

You can see from the below output that you do not need to make any change in the linear regression algorithm to make predictions on the dataset without multiple regression outputs.

Script 22:

```
1.  #importing linear regression model from sklearn
2.  from sklearn.linear_model import LinearRegression
3.
4.  lin_reg = LinearRegression()
5.
6.  #training the model
7.  regressor = lin_reg.fit(X_train, y_train)
8.
9.  #making predictions on the test set
10. y_pred = regressor.predict(X_test)
11.
12. #evaluating model performance
13. from sklearn import metrics
14.
15. print('Mean Absolute Error:', metrics.mean_absolute_
    error(y_test, y_pred))
16. print('Mean Squared Error:', metrics.mean_squared_error(y_
    test, y_pred))
17. print('Root Mean Squared Error:', np.sqrt(metrics.mean_
    squared_error(y_test, y_pred)))
```

Output:

```
Mean Absolute Error: 0.24400622004095515
Mean Squared Error: 0.09288200051053495
Root Mean Squared Error: 0.3047654844475256
```

The following script makes a prediction on a single test point.

Script 23:
```
1.  #making predictions on the 51st record from the test set
2.  single_record = sc.transform (X_test[50].reshape(1, -1))
3.  predicted_val = regressor.predict(single_record)
4.
5.  #printing the predicted value
6.  print(predicted_val)
7.
8.  #printing the actual value
9.  print(y_test[50])
```

The output shows the predicted output and actual output. You can see that there are three values in the output now since this is a multi-output regression problem.

Output:
```
[[ 52.14499321  154.07153888   29.65411176]]
 [ 50.3331556   155.43458476   26.52621361]
```

5.3.2 Random Forest for Multi-output Regression

The following script shows how you can use a Random Forest Regressor for multi-output regression. You can see that the script is no different than the one for single output regression problems.

Script 24:

```
1.  #importing the random forest algorithm from Sklearn
2.  from sklearn.ensemble import RandomForestRegressor
3.  rf_reg = RandomForestRegressor(random_state=42, n_
    estimators=500)
4.
5.  #training the model
6.  regressor = rf_reg.fit(X_train, y_train)
7.
8.  #making predictions on the test set
9.  y_pred = regressor.predict(X_test)
10.
11.
12. #evaluating the model performance
13. from sklearn import metrics
14.
15. print('Mean Absolute Error:', metrics.mean_absolute_
    error(y_test, y_pred))
16. print('Mean Squared Error:', metrics.mean_squared_error(y_
    test, y_pred))
17. print('Root Mean Squared Error:', np.sqrt(metrics.mean_
    squared_error(y_test, y_pred)))
```

Output:

```
Mean Absolute Error: 17.578462377518566
Mean Squared Error: 737.569952450891
Root Mean Squared Error: 27.158239126476722
```

The following script uses a trained Random Forest Regressor algorithm to make predictions on a single data point.

Script 25:

```
1.  #making predictions on the 51st record from the test set
2.  single_record = sc.transform (X_test[50].reshape(1, -1))
3.  predicted_val = regressor.predict(single_record)
4.
5.  #printing the predicted value
6.  print(predicted_val)
7.
8.  #printing the actual value
9.  print(y_test[50])
```

Output:

```
[[ 15.29925902  114.41624666   12.90183432]]
 [ 50.3331556   155.43458476   26.52621361]
```

Some algorithms, such as support vector machines, also known as support vector regressor (SVR) for regression problems, cannot by default make predictions on datasets with multiple regression outputs. In such cases, you have two options. You can use either direct multiclass output wrapper algorithms for regression or chained multi-output wrapper algorithms for regression.

5.3.3. Direct Multioutput Regression with Wrapper Algorithms

In direct multiclass output regression wrapper algorithms, each one of the multiple output regression labels is treated as an individual label. So, if you have three outputs labels y1, y2, and y3, and one feature set X, the direct wrapper algorithm will train three individual models behind the scene where each model predicts output labels y1, y2, and y3 using feature set X.

To implement direct multi-output regression, you can use the `Multi-outputRegressor` class from the `multi-output` module of the Sklearn library. The algorithm that you want to train is passed as a parameter to the `Multi-outputRegressor` class.

The following script uses `MultoutputRegressor` class to make predictions on a multi-output dataset using the `SVR` regressor model.

Once you pass the `SVR` class to the `Multi-outputRegressor` class object, the rest of the process is similar to making predictions using a common algorithm. You have to pass the feature and label set to the fit method of the `Multi-outputRegressor` class.

Script 26:

```
1.  #importing MultiputputRegressor and LinearSVR from the Sklearn library
2.  from sklearn.multi-output import Multi-outputRegressor
3.  from sklearn.svm import LinearSVR
4.
5.  svr_reg = LinearSVR()
6.  # define the direct multi-output wrapper model
7.  wrap_clf = Multi-outputRegressor(svr_reg)
8.
9.  #training the model
10. regressor = wrap_clf.fit(X_train, y_train)
11.
12. #making predictions on the test set
13. y_pred = regressor.predict(X_test)
14.
15.
16. #evaluating the model performance
17. from sklearn import metrics
18.
19. print('Mean Absolute Error:', metrics.mean_absolute_error(y_test, y_pred))
20. print('Mean Squared Error:', metrics.mean_squared_error(y_test, y_pred))
21. print('Root Mean Squared Error:', np.sqrt(metrics.mean_squared_error(y_test, y_pred)))
```

Output:

```
Mean Absolute Error: 0.24566521365979566
Mean Squared Error: 0.09412825912574384
Root Mean Squared Error: 0.30680329060449113
```

Finally, you can also make predictions on a single data point using direct multi-output regressor wrapper algorithms, as shown in the following script.

Script 27:

```
1.  #making predictions on the 51st record from the test set
2.  single_record = sc.transform (X_test[50].reshape(1, -1))
3.  predicted_val = regressor.predict(single_record)
4.
5.  #printing the predicted value
6.  print(predicted_val)
7.
8.  #printing the actual value
9.  print(y_test[50])
```

Output:

```
[[ 52.10616073 154.0113967    29.64235478]]
 [ 50.3331556   155.43458476  26.52621361]
```

5.3.4. Chained Multioutput Regression with Wrapper Algorithms

In chained multiclass output regression, the output predictions for each class are incremental. For instance, if you have a feature set X and output labels y1, y2, and y3, in the first increment, the algorithm predicts y1 using the feature set X.

In the next iteration, the feature set X and the previously predicted values of y1 are concatenated and used to predict y2. In the next iteration, the feature set X and the predicted value of y2 are used to predict y3.

To make predictions for multi-output regression problems, you can use the `RegressorChain` class from the multi-output module of the Sklearn library, as shown below.

The base algorithm is passed to the `RegressorChain` class along with the order of the output classes that you want to predict in a sequence or chain. The following script uses the `LinearSVR` algorithm to make predictions for multiclass output regression using the `RegressorChain` wrapper.

Script 28:

```
1.  #importing Multi-output Regressor and LinearSVR from the Sklearn library
2.  from sklearn.multi-output import RegressorChain
3.  from sklearn.svm import LinearSVR
4.
5.  svr_reg = LinearSVR()
6.  # define the direct multi-output wrapper model
7.  wrap_clf = RegressorChain(svr_reg, order=[0,1,2])
8.
9.  #training the model
10. regressor = wrap_clf.fit(X_train, y_train)
11.
12. #making predictions on the test set
13. y_pred = regressor.predict(X_test)
14.
15.
16. #evaluating the model performance
17. from sklearn import metrics
18.
19. print('Mean Absolute Error:', metrics.mean_absolute_error(y_test, y_pred))
20. print('Mean Squared Error:', metrics.mean_squared_error(y_test, y_pred))
21. print('Root Mean Squared Error:', np.sqrt(metrics.mean_squared_error(y_test, y_pred)))
```

Output:
```
Mean Absolute Error: 0.2999883276581629
Mean Squared Error: 0.14873277575291557
Root Mean Squared Error: 0.3856588852249039
```

Finally, the following script shows how you can use the `LinearSVR` algorithm along with the `RegressorChain` wrapper to make predictions on a single data point.

Script 29:
```
1.  #making predictions on the 51st record from the test set
2.  single_record = sc.transform (X_test[50].reshape(1, -1))
3.  predicted_val = regressor.predict(single_record)
4.
5.  #printing the predicted value
6.  print(predicted_val)
7.
8.  #printing the actual value
9.  print(y_test[50])
```

Output:
```
[[ 52.11002869  154.00609972   29.12383881]]
 [ 50.3331556   155.43458476   26.52621361]
```

In the next chapter, you will see how to solve classification problems using machine learning algorithms in Scikit (Sklearn) library.

> **Hands-on Time – Exercise**
>
> Now, it is your turn. Follow the instruction in **the exercises below** to check your understanding of the about regression algorithms in machine learning. The answers to these questions are given at the end of the book.

Exercise 5.1

Question 1

Which one of the following is an example of a regression output?

    A- True

    B- Red

    C- 2.5

    D- None of the above

Question 2

Which one of the following algorithms is a lazy algorithm?

    A- Random Forest

    B- KNN

    C- SVM

    D- Linear Regression

Question 3

Which one of the following algorithms is not a regression metric?

    A- Accuracy

    B- Recall

    C- F1 Measure

    D- All of the above

Exercise 5.2

Using the `Diamonds` dataset from the Seaborn library, train a regression algorithm of your choice, which predicts the price of the diamond. Perform all the preprocessing steps.

6

Solving Classification Problems in Machine Learning Using Sklearn Library

In the previous chapter, you saw how to solve regression problems with machine learning using the Sklearn library (https://bit.ly/2Zvy2Sm). In this chapter, you will see how to solve classification problems. Classification problems are the type of problems where you have to predict a discrete value, i.e., whether or not a tumor is malignant, whether the condition of a car is good, whether or not a student will pass an exam, and so on.

6.1 Preparing Data for Classification Problems

Like regression, you have to first convert data into a specific format before it can be used to train classification algorithms.

The following script imports the Pandas, Seaborn, and NumPy libraries.

Script 1:

```
1.  # importing required libraries
2.  import pandas as pd
3.  import numpy as np
```

The following script uses the `read_csv()` method from the Pandas library to read the customer_churn.csv file, which contains records of customers who left the bank six months after various information about them is recorded. You can find the "customer_churn.csv" file in the data folder of the book resources. The `head()` method prints the first five rows of the dataset.

Script 2:

```
1.  # importing the dataset
2.  churn_df = pd.read_csv("E:\Hands on Python for Data
    Science and Machine Learning\Datasets\customer_churn.csv")
3.  churn_df.head()
```

The output shows that the dataset contains information, such as surname, customer id, geography, gender, age, etc., as shown below. The Exited column contains information regarding whether or not the customer exited the bank after six months.

Output:

Number	CustomerId	Surname	CreditScore	Geography	Gender	Age	Tenure	Balance	NumOfProducts	HasCrCard	IsActiveMember	EstimatedSalary	Exited
1	15634602	Hargrave	619	France	Female	42	2	0.00	1	1	1	101348.88	1
2	15647311	Hill	608	Spain	Female	41	1	83807.86	1	0	1	112542.58	0
3	15619304	Onio	502	France	Female	42	8	159660.80	3	1	0	113931.57	1
4	15701354	Boni	699	France	Female	39	1	0.00	2	0	0	93826.63	0
5	15737888	Mitchell	850	Spain	Female	43	2	125510.82	1	1	1	79084.10	0

We do not need RowNumber, CustomerId, and Surname columns in our dataset since they do not help to predict if a customer will churn or not. To remove these columns, you can use the `drop()` method, as shown below:

Script 3:

```
1.  #removing unnecessary columns
2.  churn_df = churn_df.drop(['RowNumber', 'CustomerId',
    'Surname'], axis=1)
```

6.1.1 Dividing Data into Features and Labels

As shown in regression, the next step in classification is to divide the data into features and labels. The features set, i.e., X, in the following script contains all the columns except the Exited column. On the other hand, the label set, i.e., y, contains values from the Exited column only.

Script 4:

```
1.  #creating feature set
2.  X = churn_df.drop(['Exited'], axis=1)
3.
4.  #creating label set
5.  y = churn_df['Exited']
```

The following script prints the first five rows of the features set.

Script 5:

```
1.  #printing feature set
2.  X.head()
```

Output:

	CreditScore	Geography	Gender	Age	Tenure	Balance	NumOfProducts	HasCrCard	IsActiveMember	EstimatedSalary
0	619	France	Female	42	2	0.00	1	1	1	101348.88
1	608	Spain	Female	41	1	83807.86	1	0	1	112542.58
2	502	France	Female	42	8	159660.80	3	1	0	113931.57
3	699	France	Female	39	1	0.00	2	0	0	93826.63
4	850	Spain	Female	43	2	125510.82	1	1	1	79084.10

And the following script prints the first five rows of the labels set, as shown below:

Script 6:

```
1.  #printing label set
2.  y.head()
```

Output:

```
0    1
1    0
2    1
3    0
4    0
Name: Exited, dtype: int64
```

6.1.2 Converting Categorical Data to Numbers

In section 5.1.2, you saw that we converted categorical columns to numerical because the machine learning algorithms in the Sklearn library only work with numbers.

For a classification problem, too, we need to convert categorical columns to numerical ones.

The first step is to create a dataframe containing only numeric values. You can do so by dropping categorical columns and creating a new dataframe.

Script 7:

```
1.  #dropping categorical columns
2.  numerical = X.drop(['Geography', 'Gender'], axis= 1)
```

The following script prints the dataframe that contains numeric columns only.

Script 8:

```
1.  #printing numerical columns only
2.  numerical.head()
```

Output:

	CreditScore	Age	Tenure	Balance	NumOfProducts	HasCrCard	IsActiveMember	EstimatedSalary
0	619	42	2	0.00	1	1	1	101348.88
1	608	41	1	83807.86	1	0	1	112542.58
2	502	42	8	159660.80	3	1	0	113931.57
3	699	39	1	0.00	2	0	0	93826.63
4	850	43	2	125510.82	1	1	1	79084.10

Next, create a dataframe that contains categorical values only. You can do so by using the `filter()` function, as shown below:

Script 9:

```
1. #filtering categorical columns
2. categorical = X.filter(['Geography', 'Gender'])
3. categorical.head()
```

The output shows that there are two categorical columns: Geography and Gender in our dataset.

Output:

	Geography	Gender
0	France	Female
1	Spain	Female
2	France	Female
3	France	Female
4	Spain	Female

In the previous chapter, you saw how to use the one-hot encoding approach in order to convert categorical features to numeric one. Here, we will use the same approach.

The following script converts categorical columns into one-hot encoded columns using the `pd.get_dummies()` method.

Script 10:

```
1. #converting categorical columns to one hot encoded columns
2. import pandas as pd
3. cat_numerical = pd.get_dummies(categorical,drop_first=True)
4. cat_numerical.head()
```

Output:

	Geography_Germany	Geography_Spain	Gender_Male
0	0	0	0
1	0	1	0
2	0	0	0
3	0	0	0
4	0	1	0

The last and final step is to join or concatenate the numeric columns and one-hot encoded categorical columns. To do so, you can use the `concat` function from the Pandas library, as shown here:

Script 11:

```
1. #concating numerical columns with one-hot encoded columns
2. X = pd.concat([numerical, cat_numerical], axis =1)
3. X.head()
```

The final dataset containing all the values in numeric form is shown below:

Output:

	CreditScore	Age	Tenure	Balance	NumOfProducts	HasCrCard	IsActiveMember	EstimatedSalary	Geography_Germany	Geography_Spain	Gender_Male
0	619	42	2	0.00	1	1	1	101348.88	0	0	0
1	608	41	1	83807.86	1	0	1	112542.58	0	1	0
2	502	42	8	159660.80	3	1	0	113931.57	0	0	0
3	699	39	1	0.00	2	0	0	93826.63	0	0	0
4	850	43	2	125510.82	1	1	1	79084.10	0	1	0

6.1.3 Divide Data into Training and Test Sets

After a machine learning algorithm has been trained, it needs to be evaluated to see how well it performs on unseen data. Like regression, in classification problems, too, we divide the dataset into two sets, i.e., train set and test set. The dataset is trained via the train set and evaluated on the test set. To split the data into training and test sets, you can use the `train_test_split()` function from the Sklearn library, as shown below. The following script divides the data into 80 percent train set and 20 percent test set.

Script 12:

```
1.  #dividing data into the training and test sets
2.  from sklearn.model_selection import train_test_split
3.
4.  X_train, X_test, y_train, y_test = train_test_split(X, y,
    test_size=0.20, random_state=0)
```

6.1.4 Data Scaling/Normalization

The last step (optional) before the data is passed to the machine learning algorithms is to scale the data. You can see that some columns of the dataset contain small values while the others contain very large values. It is better to convert all values to a uniform scale. To do so, you can use the `StandardScaler()` function from the `sklearn.preprocessing` module, as shown below:

Script 13:

```
1.  #applying standard scaling to the dataset
2.  from sklearn.preprocessing import StandardScaler
3.  sc = StandardScaler()
4.  X_train = sc.fit_transform(X_train)
5.  X_test = sc.transform (X_test)
```

We have converted data into a format that can be used to train machine learning algorithms for classification from the Sklearn library. Details, including functionalities and usage of all the machine learning algorithms, are available at this link. You can check all the classification algorithms by going to that link.

In the following section, we will review some of the most commonly used classification algorithms for binary, multiclass, and multilabel classification.

6.2 Solving Binary Classification Problems

Binary classification problems are those classification problems where there are only two possible values for the output label. For example, predicting whether a tumor is benign or malignant, whether a student will pass or fail, whether a customer will leave the bank after a certain period or not. In this section, you will see some of the most commonly used algorithms for binary classification.

6.2.1 Logistic Regression

Logistic regression is a linear model, which makes classification by passing the output of linear regression through a sigmoid function. The pros and cons of logistic regression algorithms are the same as linear regression algorithms explained already in chapter 5, section 5.2.1.

To implement the logistic regression with Sklearn, you can use the `LogisticRegression` class from the `sklearn.linear_model` module. To train the algorithm, the training and test sets, i.e., `X_train` and `X_test` in our case, are passed to the fit() method of the object of the `LogisticRegression` class.

To make predictions, the test set is passed to the `predict()` method of the class. The process of training and making predictions with the linear regression algorithm is as follows:

Script 14:

```
1.  #importing logistic regression classifier from sklearn
2.  from sklearn.linear_model import LogisticRegression
3.
4.  log_clf = LogisticRegression()
5.
6.  #training the logistic regression classifier
7.  classifier = log_clf.fit(X_train, y_train)
8.
9.  #making predictions on the test set
10. y_pred = classifier.predict(X_test)
```

Once you have trained a model and have made predictions on the test set, the next step is to know how well your model has performed for making predictions on the unknown test set. There are various metrics to evaluate a classification method. Some of the most commonly used classification metrics are F1, recall, precision, accuracy, and confusion matrix. Before you see the equations for these terms, you need to understand the concept of true positive, true negative, and false positive, and false negative outputs:

True Negatives: (TN/tn): True negatives are those output labels that are actually false, and the model also predicted them as false.

True Positive: True positives are those labels that are actually true and also predicted as true by the model.

False Negative: False negatives are labels that are actually true but predicted as false by machine learning models.

False Positive: Labels that are actually false but predicted as true by the model are called false positive.

One way to analyze the results of a classification algorithm is by plotting a confusion matrix, such as the one shown below:

§ Confusion Matrix

		Predicted Class	
	Total Population n = a number	False (0)	True (1)
Actual Class	False (0)	TN True Negative	FP False Positive
	True (1)	FN False Negative	TP True Positive

§ Precision

Another way to analyze a classification algorithm is by calculating precision, which is basically obtained by dividing true positives by the sum of true positive and false positive, as shown below:

$$\text{Precision} = \frac{tp}{tp + fp}$$

§ Recall

Recall is calculated by dividing true positives by the sum of true positive and false negative, as shown below:

$$\text{Recall} = \frac{tp}{tp + fn}$$

§ F1 Measure

F1 measure is simply the harmonic mean of precision and recall and is calculated as follows:

$$F_1 = \left(\frac{2}{\text{recall}^{-1} + \text{precision}^{-1}} \right) = 2 \cdot \frac{\text{precision} \cdot \text{recall}}{\text{precision} + \text{recall}}$$

§ Accuracy

Accuracy refers to the number of correctly predicted labels divided by the total number of observations in a dataset.

$$\text{Accuracy} = \frac{tp + tn}{tp + tn + fp + fn}$$

The choice of using a metric for classification problems depends totally upon you. However, as a rule of thumb, in the case of balanced datasets, i.e., where the number of labels for each class is balanced, accuracy can be used as an evaluation metric. For imbalanced datasets, you can use the F1 measure as the classification metric.

The methods used to find the value for these metrics are available in `sklearn.metrics` class. The predicted and actual values have to be passed to these methods, as shown in the output.

Script 15:

```
1.  #evaluating the algorithm on test set
2.  from sklearn.metrics import classification_report, confusion_matrix, accuracy_score
3.
4.  print(confusion_matrix(y_test,y_pred))
5.  print(classification_report(y_test,y_pred))
6.  print(accuracy_score(y_test, y_pred))
```

Output:

```
[[1526   69]
 [ 309   96]]
              precision    recall  f1-score   support

           0       0.83      0.96      0.89      1595
           1       0.58      0.24      0.34       405
    accuracy                           0.81      2000
   macro avg       0.71      0.60      0.61      2000
weighted avg       0.78      0.81      0.78      2000

0.811
```

The output shows that for 81 percent of the records in the test set, logistic regression correctly predicted whether or not a customer will leave the bank.

Further Readings – Logistic Regression
To study more about logistic regression, please check these links: 1. https://bit.ly/3mjFV76 2. https://bit.ly/2FvcU7B

6.2.2 KNN Classifier

As discussed in section 5.2 of the Chapter 5, KNN stands for K-nearest neighbors. KNN is a lazy learning algorithm, which is based on finding the Euclidean distance between different data points.

The pros and cons of the KNN classifier algorithm are the same as the KNN regression algorithm, which has been explained already in chapter 5, section 5.2.2.

KNN algorithm can be used both for classification and regression. With Sklearn, it is extremely easy to implement KNN classification. To do so, you can use the KNeighborsClassifiers class. The process of training and testing is the same as linear regression. For training, you need to call the fit() method, and for testing, you need to call the predict() method.

The following script shows the process of training, testing, and evaluating the KNN classification algorithm for predicting the values for the *tip* column from the Tips dataset.

Script 16:

```
1.  #importing KNN classifier from sklearn
2.  from sklearn.neighbors import KNeighborsClassifier
3.  knn_clf = KNeighborsClassifier(n_neighbors=5)
4.
5.  #training the KNN classifier
6.  classifier = knn_clf.fit(X_train, y_train)
7.
8.  #making predictions on the test set
9.  y_pred = classifier.predict(X_test)
10.
11. #evaluating the algorithm on test set
12. from sklearn.metrics import classification_report, confusion_matrix, accuracy_score
13.
14. print(confusion_matrix(y_test,y_pred))
15. print(classification_report(y_test,y_pred))
16. print(accuracy_score(y_test, y_pred))
```

Output:

```
[[1486  109]
 [ 237  168]]
              precision    recall  f1-score   support

           0       0.86      0.93      0.90      1595
           1       0.61      0.41      0.49       405
    accuracy                           0.83      2000
   macro avg       0.73      0.67      0.69      2000
weighted avg       0.81      0.83      0.81      2000

0.827
```

> **Further Readings – KNN Classification**
>
> To study more about KNN classification, please check these links:
>
> 1. https://bit.ly/33pXWIj
> 2. https://bit.ly/2FqNmZx

6.2.3 Random Forest Classifier

Like a random forest regressor, a random forest classifier is a tree-based algorithm, which converts features into tree nodes and then uses entropy loss to make classification predictions.

The pros and cons of the random forest classifier algorithm are the same as the random forest regression algorithm, which has been explained already in chapter 5, section 5.2.3.

The `RandomForestClassifier` class from the `Sklearn.ensemble` module can be used to implement the random forest regressor algorithm in Python, as shown below.

Script 17:

```
1.  #importing random forest classifier from sklearn
2.  from sklearn.ensemble import RandomForestClassifier
3.  rf_clf = RandomForestClassifier(random_state=42,n_
    estimators=500)
4.
5.  #training the random forest classifier
6.  classifier = rf_clf.fit(X_train, y_train)
7.
8.  #making predictions on the test set
9.  y_pred = classifier.predict(X_test)
10.
11.
12. #evaluating the algorithm on test set
13. from sklearn.metrics import classification_report,
    confusion_matrix, accuracy_score
14.
15. print(confusion_matrix(y_test,y_pred))
16. print(classification_report(y_test,y_pred))
17. print(accuracy_score(y_test, y_pred))
```

Output:

```
[[1521   74]
 [ 196  209]]
              precision    recall  f1-score   support

           0       0.89      0.95      0.92      1595
           1       0.74      0.52      0.61       405
    accuracy                           0.86
2000
   macro avg       0.81      0.73      0.76
2000
weighted avg       0.86      0.86      0.86
2000

0.865
```

> **Further Readings – Random Forest Classification**
>
> To study more about random forest classification, please check these links:
> 1. https://bit.ly/2V1G0k0
> 2. https://bit.ly/2GTyqDH

6.2.4 K-Fold Cross-validation

You can also perform K-fold cross-validation for classification models, just like regression models. You can use `cross_val_score()` function from the `sklearn.model_selection` module to perform cross-validation, as shown below. For the classification algorithm, you need to pass a classification metric, e.g., accuracy, to the `scoring` attribute. Further details of K-Fold cross-validation are presented in chapter 9.

Script 18:

```
1. #importing cross-validation model from the sklearn
2. from sklearn.model_selection import cross_val_score
3.
4. #applying 5 fold cross-validation
5. print(cross_val_score(classifier, X, y, cv=5, scoring
   ="accuracy"))
```

Output:

```
[0.796  0.796  0.7965 0.7965 0.7965]
```

6.2.5 Predicting a Single Value

Let's make a prediction on a single customer record and see if he will leave the bank after six months or not. The following script prints details of the 100th record.

Script 19:

```
1.  #printing information about the 101th record in the
    dataset
2.  churn_df.loc[100]
```

Output:

```
CreditScore             665
Geography               France
Gender                  Female
Age                     40
Tenure                  6
Balance                 0
NumOfProducts           1
HasCrCard               1
IsActiveMember          1
EstimatedSalary         161848
Exited                  0
Name: 100, dtype: object
```

The output above shows that the customer did not exit the bank after six months since the value for the Exited attribute is 0. Let's see what our classification model predicts:

Script 20:

```
1.  # importing random forest classifier from sklearn
2.  from sklearn.ensemble import RandomForestClassifier
3.  rf_clf = RandomForestClassifier(random_state=42,n_
    estimators=500)
4.
5.  #training the algorithm on the training set
6.  classifier = rf_clf.fit(X_train, y_train)
7.
8.  # scaling single record
9.  single_record = sc.transform (X.values[100].reshape(1,
    -1))
10.
11. #making predictions on the 101st record from thedataset
12. predicted_churn = classifier.predict(single_record)
13. print(predicted_churn)
```

The output is 0, which shows that our model correctly predicted that the customer will not churn after six months.

Output:

```
[0]
```

6.3 Solving Multiclass Classification Problems

In the previous section, you studied how to solve binary classification problems. In this section, you will see how to solve multiclass classification problems. Multiclass classification problems are classification problems in which there are three or more possible classes for the output.

However, at a time, one record can belong to only one class. An example of a multiclass classification is sentiment classification, where the sentiment of a tweet or text can be positive, negative, or neutral.

In this section, you will see how to solve multiclass classification problems.

The first step is to create a dummy dataset where there are three or more classes in the output. To do so, you can use the `make_classification()` method from the `datasets` module of the Sklearn library.

The following script creates a dummy dataset with 2,000 records and 12 features. The number of output classes is four. One record can belong to one of these four classes. The script also prints the shape of the features (X) and labels (y).

Script 21:

```
1.  # example of multiclass classification problem
2.
3.  from sklearn.datasets import make_classification
4.
5.  # create dummy dataset
6.  X, y = make_classification(n_samples=2000, n_features=12,
    n_informative=8, n_redundant=4, n_classes=4, random_
    state=42)
7.
8.  # print dataset shape
9.  print(X.shape, y.shape)
```

Output:

```
(2000, 12) (2000,)
```

Let's print the number of unique labels. Run the following script.

Script 22:

```
1.  np.unique(y)
```

The output below shows that there are four unique labels in the output corresponding to four output classes.

Output:

```
array([0, 1, 2, 3])
```

Before we train our algorithms, let's divide the dataset into training and test sets and apply feature scaling on the dataset.

Script 23:

```
1.  #dividing data into training and test sets
2.  from sklearn.model_selection import train_test_split
3.
4.  X_train, X_test, y_train, y_test = train_test_split(X, y,
    test_size=0.20, random_state=0)
5.
6.  # feature scaling using standard scaler
7.  from sklearn.preprocessing import StandardScaler
8.  sc = StandardScaler()
9.  X_train = sc.fit_transform(X_train)
10. X_test = sc.transform (X_test)
```

There are three possibilities to solve multiclass classification problems with Scikit-learn. Some of the classification algorithms, such as the Random Forest Classifier, can by default solve a multiclass classification problem. The other option is to use one-vs-rest classification or one-vs-one classification.

Let's first see the first technique. The following script uses a random forest classifier for multiclass classification. You can see that no change has been made in the script that you used for binary classification.

Script 24:

```
1.  #importing random forest classifier from sklearn
2.  from sklearn.ensemble import RandomForestClassifier
3.  rf_clf = RandomForestClassifier(random_state=42,n_
    estimators=500)
4.
5.  #training the random forest classifier
6.  classifier = rf_clf.fit(X_train, y_train)
7.
8.  #making predictions on the test set
9.  y_pred = classifier.predict(X_test)
10.
11.
12. #evaluating the algorithm on test set
```

```
13. from sklearn.metrics import classification_report,
    confusion_matrix, accuracy_score
14.
15. print(confusion_matrix(y_test,y_pred))
16. print(classification_report(y_test,y_pred))
17. print(accuracy_score(y_test, y_pred))
```

Output:

```
[[74  7  6  4]
 [ 5 92  8  4]
 [ 5  7 82 14]
 [11  3  6 72]]
              precision    recall  f1-score   support

           0       0.78      0.81      0.80        91
           1       0.84      0.84      0.84       109
           2       0.80      0.76      0.78       108
           3       0.77      0.78      0.77        92
    accuracy                           0.80       400
   macro avg       0.80      0.80      0.80       400
weighted avg       0.80      0.80      0.80       400

0.8
```

6.3.1 One-vs-Rest for Multiclass Classification

In the One-vs-Rest classifier, you split the multiclass classification problem into N number of binary classification problems where N is the number of output classes.

For instance, if there are three possible output classes A, B, and C, a binary classification algorithm is trained, which makes predictions between A and the rest of the classes. Another binary classification is made between B and other classes, and so on. In the end, the algorithm with the highest prediction confidence is selected.

You can implement one vs. rest classifier using the Scikit-learn library. To do so, you can use the `OneVsRestClassifier` class from the `multiclass` module. The base algorithm that you want to train multiple binary classification algorithms is passed as a parameter value to the constructor of the OneVsRestClassifier class. For instance, the following script uses the logistic regression algorithm as a base classifier to make multiclass classification using the `OneVsRestClassifier` class. The process is straightforward. The training data is passed to the `fit()` method of the `OneVsRestClassifier` class. To make predictions, you can use the `predict()` method.

Script 25:

```
1.  # import one vs. rest and logistic regression model from sklearn
2.  from sklearn.multiclass import OneVsRestClassifier
3.  from sklearn.linear_model import LogisticRegression
4.
5.  log_clf = LogisticRegression()
6.
7.  # define the ovr strategy
8.  clf = OneVsRestClassifier(log_clf)
9.
10. #training the logistic regression classifier
11. classifier = clf.fit(X_train, y_train)
12.
13. #making predictions on the test set
14. y_pred = classifier.predict(X_test)
15.
16. #evaluating the algorithm on test set
17. from sklearn.metrics import classification_report, confusion_matrix, accuracy_score
18.
19. print(confusion_matrix(y_test,y_pred))
20. print(classification_report(y_test,y_pred))
21. print(accuracy_score(y_test, y_pred))
```

Output:

```
[[58 11 15  7]
 [ 9 71  9 20]
 [ 9 23 53 23]
 [17 11 11 53]]
              precision    recall  f1-score   support

           0       0.62      0.64      0.63        91
           1       0.61      0.65      0.63       109
           2       0.60      0.49      0.54       108
           3       0.51      0.58      0.54        92
    accuracy                           0.59       400
   macro avg       0.59      0.59      0.59       400
weighted avg       0.59      0.59      0.59       400

0.5875
```

6.3.2 One-vs-One for Multiclass Classification

In one-vs-one classification, a model is trained, which makes a binary classification between each pair of classes. The class with the highest number of classifications is selected on the basis of voting and is labeled as the final predicted output class. For example, if you have four output classes, y1, y2, y3, and y4, the following binary classification models will be trained:

- Models that classify y1 and y2
- Model that classifies y1 and y3
- Model that classifies y1 and y4
- Model that classified y2 and y3
- Model that classifies y2 and y4
- Model that classifies y3 and y4

If the number of output classes is n, then the number of binary classification models is given by the following formula:

$$No.\ of\ Binary\ Classifiers = \frac{(n-1)}{2}$$

Scikit-learn library contains a class OneVsOneClassifier in the multiclass module. Like OneVsRestClassifier, you need to pass the base model to the OneVsOneClassifier, which trains multiple binary classification models on the training set. Look at the following script for reference.

Script 26:

```
1.  # import one vs. one and logistic regression model from sklearn
2.  from sklearn.multiclass import OneVsOneClassifier
3.  from sklearn.linear_model import LogisticRegression
4.
5.  log_clf = LogisticRegression()
6.
7.  # define the ovr strategy
8.  clf = OneVsOneClassifier(log_clf)
9.
10. #training the logistic regression classifier
11. classifier = clf.fit(X_train, y_train)
12.
13. #making predictions on the test set
14. y_pred = classifier.predict(X_test)
15.
16. #evaluating the algorithm on test set
17. from sklearn.metrics import classification_report, confusion_matrix, accuracy_score
18.
19. print(confusion_matrix(y_test,y_pred))
20. print(classification_report(y_test,y_pred))
21. print(accuracy_score(y_test, y_pred))
```

Output:

```
[[59  8 15  9]
 [ 8 75 10 16]
 [ 6 23 54 25]
 [ 9  8 10 65]]
              precision    recall  f1-score   support

           0       0.72      0.65      0.68        91
           1       0.66      0.69      0.67       109
           2       0.61      0.50      0.55       108
           3       0.57      0.71      0.63        92
    accuracy                           0.63       400
   macro avg       0.64      0.64      0.63       400
weighted avg       0.64      0.63      0.63       400

0.6325
```

6.4 Solving Multilabel Classification Problems

Multilabel classification is a type of multiclass classification. However, in multilabel classification, one record can belong to more than one output class.

For instance, a text comment on a social media platform can be labeled as abusive, spam, and threatening at the same time, which means that the comment may belong to multiple classes at the same time. Such a type of classification is called multilabel classification.

Let's first create a dummy multilabel dataset. You can use the `make_multilabel_classifcation` method from the `datasets` module of the Sklearn library to create a dummy multilabel dataset. The following script creates a dummy multilabel classification dataset, which contains 2,000 records, 10 features, and 5 classes.

Script 27:

```
1.  # example of multiclass classification problem
2.
3.  from sklearn.datasets import make_multilabel_classification
4.
5.  # create dummy dataset
6.  X, y = make_multilabel_classification(n_samples=2000, n_
    features=10, n_classes=5, n_labels=3, random_state=42)
7.
8.  # print dataset shape
9.  print(X.shape, y.shape)
```

Output:

```
(2000, 10) (2000, 5)
```

Let's print one of the output labels and see what it contains.

Script 28:

```
1.  y[200]
```

The output for the record at index 200 shows that there can be three possible output classes for the record, as marked by digit 1 at three different indexes belonging to different classes.

Output:

```
array([0, 1, 0, 1, 1])
```

The following script divides the dummy data into the training and test sets and also applies feature scaling on the dataset.

Script 29:

```
1.  #dividing data into training and test sets
2.  from sklearn.model_selection import train_test_split
3.
4.  X_train, X_test, y_train, y_test = train_test_split(X, y,
    test_size=0.20, random_state=0)
5.
6.  # feature scaling using standard scaler
7.  from sklearn.preprocessing import StandardScaler
8.  sc = StandardScaler()
9.  X_train = sc.fit_transform(X_train)
10. X_test = sc.transform (X_test)
```

Like multiclass classification, you can use some algorithms by default for multilabel classification. For example, the random forest classifier can be used as it is without any modification for multilabel classification, as shown in the following script.

Script 30:

```
1.  #importing random forest classifier from sklearn
2.  from sklearn.ensemble import RandomForestClassifier
3.  rf_clf = RandomForestClassifier(random_state=42,n_
    estimators=500)
4.
5.  #training the random forest classifier
6.  classifier = rf_clf.fit(X_train, y_train)
7.
8.  #making predictions on the test set
9.  y_pred = classifier.predict(X_test)
10.
11.
12. #evaluating the algorithm on test set
13. from sklearn.metrics import classification_report,
    confusion_matrix, accuracy_score
14.
15. print(classification_report(y_test,y_pred))
16. print(accuracy_score(y_test, y_pred))
```

Output:

```
precision    recall  f1-score   support

0              0.78      0.75      0.77       189
1              0.87      0.94      0.90       294
2              0.81      0.93      0.87       239
3              0.73      0.90      0.81       230
4              0.73      0.36      0.48       100
micro avg      0.80      0.84      0.82      1052
macro avg      0.79      0.78      0.77      1052
weighted avg   0.80      0.84      0.81      1052
samples avg    0.82      0.83      0.80      1052

0.37
```

Apart from default algorithms, you can use one vs. rest classifier for multilabel classification, as well. The final prediction is calculated as a result of the union of individual one vs. the rest binary classifiers. The following script uses logistic regression as the base algorithm to perform multilabel classification using the one vs. the rest classifier.

Script 31:

```
1.  # imoport one vs. rest and logistic regression model from
    sklearn
2.  from sklearn.multiclass import OneVsRestClassifier
3.  from sklearn.linear_model import LogisticRegression
4.
5.  log_clf = LogisticRegression()
6.
7.  # define the ovr strategy
8.  clf = OneVsRestClassifier(log_clf)
9.
10. #training the logistic regression classifier
11. classifier = clf.fit(X_train, y_train)
12.
```

```
13. #making predictions on the test set
14. y_pred = classifier.predict(X_test)
15.
16. #evaluating the algorithm on test set
17. from sklearn.metrics import classification_report,
    confusion_matrix, accuracy_score
18.
19. print(classification_report(y_test,y_pred))
20. print(accuracy_score(y_test, y_pred))
```

Output:

```
precision     recall   f1-score    support

0         0.76      0.77     0.77       189
1         0.88      0.90     0.89       294
2         0.78      0.86     0.82       239
3         0.71      0.81     0.75       230
4         0.71      0.37     0.49       100
micro avg        0.78     0.80     0.79      1052
macro avg        0.77     0.74     0.74      1052
weighted avg     0.78     0.80     0.78      1052
samples avg      0.79     0.81     0.76      1052

0.2725
```

> **Hands-on Time – Exercise**
>
> Now, it is your turn. Follow the instructions in **the exercises below** to check your understanding of the about classification algorithms in machine learning. The answers to these questions are given at the end of the book.

Exercise 6.1

Question 1

Which of the following is not an example of classification outputs?

A. True
B. Red
C. Male
D. None of the above

Question 2

Which of the following metrics is used for unbalanced classification datasets?

A. Accuracy
B. F1
C. Precision
D. Recall

Question 3

Which one of the following functions is used to convert categorical values to one-hot encoded numerical values?

A. pd.get_onehot()
B. pd.get_dummies()
C. pd.get_numeric()
D. All of the above

Exercise 6.2

Using the `iris` dataset from the Seaborn library, train a classification algorithm of your choice, which predicts the specie of the iris plant. Perform all the preprocessing steps.

7

Clustering Data with Scikit-Learn Library

In chapters 5 and 6, you studied how to solve regression and classification problems, respectively, using machine learning algorithms in Sklearn. Regression and Classification are types of supervised machine learning problems. In this chapter, you are going to study data clustering algorithms.

Clustering algorithms are unsupervised algorithms where the training data is not labeled. Rather, the algorithms cluster or group the data sets based on common characteristics. In this chapter, you will study two of the most common types of clustering algorithms:

1. K-Means Clustering
2. Hierarchical Clustering.

You will see how Python's Sklearn library can be used to implement the two clustering algorithms. So, let's begin without much ado.

7.1 K-Means Clustering

K-Means clustering is one of the most commonly used algorithms for clustering unlabeled data. In K-Means Clustering,

K refers to the number of clusters that you want your data to be grouped into. In K-Means clustering, the number of clusters has to be defined before K clustering can be applied to the data points.

Steps for K-Means Clustering

The following are the steps that are needed to be performed in order to perform K-Means clustering of data points.

1. Randomly assign centroid values for each cluster.
2. Calculate the distance (Euclidean or Manhattan) between each data point and centroid values of all the clusters.
3. Assign the data point to the cluster of the centroid with the shortest distance.
4. Calculate and update centroid values based on the mean values of the coordinates of all the data points of the corresponding cluster.
5. Repeat steps 2–4 until new centroid values for all the clusters are different from the previous centroid values.

Why Use K-Means Clustering?

K-Means clustering is particularly useful when:

1. K-Means clustering is a simple to implement algorithm
2. Can be applied to large datasets
3. Scales well to unseen data points
4. Generalizes well to clusters of various sizes and shapes.

Disadvantages of K-Means Clustering Algorithm

The following are some of the disadvantages of the K- Means clustering algorithm:

1. The value of K has to be chosen manually.
2. Convergence or training time depends on the initial value of K
3. Clustering performance is affected greatly by outliers.

Enough of theory. Let's see how to perform K-Means clustering with Scikit-learn. You will see two examples of K-Means clustering in this chapter. You will first see how to apply K-Means clustering to group dummy datasets. Next, you will see how K-Means clustering can be used to solve a real-world problem where you will identify customers who are more likely to spend money on shopping items in a mall.

Let's first see how to cluster dummy data using the K-Means clustering.

7.1.1 Clustering Dummy Data with K-Means Clustering

The first step is importing the required libraries, as shown in the following script:

Script 1:

```
1. import numpy as np
2. import pandas as pd
3. from sklearn.datasets.samples_generator import make_blobs
4. from sklearn.cluster import KMeans
5. from matplotlib import pyplot as plt
6. %matplotlib inline
```

Next, we create a dummy dataset containing 500 records and 4 cluster centers. The average standard deviation between the records is 2.0.

The following script creates a dummy dataset and plots data points on a plot.

Script 2:

```
1.  # generating dummy data of 500 records with 4 clusters
2.  features, labels = make_blobs(n_samples=500, centers=4,
    cluster_std = 2.00)
3.
4.  #plotting the dummy data
5.  plt.scatter(features[:,0], features[:,1] )
```

The output looks like this. Using K-Means clustering, you will see how you can create four clusters in this dataset.

Output:

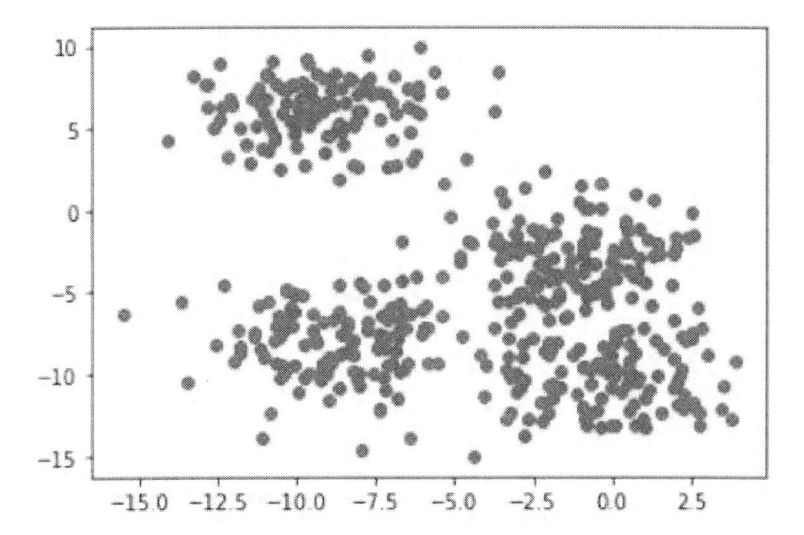

Note: It is important to mention that dummy data is generated randomly, and, hence, you can have a slightly different plot than the one in the above figure.

To implement K-Means clustering, you can use the K-Means class from the sklearn.cluster module. You have to pass the number of clusters as an attribute to the K-Means class constructor. To train the K-Means model, simply pass the dataset to the fit() method of the K-Means class, as shown below.

Script 3:

```
1.  # performing kmeans clustering using KMeans class
2.  km_model = KMeans(n_clusters=4)
3.  km_model.fit(features)
```

Once the model is trained, you can print the cluster centers using the `cluster_centers_` attribute of the `K-Means` class object.

Script 4:

```
1.  #printing centroid values
2.  print(km_model.cluster_centers_)
```

The four cluster centers, as predicted by our K-Means model, have the following coordinates.

Output:

```
[[ -1.43956092  -2.89493362]
 [ -8.7477121   -8.06593055]
 [ -9.25770944   6.1927544 ]
 [ -0.21911049 -10.22506455]]
```

In addition to finding cluster centers, the `K-Means` class also assigns a cluster label to each data point. The cluster labels are numbers that basically serve as cluster id. For instance, in the case of the four clusters, the cluster ids are 0,1,2, and 3.

To print the cluster ids for all the labels, you can use the `labels_` attribute of the `K-Means` class, as shown below.

Script 5:

```
1.  #printing predicted label values
2.  print(km_model.labels_)
```

Output:

```
[2 0 3 1 3 2 2 3 0 1 0 3 2 1 2 1 3 1 3 2 2 3 3
 1 2 3 3 2 3 2 0 2 2 0 3 1 2 2
 1 2 3 1 2 2 2 3 0 0 0 0 3 3 3 3 2 1 1 3 2 2
 0 0 1 1 1 1 1 3 3 1 0 1 1 1 0
 1 1 1 3 1 3 0 0 0 3 3 0 3 0 2 0 3 3 1 2 3 1
 2 0 1 3 0 0 1 2 3 3 3 0 1 2 0
 0 0 1 1 3 1 2 0 0 0 3 1 0 3 0 0 3 3 1 0 3 3
 0 3 1 3 0 3 1 0 3 1 3 3 2 3 2
 1 0 3 3 0 2 1 3 3 3 0 3 2 2 1 2 2 3 0 1 3 1
 1 1 1 0 2 1 2 3 3 1 1 1 0 0 2
 2 2 2 1 0 0 2 2 3 1 0 0 2 2 2 1 0 0 2 2 0 3
 1 0 2 3 1 3 1 0 1 2 0 1 2 2 0
 0 3 2 3 2 2 3 2 3 0 0 0 3 1 0 2 3 1 2 2 3 1
 0 3 0 0 0 1 0 1 3 2 0 0 1 3 1
 3 3 2 0 2 2 0 0 1 0 3 0 3 3 1 0 3 1 1 1 1 1
 0 1 0 1 2 0 3 2 2 0 1 0 2 1 2
 1 2 0 2 1 0 1 3 2 2 2 2 0 1 2 2 2 1 2 1 3 1
 3 2 1 1 3 1 0 0 0 0 3 1 2 2 1
 0 0 1 3 1 3 1 3 2 0 3 0 1 0 2 2 2 0 2 2 0 3
 0 0 2 1 3 2 3 1 0 3 1 2 3 2 3
 0 2 1 0 1 3 1 1 3 2 3 1 1 2 1 0 0 2 2 2 2 1
 3 1 3 1 3 0 0 0 2 1 0 2 2 2 3
 3 0 2 1 0 1 0 2 2 0 2 0 0 1 3 2 0 1 3 0 0 2
 0 1 3 0 0 3 1 1 3 0 3 3 3 0 2
 1 3 2 2 3 3 0 3 2 0 3 0 3 3 3 2 2 1 3 0 2 3
 2 2 1 0 2 0 0 1 0 2 1 2 3 1 3
 1 1 0 2 1 1 1 2 2 0 2 2 0 2 0 0 0 3 0]
```

The following script prints the clusters in different colors along with the cluster centers as black data points, as shown below.

Script 6:

```
1.  #print the data points
2.  plt.scatter(features[:,0], features[:,1], c= km_model.
    labels_, cmap='rainbow' )
3.
4.  #print the centroids
5.  plt.scatter(km_model.cluster_centers_[:, 0], km_model.
    cluster_centers_[:, 1], s=100, c='black')
```

The following output shows the four clusters identified by the K-Means clustering algorithm.

Output:

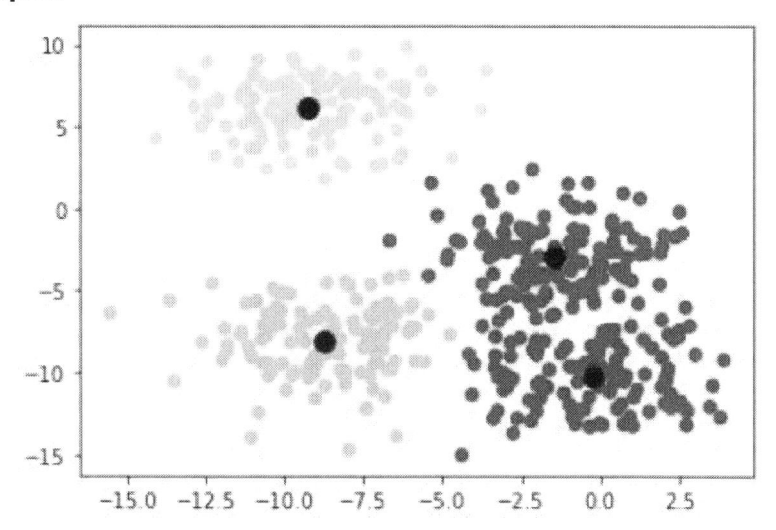

The following script prints the actual four clusters in the dataset.

Script 7:

```
1.  #print actual datapoints
2.  plt.scatter(features[:,0], features[:,1], c= labels,
    cmap='rainbow' )
```

The output shows that in the actual dataset, the clusters represented by red and blue data points slightly overlap. However, the predicted clusters do not contain any overlapping data points.

Output:

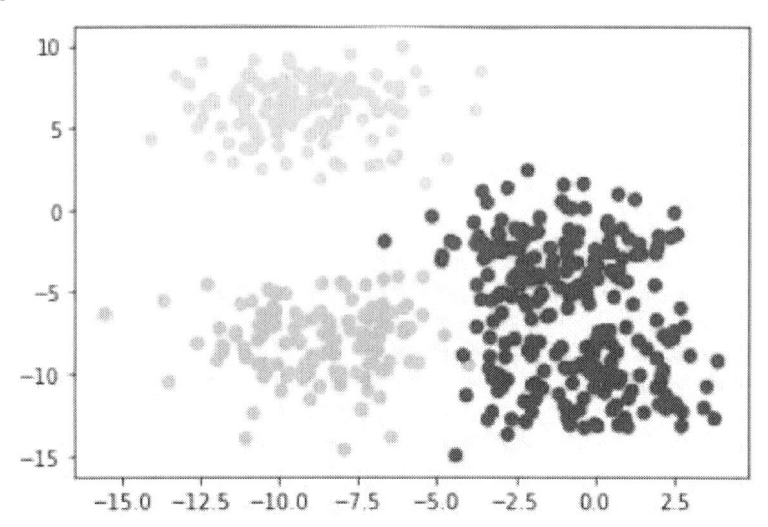

[Scatter plot showing clustered data points ranging from -15.0 to 2.5 on x-axis and -15 to 10 on y-axis]

Note: The color of the clusters doesn't have to be the same since cluster colors are randomly generated at runtime. Only the cluster positions matter.

7.1.2 Customer Segmentation Using K-Means Clustering

In this section, you will use K-Means clustering for customer segmentation. You will see how to segment customers based on their incomes and past spending habits. You will then identify customers who have high incomes and higher spending.

Importing Required Libraries

The first step is importing the required libraries, as shown in the following script:

Script 8:

```
1.  import numpy as np
2.  import pandas as pd
3.  from sklearn.datasets.samples_generator import make_blobs
4.  from sklearn.cluster import KMeans
5.  from matplotlib import pyplot as plt
6.  import seaborn as sns
7.  %matplotlib inline
```

Importing the Dataset

The CSV dataset file for this project is freely available at this link (https://bit.ly/3kxXvCl). The CSV file for the dataset Mall_Customers.csv can also be downloaded from the *Datasets* folder of GitHub and SharePoint repositories.

The following script imports the dataset.

Script 9:

```
1.  #importing the dataset
2.  dataset = pd.read_csv('E:\Datasets\Mall_Customers.csv')
```

The following script prints the first five rows of the dataset.

Script 10:

```
1.  # printing the first five rows of the dataset
2.  dataset.head()
```

The below output shows that the dataset has five columns: CustomerID, Genre, Age, Annual Income (K$), and Spending Score (1-100). The spending score is the score assigned to customers based on their previous spending habits. Customers with higher spending in the past have higher scores.

Output:

	CustomerID	Genre	Age	Annual Income (k$)	Spending Score (1-100)
0	1	Male	19	15	39
1	2	Male	21	15	81
2	3	Female	20	16	6
3	4	Female	23	16	77
4	5	Female	31	17	40

Let's see the shape of the dataset.

Script 11:

```
1.  #printing the number of rows and columns of the dataset
2.  dataset.shape
```

The output below shows that the dataset contains 200 records and 5 columns.

Output

```
(200, 5)
```

Data Analysis

Before we do actual customer segmentation, let's briefly analyze the dataset. Let's plot a histogram showing the annual income of the customers.

Script 12:

```
1.  # plotting the histogram for the annual income column
2.  sns.distplot(dataset['Annual Income (k$)'], kde=False,
    bins = 50)
```

The output shows that most of the customers have incomes between 60 and 90K per year.

Output:

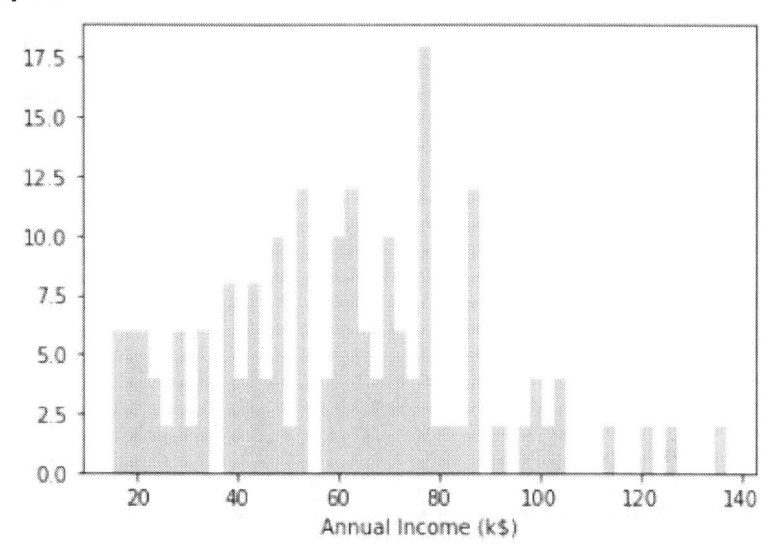

Similarly, we can plot a histogram for the spending scores of the customers, as well.

Script 13:

```
1.  # plotting the histogram for the spending score colummn in
    red color with 50 bins
2.  sns.distplot(dataset['Spending Score (1-100)'], kde=False,
    bins = 50, color = "red")
```

The output shows that most of the customers have a spending score between 40 and 60.

Output:

[Histogram of Spending Score (1-100)]

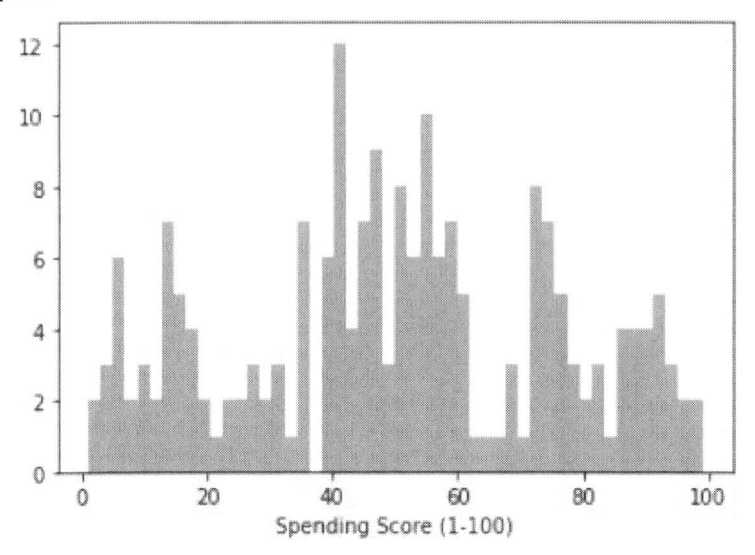

We can also plot a regression line between annual income and spending score to see if there is any linear relationship between the two or not.

Script 14:

```
1.  # plotting regression plot for annual income against
    spending score
2.  sns.regplot(x="Annual Income (k$)", y="Spending Score (1-
    100)", data=dataset)
```

From the straight line in the below output, you can infer that there is no linear relationship between annual income and spending.

Output:

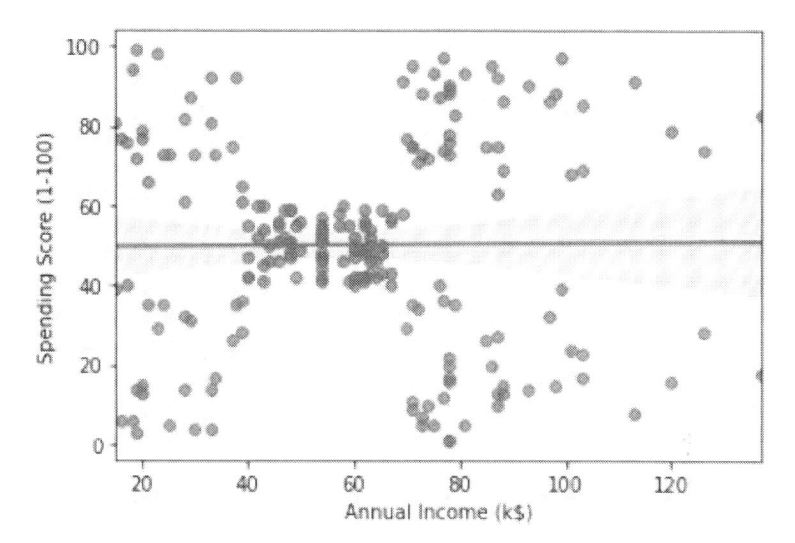

Finally, you can also plot a linear regression line between the age column and the spending score.

Script 15:

```
1.  # plotting regression plot for age against spending score
2.  sns.regplot(x="Age", y="Spending Score (1-100)",
    data=dataset);
```

The output confirms an inverse linear relationship between age and spending score. It can be inferred from the output that young people have higher spending compared to older people.

Output:

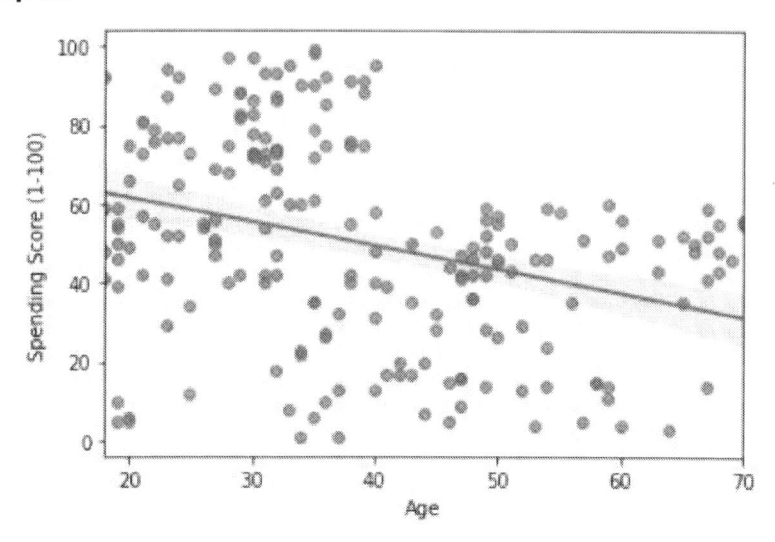

Enough of the data analysis. We are now ready to perform customer segmentation on our data using the K-Means algorithm.

Performing K-Means Clustering

We want to perform K-Means clustering based on the annual income and spending score columns because we want to target a customer base with high income and high spending scores. Therefore, we will filter these two columns, and we will remove the remaining columns from our dataset. Here is the script to do so:

Script 16:

```
1.  # filtering annual income and spending score columns and
    removing remaining columns
2.  dataset = dataset.filter(["Annual Income (k$)", "Spending
    Score (1-100)" ], axis = 1)
3.
4.  #printingt he first five rows of the filtered dataset
5.  dataset.head()
```

The output shows that we now have only annual income and spending score columns in our dataset.

Output:

	Annual Income (k$)	Spending Score (1-100)
0	15	39
1	15	81
2	16	6
3	16	77
4	17	40

To implement K-Means clustering, you can use the K-Means class from the sklearn.cluster module of the Sklearn library. You have to pass the number of clusters as an attribute to the K-Means class constructor. To train the K-Means model, simply pass the dataset to the fit() method of the K-Means class, as shown below.

Script 17:

```
1. # performing kmeans clustering using KMeans class
2. km_model = KMeans(n_clusters=4)
3. km_model.fit(dataset)
```

Output

```
KMeans(n_clusters=4)
```

Once the model is trained, you can print the cluster centers using the cluster_centers_ attribute of the K-Means class object.

Script 18:

```
1. #printing centroid values
2. print(km_model.cluster_centers_)
```

The four cluster centers, as predicted by our K-Means model, has the following values:

Output

```
[[86.53846154 82.12820513]
 [48.26 56.48    ]
 [26.30434783 20.91304348]
 [87.   18.63157895]]
```

In addition to finding cluster centers, the K-Means class also assigns a cluster label to each data point. The cluster labels are numbers that basically serve as cluster id. For instance, in the case of the four clusters, the cluster ids are 0,1,2, and 3.

To print the cluster ids for all the labels, you can use the `labels_` attribute of the K-Means class, as shown below.

Script 19:

```
1. #printing predicted label values
2. print(km_model.labels_)
```

Output

```
[2 1 2 1 2 1 2 1 2 1 2 1 2 1 2 1 2 1 2 1 2 1
 2 1 2 1 2 1 2 1 2 1 2 1 2 1 2
 1 2 1 2 1 2 1 2 1 1 1 1 1 1 1 1 1 1 1 1 1 1
 1 1 1 1 1 1 1 1 1 1 1 1 1 1 1
 1 1 1 1 1 1 1 1 1 1 1 1 1 1 1 1 1 1 1 1 1 1
 1 1 1 1 1 1 1 1 1 1 1 1 1 1 1
 1 1 1 1 1 1 1 1 1 1 1 0 3 0 3 0 3 0 3 0 3
 0 3 0 3 0 3 0 3 0 3 0 3 0 3 0
 3 0 3 0 3 0 3 0 3 0 3 0 3 0 3 0 3 0 3 0 3 0
 3 0 3 0 3 0 3 0 3 0 3 0 3 0 3
 0 3 0 3 0 3 0 3 0 3 0 3 0 3 0]
```

The following script prints the clusters in different colors along with the cluster centers as black data points, as shown below.

Note: The colors are assigned randomly, so you might get clusters of different colors.

Script 20:
```
1.  #print the data points
2.  plt.scatter(dataset.values[:,0], dataset.values[:,1], c=
    km_model.labels_, cmap='rainbow' )
3.
4.
5.  #print the centroids
6.  plt.scatter(km_model.cluster_centers_[:, 0], km_model.
    cluster_centers_[:, 1], s=100, c='black')
```

Output:

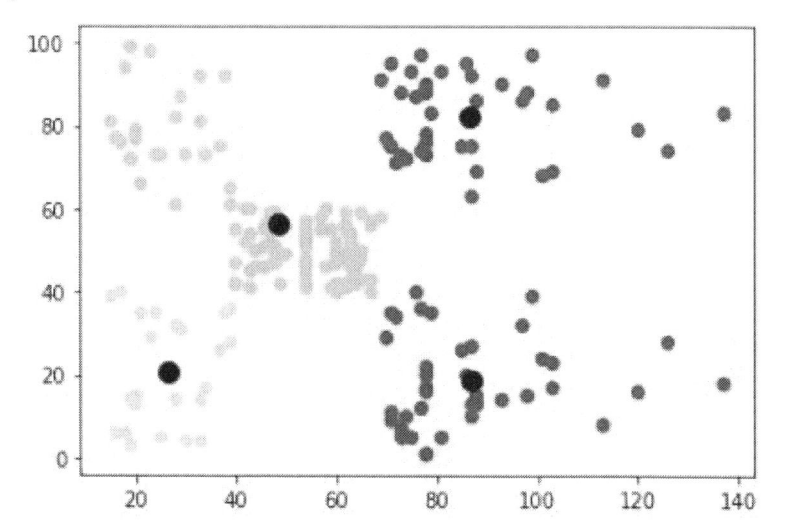

Till now, in this section, we have been randomly initializing the value of K or the number of clusters. However, we do not exactly know how many segments of customers are there in our dataset. To find the optimal number of customer segments, we need to find the optimal number of K because K defines the number of clusters.

There is a way to find the ideal number of clusters. The method is known as the *elbow method*.

Elbow Method for Finding K Value

In the elbow method, the value of inertia obtained by training K-Means clusters with different number of K is plotted on a graph.

The inertia represents the total distance between the data points within a cluster. Smaller inertia means that the predicted clusters are robust and close to the actual clusters.

To calculate the inertia value, you can use the `inertia_` attribute of the `K-Means` class object. The following script creates inertial values for K=1 to 10, and plots in the form of a graph.

Script 21:

```
1.  # training KMeans on K values from 1 to 10
2.  loss =[]
3.  for i in range(1, 11):
4.    km = KMeans(n_clusters = i).fit(dataset)
5.    loss.append(km.inertia_)
6.
7.  #printing loss against number of clusters
8.
9.  import matplotlib.pyplot as plt
10. plt.plot(range(1, 11), loss)
11. plt.title('Finding Optimal Clusters via Elbow Method')
12. plt.xlabel('Number of Clusters')
13. plt.ylabel('loss')
14. plt.show()
```

From the output below, it can be seen that the value of inertia didn't decrease much after five clusters.

Output:

Finding Optimal Clusters via Elbow Method

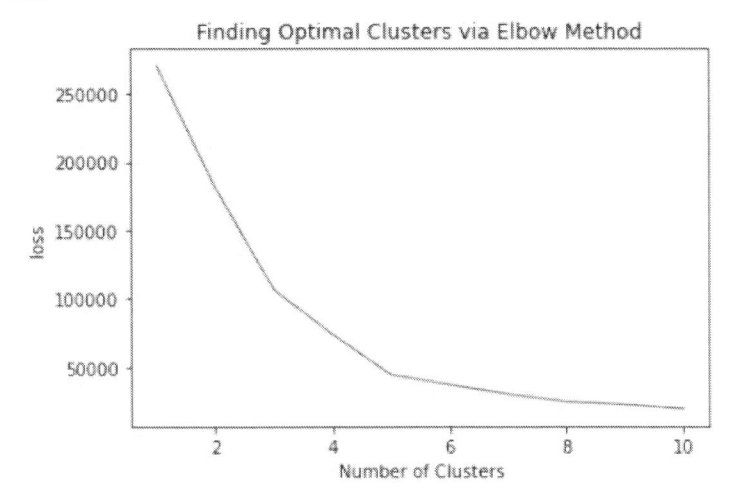

Let's now segment our customer data into five groups by creating five clusters.

Script 22:

```
1.  # performing kmeans clustering using KMeans class
2.  km_model = KMeans(n_clusters=5)
3.  km_model.fit(dataset)
```

Output

```
KMeans(n_clusters=5)
```

Script 23:

```
1.  #print the data points
2.  plt.scatter(dataset.values[:,0], dataset.values[:,1], c=
    km_model.labels_, cmap='rainbow' )
3.
4.
5.  #print the centroids
6.  plt.scatter(km_model.cluster_centers_[:, 0], km_model.
    cluster_centers_[:, 1], s=100, c='black')
```

With K = 5, the clusters predicted by the K-Means clustering algorithm are as follows:

Output:

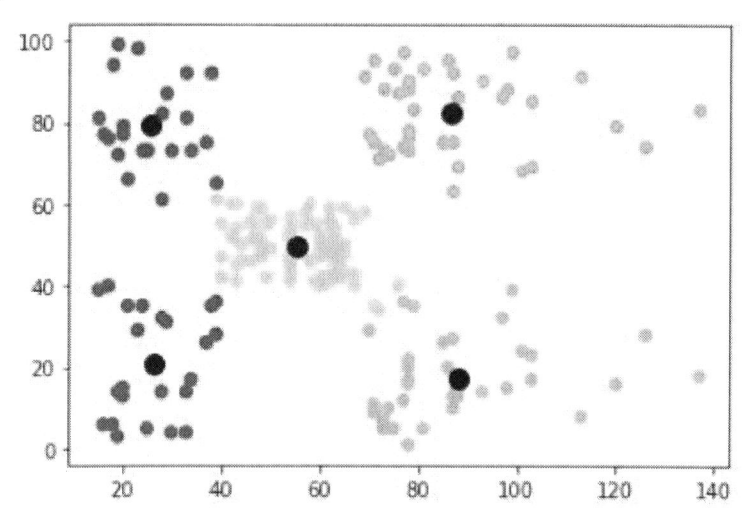

From the above output, you can see that the customers are divided into five segments. The customers in the middle of the plot (in purple) are the customers with average income and average spending. The customers belonging to the red cluster are the ones with low income and low spending. You need to target the customers who belong to the top right cluster (sky blue). These are the customers with high incomes and high spending in the past, and they are more likely to spend in the future, as well. So any new marketing campaigns or advertisements should be directed to these customers.

Finding Customers to Target for Marketing

The last step is to find the customers who belong to the sky-blue cluster. To do so, we will first plot the centers of the clusters.

Script 24:

```
1. #printing centroid values
2. print(km_model.cluster_centers_)
```

Here is the output. From the output, it seems that the coordinates of the centroid for the top right cluster are 86.53 and 82.12. The centroid values are located at index 1, which is also the id of the cluster.

Output

```
[[26.30434783 20.91304348]
 [86.53846154 82.12820513]
 [55.2962963  49.51851852]
 [88.2        17.11428571]
 [25.72727273 79.36363636]]
```

To fetch all the records from the cluster with id 1, we will first create a dataframe containing index values of all the records in the dataset and their corresponding cluster labels, as shown below.

Script 25:

```
1. cluster_map = pd.DataFrame()
2. cluster_map['data_index'] = dataset.index.values
3. cluster_map['cluster'] = km_model.labels_4.  cluster_map
```

Output:

	data_index	cluster
0	0	4
1	1	2
2	2	4
3	3	2
4	4	4
...	...	...
195	195	1
196	196	3
197	197	1
198	198	3
199	199	1

Next, we can simply filter all the records from the cluster_map dataframe, where the value of the *cluster* column is 1. Execute the following script to do so.

Script 26:
```
1. cluster_map = cluster_map[cluster_map.cluster==1]
2. cluster_map.head()
```

Here are the first five records that belong to cluster 1. These are the customers who have high incomes and high spending, and these customers should be targeted during marketing campaigns.

Output:

	data_index	cluster
123	123	1
125	125	1
127	127	1
129	129	1
131	131	1

7.2 Hierarchical Clustering

Like K-Means clustering, hierarchical clustering is another commonly used unsupervised machine learning technique for data clustering.

Hierarchical clustering can be divided into two types: agglomerative clustering and divisive clustering. Agglomerative clustering follows a bottom-up approach where individual data points are clustered together to form multiple small clusters leading to a big cluster, which can then be divided into small clusters using dendrograms. On the other hand, in the case of divisive clustering, you have one big cluster, which you divide into N number of small clusters.

In this section, you will perform agglomerative clustering using the Sklearn library.

Steps for Hierarchical Agglomerative Clustering

The steps required to perform agglomerative clustering are as follows:

1. Consider each data point in the dataset as one cluster. Hence, the number of clusters in the beginning is equal to the number of data points.
2. Form a cluster by joining the two closest data points.
3. Form more clusters by joining the closest clusters. Repeat this process until one big cluster is formed.
4. Use dendrograms to divide the one big cluster into multiple small clusters. (The concept of dendrograms is explained later in the chapter.)

Why Use Hierarchical Clustering?

Hierarchical clustering has the following advantages:

1. Unlike K-Means clustering, for hierarchical clustering, you do not have to specify the number of centroids clustering.
2. With dendrograms, it is easier to interpret how data has been clustered.

Disadvantages of the Hierarchical Clustering Algorithm

The following are some of the disadvantages of the hierarchical clustering algorithm.

1. Doesn't scale well on unseen data.

2. Has higher time complexity compared to K-Means clustering?
3. Difficult to determine the number of clusters in the case of a large dataset.

In the next section, you will see how to perform agglomerative clustering via Sklearn.

7.2.1 Hierarchical Clustering Example using Dummy Data

First, we will see how to perform hierarchical clustering on dummy data, and then we will perform hierarchical clustering on Iris data.

Example 1

In the first example, we will perform agglomerative clustering of 10 two-dimensional data points only.

The following script imports the required libraries:

Script 27:

```
1. import numpy as np
2. import pandas as pd
3. from sklearn.datasets.samples_generator import make_blobs
4. from matplotlib import pyplot as plt
5. %matplotlib inline
```

The following script randomly creates data points and then labels the data points from 1 to 10. The data points are plotted as a scatter plot.

Script 28:

```
1.  # generating dummy data of 10 records with 2 clusters
2.  features, labels = make_blobs(n_samples=10, centers=2,
    cluster_std = 2.00)
3.
4.  #plotting the dummy data
5.  plt.scatter(features[:,0], features[:,1], color ='r' )
6.
7.  #adding numbers to data points
8.  annots = range(1, 11)
9.  for label, x, y  in zip(annots, features[:, 0],
    features[:, 1]):
10. plt.annotate(
11. label,
12. xy=(x, y), xytext=(-3, 3),
13. textcoords='offset points', ha='right', va='bottom')
14. plt.show()
```

The output is as follows. From the output below, it can be clearly seen that data points 1, 4, 7, 8, and 9 belong to one cluster, and data points 2, 3, 5, 6, and 10 belong to the other cluster.

Output:

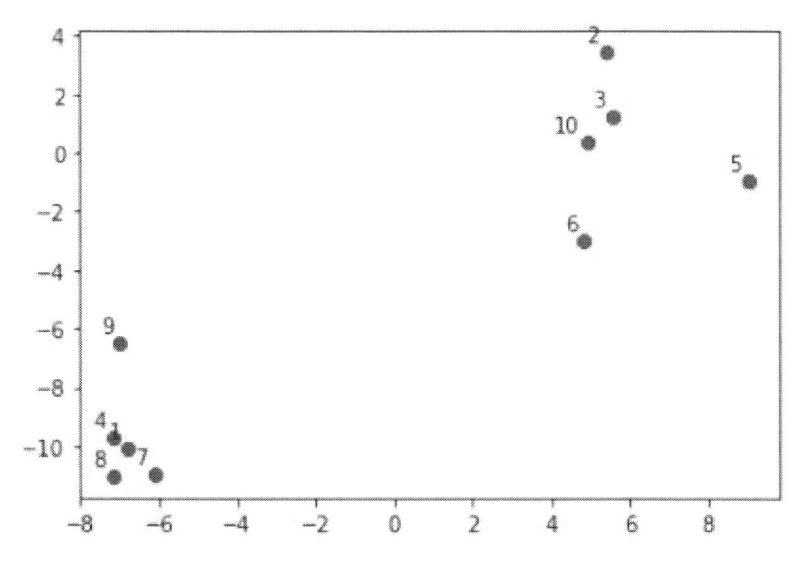

Note: You might get different data points because the points are randomly generated.

Let's now plot dendrograms for the above 10 data points. To plot dendrograms, you can use the `dendrogram` and `linkage` classes from the `scipy.cluster.hierarchy` module.

The features are passed to the `linkage` class. And the object of the linkage class is passed to the `dendrogram` class to plot dendrogram for the features, as shown in the following script:

Script 29:

```
1.  #importing dendrogram and linkage classes from scipy
2.  from scipy.cluster.hierarchy import dendrogram, linkage
3.
4.
5.  #creating an object of linkage class
6.  dendos = linkage(features, 'single')
7.
8.  annots = range(1, 11)
9.
10. # creating dendrograms
11. dendrogram(dendos,
12.     orientation='top',
13.     labels=annots,
14.     distance_sort='descending',
15.     show_leaf_counts=True)
16.
17. #printing dendrograms
18. plt.show()
```

Here is the output of the above script.

Output:

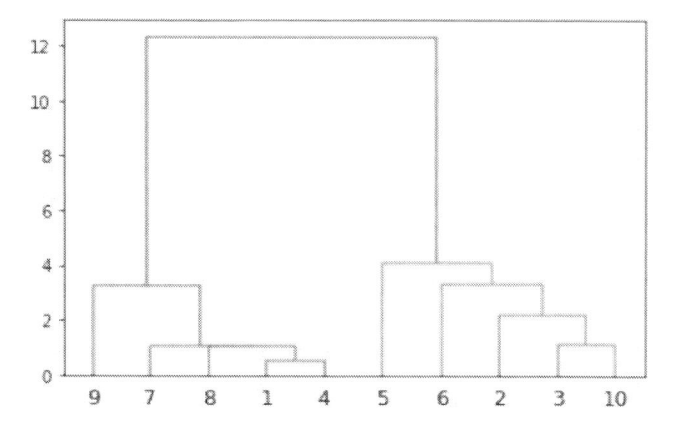

From the figure, it can be seen that points 1 and 4 are closest to each other. Hence, a cluster is formed by connecting these points. The cluster of points 1 and 4 is closest to data point 8, resulting in a cluster containing points 1, 4, and 8. In the same way, the remaining clusters are formed until a big cluster is formed.

Once one big cluster is formed, the longest vertical line is selected, and a horizontal line is drawn through it. The number of vertical lines this newly created horizontal line passes is equal to the number of clusters.

For instance, in the following figure, two clusters are formed.

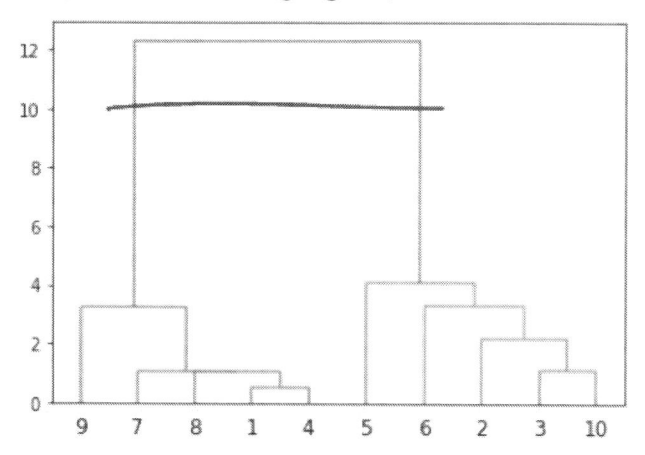

In real-world scenarios, there can be thousands of data points, and, hence, the dendrogram method cannot be used to manually cluster the data. This is where we can use the `AgglomerativeClustering` class from the `sklearn.cluster` module.

The number of clusters and the distance types are passed as parameters to the `AgglomerativeClustering` class. The following script applies agglomerative clustering to our dummy dataset.

Script 30:

```
1.  from sklearn.cluster import AgglomerativeClustering
2.
3.  # training agglomerative clustering model
4.  hc_model = AgglomerativeClustering(n_clusters=2, affinity='euclidean', linkage='ward')
5.  hc_model.fit_predict(features)
```

Output:

```
array([1, 0, 0, 1, 0, 0, 1, 1, 1, 0], dtype=int64)
```

And the following script plots the predicted clusters.

Script 31:

```
1.  #print the data points
2.  plt.scatter(features[:,0], features[:,1], c= hc_model.labels_, cmap='rainbow' )
```

The output shows that our clustering algorithm has successfully clustered the data points.

Output:

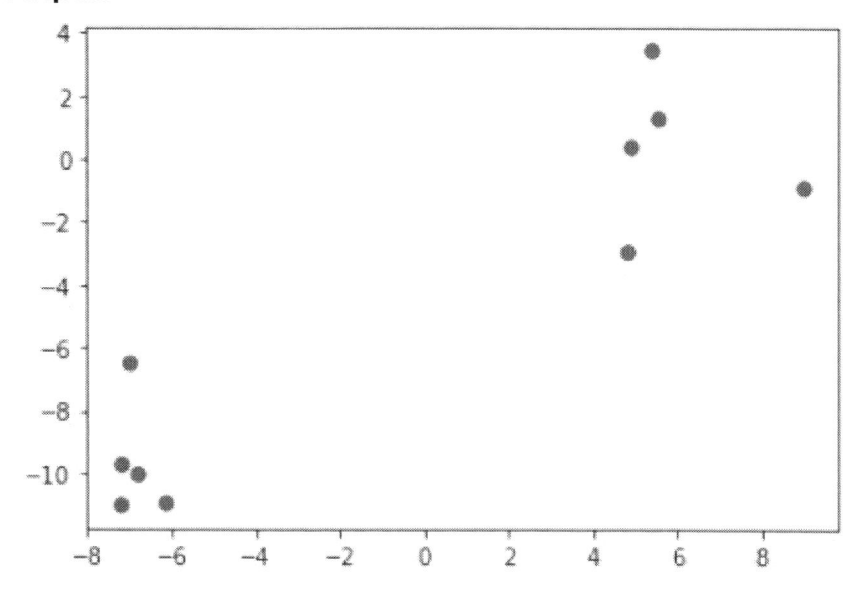

Example 2

In the previous example, we had 10 data points with 2 clusters. Let's now see an example with 500 data points. The following script creates 500 data points with 4 cluster centers.

Script 32:

```
1.  # generating dummy data of 500 records with 4 clusters
2.  features, labels = make_blobs(n_samples=500, centers=4,
    cluster_std = 2.00)
3.
4.  #plotting the dummy data
5.  plt.scatter(features[:,0], features[:,1] )
```

Output:

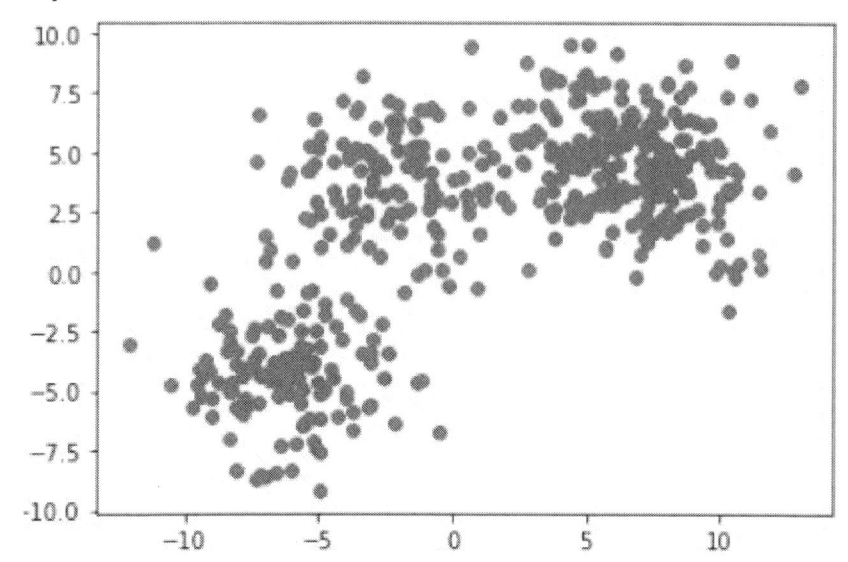

The following script applies agglomerative hierarchical clustering on the dataset. The number of predicted clusters is 4.

Script 33:

```
1. # performing kmeans clustering using
   AgglomerativeClustering class
2. hc_model = AgglomerativeClustering(n_
   clusters=4,affinity='euclidean', linkage='ward')
3. hc_model.fit_predict(features)
```

The output shows the labels of some of the data points in our dataset. You can see that since there are four clusters, there are four unique labels, i.e., 0, 1, 2, and 3.

Output:

```
([2, 1, 0, 0, 1, 2, 2, 1, 2, 2, 3, 3, 1, 2, 0, 0, 2, 0, 1, 0,
1, 2, 2, 1], dtype=int64)
```

To plot the predicted clusters, execute the following script.

Script 34:

```
1.  #print the clustered data points
2.  plt.scatter(features[:,0], features[:,1], c= hc_model.
    labels_, cmap='rainbow' )
```

Output:

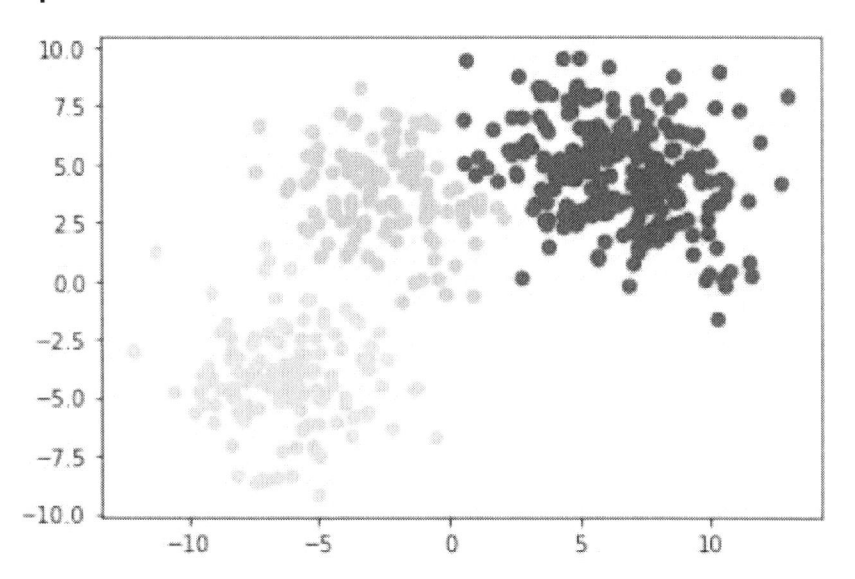

Similarly, to plot the actual clusters in the dataset (for the sake of comparison), execute the following script.

Script 35:

```
1.  #print actual datapoints
2.  plt.scatter(features[:,0], features[:,1], c= labels,
    cmap='rainbow' )
```

Output:

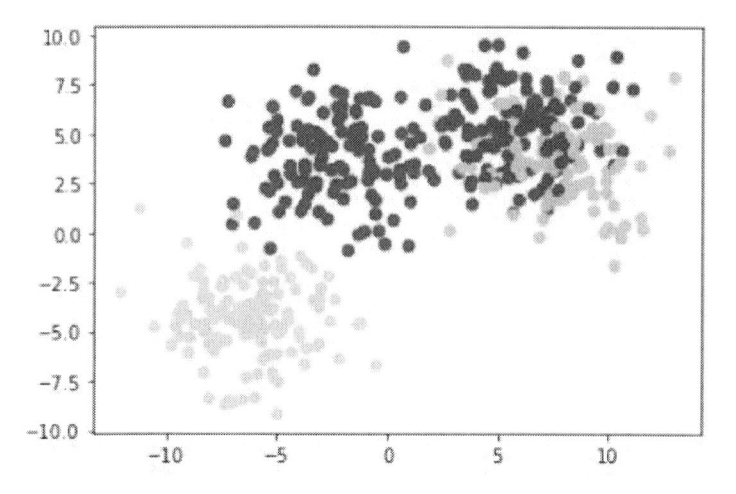

7.2.2 Clustering the Iris Plant Dataset

In this section, you will see how to cluster the Iris dataset using hierarchical agglomerative clustering.

The following script imports the Iris dataset and displays the first five rows of the dataset.

Script 36:

```
1. #importing iris dataset
2. import seaborn as sns
3.
4. iris_df = sns.load_dataset("iris")
5. iris_df.head()
```

Output:

	sepal_length	sepal_width	petal_length	petal_width	species
0	5.1	3.5	1.4	0.2	setosa
1	4.9	3.0	1.4	0.2	setosa
2	4.7	3.2	1.3	0.2	setosa
3	4.6	3.1	1.5	0.2	setosa
4	5.0	3.6	1.4	0.2	setosa

The following script divides the data into features and labels sets and displays the first five rows of the labels set.

Script 37:
```
1.  # dividing data into features and labels
2.  features = iris_df.drop(["species"], axis = 1)
3.  labels = iris_df.filter(["species"], axis = 1)
4.  features.head()
```

Output:

	sepal_length	sepal_width	petal_length	petal_width
0	5.1	3.5	1.4	0.2
1	4.9	3.0	1.4	0.2
2	4.7	3.2	1.3	0.2
3	4.6	3.1	1.5	0.2
4	5.0	3.6	1.4	0.2

Similarly, the following script applies the agglomerative clustering on the features set using the `Agglomerative-Clustering` class from the `sklearn.cluster` module.

Script 38:
```
1.  # training Hierarchical clustering model
2.  from sklearn.cluster import AgglomerativeClustering
3.
4.  # training agglomerative clustering model
5.  features = features.values
6.  hc_model = AgglomerativeClustering(n_
    clusters=3,affinity='euclidean', linkage='ward')
7.  hc_model.fit_predict(features)
```

The output below shows the predicted cluster labels for the features set in the Iris dataset.

Output:

```
array([1, 1, 1, 1, 1, 1, 1, 1, 1, 1, 1, 1, 1, 1, 1, 1, 1, 1,
1, 1, 1, 1, 1, 1, 1, 1, 1, 1, 1, 1, 1, 1, 1, 1, 1, 1, 1, 1,
1, 1, 1, 1, 1, 1, 1, 1, 1, 1, 1, 0, 0, 0, 0, 0, 0, 0, 0, 0, 0,
0, 0, 0, 0, 0, 0, 0, 0, 0, 0, 0, 0, 0, 0, 0, 0, 0, 2, 0, 0, 0,
0, 0, 0, 0, 0, 0, 0, 0, 0, 0, 0, 0, 0, 0, 0, 0, 0, 2, 0,
2, 2, 2, 2, 0, 2, 2, 2, 2, 2, 2, 0, 0, 2, 2, 2, 2, 0, 2, 0, 2,
0, 2, 2, 0, 0, 2, 2, 2, 2, 2, 0, 0, 2, 2, 2, 0, 2, 2, 2, 0, 2,
2, 2, 0, 2, 2, 0], dtype=int64)
```

The predicted clusters are printed via the following script.

Script 39:

```
1. #print the predicted cluster data points
2. plt.scatter(features[:,0], features[:,1], c= hc_model.
   labels_, cmap='rainbow' )
```

Output:

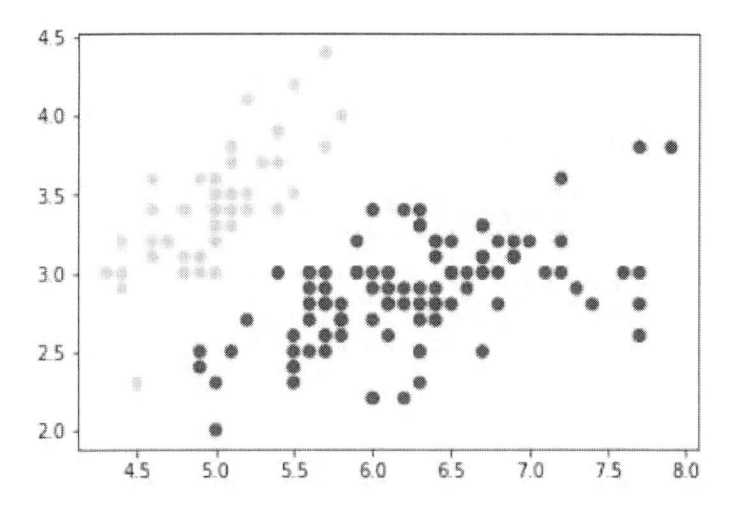

You can also create dendrograms using the features set using the shc module from the scipy.cluster.hierarchy library. You have to pass the features set to the linkage class of the shc module, and then the object of the linkage class is passed to the dendrogram class to plot the dendrograms, as shown in the following script.

Script 40:

```
1.  import scipy.cluster.hierarchy as shc
2.
3.  plt.figure(figsize=(10, 7))
4.  plt.title("Iris Dendograms")
5.  dend = shc.dendrogram(shc.linkage(features,
    method='ward'))
```

Here is the output of the script above.

Output:

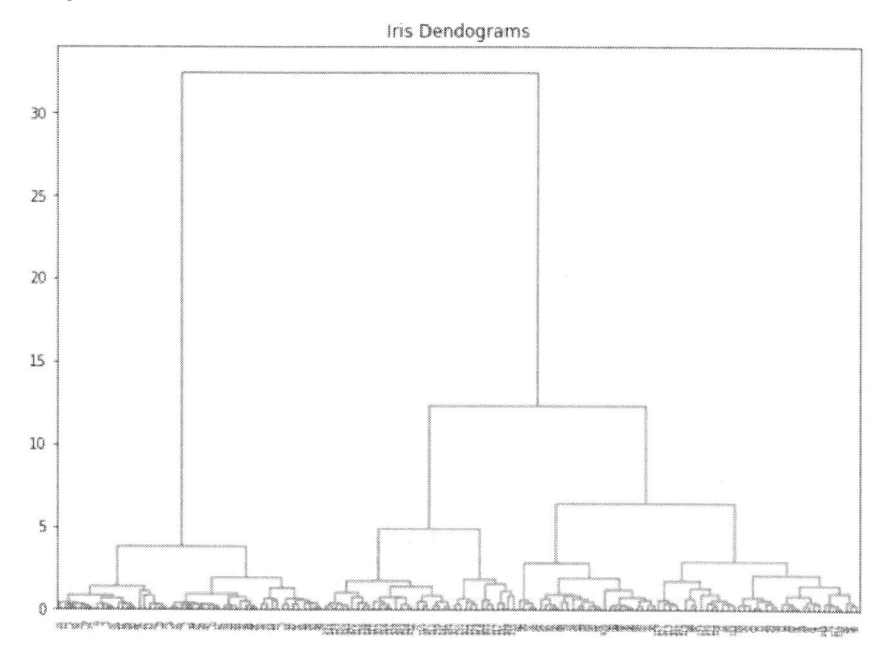

If you want to cluster the dataset into three clusters, you can simply draw a horizontal line that passes through the three vertical lines, as shown below. The clusters below the horizontal line are the resultant clusters. In the following figure, we form three clusters.

Iris Dendograms

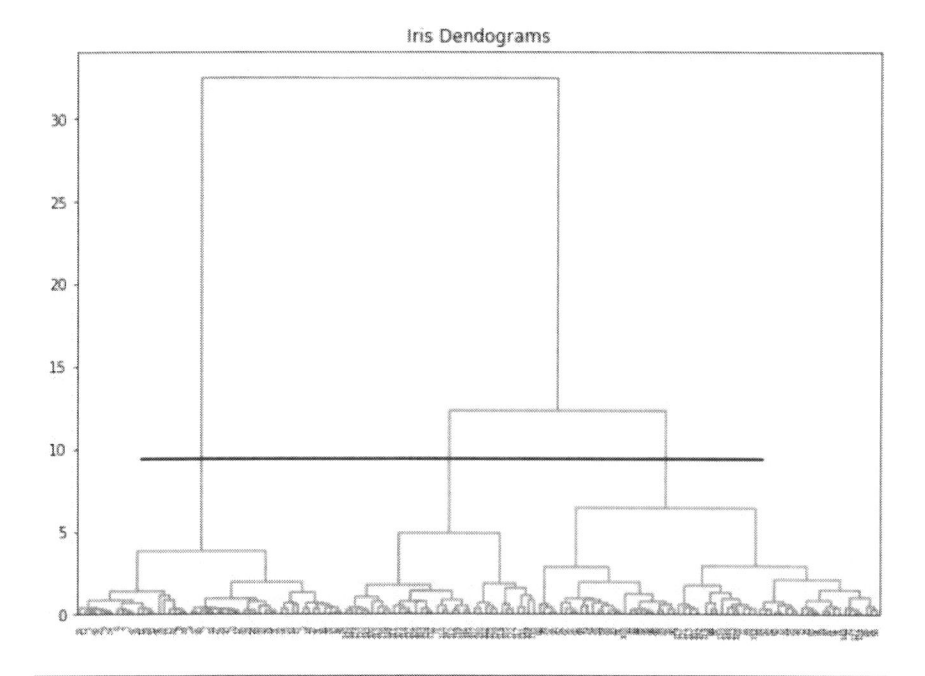

Hands-on Time – Exercise

Now, it is your turn. Follow the instruction in **the exercises below** to check your understanding of clustering algorithms. The answers to these questions are given at the end of the book.

Exercise 7.1

Question 1

Which of the following is a supervised machine learning algorithm?

    A. K-Means Clustering

    B. Hierarchical Clustering

    C. All of the above

    D. None of the above

Question 2

In K-Means clustering, what does the inertia tell us?

    A. the distance between data point within a cluster

    B. output labels for the data points

    C. the number of clusters

    D. None of the above

Question 3

In hierarchical clustering, in the case of vertical dendrograms, the number of clusters is equal to the number of _____ lines that the _____ line passes through?

    A. horizontal, vertical

    B. vertical, horizontal

    C. none of the above

    D. All of the above

Exercise 7.2

Apply K-Means clustering on the banknote.csv dataset available in the *Data* folder in the book resources. Find the optimal number of clusters and then print the clustered dataset. The following script imports the dataset and prints the first five rows of the dataset.

8

Dimensionality Reduction with PCA and LDA using Sklearn

Dimensionality reduction refers to reducing the number of features in a dataset in such a way that the overall performance of the algorithms trained on the dataset is minimally affected. With dimensionality reduction, the training time of the statistical algorithm can significantly be reduced, and data can be visualized more easily since it is not easy to visualize datasets in higher dimensions.

There are three main approaches used for dimensionality reduction: Principal Component Analysis (PCA), Linear Discriminant Analysis (LDA), and Singular Value Decomposition (SVD). In this chapter, you will study these approaches and see how to implement them using Python's Sklearn library with the help of examples. So, let's begin without much ado.

8.1 Principal Component Analysis

Principal component analysis is an unsupervised dimensionality reduction technique that doesn't depend on the labels of a dataset. Principal component analysis prioritizes features on the basis of their ability to cause maximum variance in the output.

The idea behind PCA is to capture those features that contain maximum features about the dataset. The feature that causes maximum variance in the output is called the first principal component, the feature that causes the second highest variance is called the second principal component, and so on.

Why Use PCA?

Following are the advantages of PCA:

1. Correlated features can be detected and removed using PCA.
2. Reduces overfitting because of a reduction in the number of features.
3. Model training can be expedited.

Disadvantages of PCA

There are two major disadvantages of PCA:

1. You need to standardize the data before you apply PCA.
2. Independent variable becomes less integrable.
3. Some amount of information is lost when you reduce features.

Implementing PCA with Python's Sklearn Library

In this section, you will see how to use PCA to select the two most important features in the Iris dataset using the Sklearn library.

The following script imports the required libraries:

Script 1:

```
1. import pandas as pd
2. import numpy as np
3. import seaborn as sns
```

The following script imports the Iris dataset using the Seaborn library and prints the first five rows of the dataset.

Script 2:

```
1. #importing the dataset
2. iris_df = sns.load_dataset("iris")
3.
4. #print dataset header
5. iris_df.head()
```

Output:

	sepal_length	sepal_width	petal_length	petal_width	species
0	5.1	3.5	1.4	0.2	setosa
1	4.9	3.0	1.4	0.2	setosa
2	4.7	3.2	1.3	0.2	setosa
3	4.6	3.1	1.5	0.2	setosa
4	5.0	3.6	1.4	0.2	setosa

The above output shows that the dataset contains four features: sepal_length, sepal_width, petal_length, petal_width, and one output label, i.e., species. For PCA, we will only use the features set.

The following script divides the data into the features and labels sets.

Script 3:

```
1.  #creating features set
2.  X = iris_df.drop(['species'], axis=1)
3.
4.
5.  #creating labels set
6.  y = iris_df["species"]
7.
8.  #converting labels to numbers
9.  from sklearn import preprocessing
10. le = preprocessing.LabelEncoder()
11. y = le.fit_transform(y)
```

Before we apply PCA on a dataset, we will divide it into the training and test sets, as shown in the following script.

Script 4:

```
1. #dividing data into 80-20% training and test sets
2. from sklearn.model_selection import train_test_split
3.
4. X_train, X_test, y_train, y_test = train_test_split(X, y,
   test_size=0.20, random_state=0)
```

Finally, both the training and test sets should be scaled before PCA could be applied to them.

Script 5:

```
1. #applying scaling on training and test data
2. from sklearn.preprocessing import StandardScaler
3. sc = StandardScaler()
4. X_train = sc.fit_transform(X_train)
5. X_test = sc.transform (X_test)
```

To apply PCA via Sklearn, all you have to do is import the PCA class from the Sklearn.decomposition module. Next, to apply PCA to the training set, pass the training set to the fit_tansform() method of the PCA class object. To apply PCA on the test set, pass the test set to the transform() method of the PCA class object. This is shown in the following script.

Script 6:

```
1.  #importing PCA class
2.  from sklearn.decomposition import PCA
3.
4.  #creating object of the PCA class
5.  pca = PCA()
6.
7.  #training PCA model on training data
8.  X_train = pca.fit_transform(X_train)
9.
10. #making predictions on test data
11. X_test = pca.transform(X_test)
```

Once you have applied PCA on a dataset, you can use the explained_variance_ratio_ feature to print the variance caused by all the features in the dataset. This is shown in the following script:

Script 7:

```
1.  #printing variance ratios
2.  variance_ratios = pca.explained_variance_ratio_
3.  print(variance_ratios)
```

Output:

```
[0.72229951 0.2397406 0.03335483 0.00460506]
```

The output above shows that 72.22 percent of the variance in the dataset is caused by the first principal component, while 23.97 percent of the variance is caused by the second principal component.

Let's now select the two principal components that collectively caused variance of 72.22% + 23.97% = 96.19%.

To select the two principal components, all you have to do is pass 2 as a value to the n_components attribute of the PCA class. The following script selects two principal components from the Iris training and test sets.

Script 8:

```
1.  #use one principal component
2.  from sklearn.decomposition import PCA
3.
4.  pca = PCA(n_components=2)
5.  X_train = pca.fit_transform(X_train)
6.  X_test = pca.transform(X_test)
```

Let's train a classification model using logistic regression, which predicts the label of the iris plant using the two principal components or features instead of the original four features.

Script 9:

```
1.  #making predictions using logistic regression
2.  from sklearn.linear_model import LogisticRegression
3.
4.  #training the logistic regression model
5.  lg = LogisticRegression()
6.  lg.fit(X_train, y_train)
7.
8.
9.  # Predicting the Test set results
10. y_pred = lg.predict(X_test)
11.
12. #evaluating results
13.
14. from sklearn.metrics import accuracy_score
15.
16. print(accuracy_score(y_test, y_pred))
```

Output:

```
0.8666666666666667
```

The output shows that even with two features, the accuracy for correctly predicting the label for the iris plant is 86.66.

Finally, with two features, you can easily visualize the dataset using the following script.

Script 10:

```
1.  from matplotlib import pyplot as plt
2.  %matplotlib inline
3.
4.  #print actual datapoints
5.
6.  plt.scatter(X_test[:,0], X_test[:,1], c= y_test,
    cmap='rainbow')
```

Output:

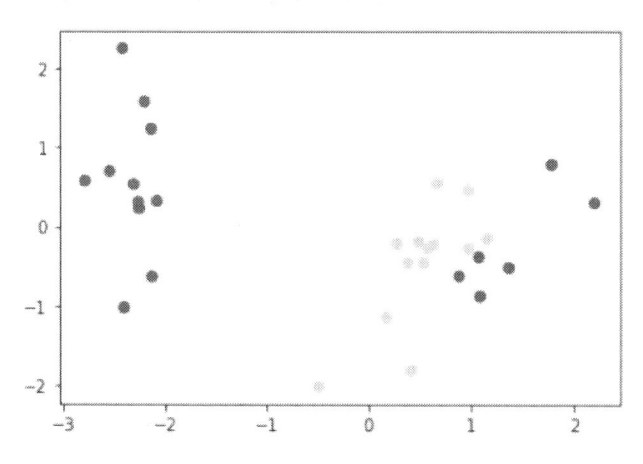

```
<matplotlib.collections.PathCollection at 0x12ea1737610>
```

8.2 Linear Discriminant Analysis

Linear Discriminant Analysis (LDA) is a supervised dimensionality reduction technique where a decision boundary is formed around the data points belonging to each cluster of a class. The data points are projected to new dimensions in a way that the distance between the data points within a cluster is minimized while the distance between the clusters is maximized. The new dimensions are ranked w.r.t their ability to (i) minimize the distance between the data points within a cluster and (ii) maximize the distance between individual clusters.

Why Use LDA?

Following are the advantages of LDA:

1. Reduces overfitting because of a reduction in the number of features.
2. Model training can be expedited.

Disadvantages of LDA

There are three major disadvantages of LDA:

1. Not able to detect correlated features.
2. Cannot be used with unsupervised or unlabeled data.
3. Some amount of information is lost when you reduce features.

Implementing LDA with Sklearn Library

Let's see how you can implement LDA using the Sklearn library. As always, the first step is to import the required libraries.

Script 11:

```
1.  import pandas as pd
2.  import numpy as np
3.  import seaborn as sns
```

You will be using the *banknote.csv* dataset from the *data* folder in the books resources). The following script imports the dataset and displays its first five rows.

Script 12:

```
1.  #importing dataset
2.  banknote_df = pd.read_csv(r"E:\Hands on Python for Data
    Science and Machine Learning\Datasets\banknote.csv")
3.
4.  #displaying dataset header
5.  banknote_df.head()
```

Output:

	variance	skewness	curtosis	entropy	class
0	3.62160	8.6661	-2.8073	-0.44699	0
1	4.54590	8.1674	-2.4586	-1.46210	0
2	3.86600	-2.6383	1.9242	0.10645	0
3	3.45660	9.5228	-4.0112	-3.59440	0
4	0.32924	-4.4552	4.5718	-0.98880	0

Let's divide the dataset into features and labels.

Script 13:

```
1.  # dividing data into features and labels
2.  X = banknote_df.drop(["class"], axis = 1)
3.  y = banknote_df.filter(["class"], axis = 1)
```

Finally, the following script divides the data into training and test sets.

Script 14:

```
1.  #dividing data into 80-20% training and test sets
2.  from sklearn.model_selection import train_test_split
3.
4.  X_train, X_test, y_train, y_test = train_test_split(X, y,
    test_size=0.20, random_state=0)
```

Like PCA, you need to scale the data before you can apply LDA on it. The data scaling is performed in the following step.

Script 15:

```
1.  #applying scaling on training and test data
2.  from sklearn.preprocessing import StandardScaler
3.  sc = StandardScaler()
4.  X_train = sc.fit_transform(X_train)
5.  X_test = sc.transform (X_test)
```

To apply LDA via Sklearn, all you have to do is import the LinearDiscriminantAnalysis class from Sklearn.

decomposition module. Next, to apply LDA to the training set, pass the training set to the `fit_tansform()` method of the LDA class object. To apply LDA on the test set, pass the test set to the `transform()` method of the LDA class object. This is shown in the following script.

Script 16:

```
1.  #importing LDA class
2.  from sklearn.discriminant_analysis import
    LinearDiscriminantAnalysis as LDA
3.
4.
5.  #creating object of the LDA class
6.  lda = LDA()
7.
8.  #training LDA model on training data
9.  X_train = lda.fit_transform(X_train, y_train)
10.
11. #making predictions on test data
12. X_test = lda.transform(X_test)
```

Like PCA, you can find variance ratios for LDA using the explained_variance_ratio attribute.

Script 17:

```
1.  #printing variance ratios
2.  variance_ratios = lda.explained_variance_ratio_
3.  print(variance_ratios)
```

Output:

```
[1.]
```

The above output shows that even with one component, the maximum variance can be achieved.

Next, we select only a single component from our dataset using LDA. To do so, you have to pass 1 as the attribute value for the n_components attribute of the LDA class, as shown below.

Script 18:

```
1.  #creating object of the LDA class
2.  lda = LDA(n_components = 1)
3.
4.  #training LDA model on training data
5.  X_train = lda.fit_transform(X_train, y_train)
6.
7.  #making predictions on test data
8.  X_test = lda.transform(X_test)
```

Next, we will try to class whether or not a banknote is fake using a single feature. We will use the Logistic Regression algorithm for that. This is shown in the following script.

Script 19:

```
1.  #making predictions using logistic regression
2.  from sklearn.linear_model import LogisticRegression
3.
4.  #training the logistic regression model
5.  lg = LogisticRegression()
6.  lg.fit(X_train, y_train)
7.
8.
9.  # Predicting the Test set results
10. y_pred = lg.predict(X_test)
11.
12. #evaluating results
13.
14. from sklearn.metrics import accuracy_score
15.
16. print(accuracy_score(y_test, y_pred))
```

Output:

```
0.9890909090909091
```

The output shows that even with a single feature, we are able to correctly predict whether or not a banknote is fake with 98.90 percent accuracy.

8.3 Singular Value Decomposition

Data for machine learning algorithms can be represented in the form of a matrix. Therefore, any technique that is used to reduce a matrix into its constituent components can be applied for dimensionality reduction since a dimension is basically a column in a matrix if you represent data features in the form of columns.

The process of reducing or describing a matrix using its constituent components is called matrix decomposition. One of the most commonly used techniques for matrix decomposition is singular value decomposition (SVD). Singular value decomposition is commonly used for dimensionality reduction in machine learning.

In this section, you will see the advantages and disadvantages of SVD for dimensionality reduction and how you can implement it with Sklearn.

Why Use SVD?

The following are some of the main advantages of SVD:

- Works better with sparse datasets, such as a bag of words representation of textual data.
- Orders the features by relevance.
- Extremely efficient for larger datasets.

Disadvantages of SVD

The following are the main disadvantages of SVD:

- SVD is relatively slower and computationally expensive.
- Results are not best for visualization; hence, difficult to interpret.
- May not work well with highly non-linear data.

Implementing SVD with Sklearn Library

Let's now see how you can implement SVD via Python's Sklearn Library.

You will be applying SVD for dimensionality reduction of the Wine dataset. The Wine dataset can be found in the Datasets folder.

The following script imports the winequality-red.csv dataset and displays its first five rows.

Script 20:

```
1.  import pandas as pd
2.  import numpy as np
3.
4.  # importing the dataset
5.  wine_data = pd.read_csv("E:/Datasets/winequality-red.csv",
    sep =";" )
6.
7.  #printing dataset header
8.  wine_data.head()
```

Output:

	fixed acidity	volatile acidity	citric acid	residual sugar	chlorides	free sulfur dioxide	total sulfur dioxide	density	pH	sulphates	alcohol	quality
0	7.4	0.70	0.00	1.9	0.076	11.0	34.0	0.9978	3.51	0.56	9.4	5
1	7.8	0.88	0.00	2.6	0.098	25.0	67.0	0.9968	3.20	0.68	9.8	5
2	7.8	0.76	0.04	2.3	0.092	15.0	54.0	0.9970	3.26	0.65	9.8	5
3	11.2	0.28	0.56	1.9	0.075	17.0	60.0	0.9980	3.16	0.58	9.8	6
4	7.4	0.70	0.00	1.9	0.076	11.0	34.0	0.9978	3.51	0.56	9.4	5

The above output shows that the dataset contains 12 columns.

The following script divides the dataset into features and labels.

Script 21:

```
1.  #creating feature set
2.  X = wine_data.drop(['quality'], axis=1)
3.
4.
5.  #creating label set
6.  y = wine_data["quality"]
```

The script below divides the data into training and test sets. The training set can be used to train the machine learning model, while the test set is used to evaluate the performance of a trained model.

Script 22:

```
1.  #dividing data into 80-20% training and test sets
2.  from sklearn.model_selection import train_test_split
3.
4.  X_train, X_test, y_train, y_test = train_test_split(X, y,
    test_size=0.20, random_state=0)
5.
6.  print(X_train.shape)
7.  print(y_train.shape)
```

The output shows that your feature set consists of 1,279 records where the total number of features is 11.

Output:

```
(1279, 11)
(1279,)
```

It is always recommended to normalize/scale the data before applying any dimensionality reduction technique. The following script scales the data using the standard scaler from the Scikit-learn library.

Script 23:

```
1.  #applying scaling on training and test data
2.  from sklearn.preprocessing import StandardScaler
3.  sc = StandardScaler()
4.  X_train = sc.fit_transform(X_train)
5.  X_test = sc.transform (X_test)
```

As a first step, you will train a regression algorithm on the complete feature set and then make predictions about the quality of the wine. Next, you will apply SVD to the Wine dataset to reduce it to two components and again predict the quality of wine.

The following script trains the Logistic Regression algorithm on the training data that contains a full feature set (11 features) and then makes a prediction on the test set containing the 11 features to predict the quality of the wine.

Script 24:

```
1.  #making predictions using logistic regression
2.  from sklearn.linear_model import LogisticRegression
3.
4.  #training the logistic regression model
5.  lg = LogisticRegression()
6.  lg.fit(X_train, y_train)
7.
8.
9.  # Predicting the Test set results
10. y_pred = lg.predict(X_test)
11.
12. #evaluating results
13.
14. from sklearn import metrics
15.
16. print('Mean Absolute Error:', metrics.mean_absolute_
    error(y_test, y_pred))
17. print('Mean Squared Error:', metrics.mean_squared_error(y_
    test, y_pred))
18. print('Root Mean Squared Error:', np.sqrt(metrics.mean_
    squared_error(y_test, y_pred)))
```

The output shows that we get a mean absolute error value of 0.40.

Output:

```
Mean Absolute Error: 0.403125
Mean Squared Error: 0.484375
Root Mean Squared Error: 0.6959705453537527
```

Next, we will apply SVD to our features set and reduce the total number of features to 2.

To apply SVD via the Sklearn Library, you can use the `TruncatedSVD` class from the `Sklearn.decomposition` module. You first need to create an object of the class and then pass the training set to the `fit_transform()` method. The test set can simply be passed to the `transform()` method. These two methods return training and test sets with reduced features (2 by default). The following script then prints the shape of the training test set.

Script 25:

```
1.  #importing TruncatedSVD class
2.  from sklearn.decomposition import TruncatedSVD
3.
4.  #creating object of the TruncatedSVD class
5.  svd = TruncatedSVD()
6.
7.  #training SVD model on training data
8.  X_train = svd.fit_transform(X_train)
9.
10. #making predictions on test data
11. X_test = svd.transform(X_test)
12.
13. print(X_train.shape)
14. print(y_train.shape)
```

From the output, you can see that the training set now consists of only two features.

Output:

```
(1279, 2)
(1279,)
```

You will now use the reduced training set to make predictions about the quality of the wine. Execute the following script.

Script 26:

```
1.  #making predictions using logistic regression
2.  from sklearn.linear_model import LogisticRegression
3.
4.  #training the logistic regression model
5.  lg = LogisticRegression()
6.  lg.fit(X_train, y_train)
7.
8.
9.  # Predicting the Test set results
10. y_pred = lg.predict(X_test)
11.
12. #evaluating results
13.
14. from sklearn import metrics
15.
16. print('Mean Absolute Error:', metrics.mean_absolute_
    error(y_test, y_pred))
17. print('Mean Squared Error:', metrics.mean_squared_error(y_
    test, y_pred))
18. print('Root Mean Squared Error:', np.sqrt(metrics.mean_
    squared_error(y_test, y_pred)))
```

The output shows that with two features, the mean absolute error is 0.51, which is slightly greater than when you used the complete feature set with 11 features. This is because when you remove nine features, you lose some information from your dataset.

Output:

```
Mean Absolute Error: 0.51875
Mean Squared Error: 0.64375
Root Mean Squared Error: 0.8023403267940606
```

However, your algorithm now runs much faster. It is up to you to find a balance between the number of features you need in your dataset and the performance of your algorithm.

> **Hands-on Time - Exercise**
>
> Now, it is your turn. Follow the instructions in **the exercises below** to check your understanding of dimensionality reduction using PCA and LDA, and SVD. The answers to these questions are given at the end of the book.

Exercise 8.1

Question 1

Which of the following are the benefits of dimensionality reduction?

    A. Data Visualization

    B. Faster training time for statistical algorithms

    C. All of the above

    D. None of the above

Question 2

In PCA, dimensionality reduction depends upon the:

    A. Features set only

    B. Labels set only

    C. Both features and labels set

    D. None of the above

Question 3

LDA is a ____ dimensionality reduction technique.

    A. Unsupervised

    B. Semi-Supervised

    C. Supervised

    D. Reinforcement

Exercise 8.2

Apply principal component analysis for dimensionality reduction on the *customer_churn.csv* dataset from the Datasets folder. Print the accuracy using two principal components. Also, plot the results on the test set using the two principal components.

9

Selecting Best Models with Scikit- Learn

The performance of a machine learning model depends upon several factors, such as the training and test sets used to train and test an algorithm, values of the hyperparameters of an algorithm, metrics used to evaluate the performance of an algorithm, etc. In this chapter, you will see different techniques for model selection in Scikit-learn.

9.1 K-Fold Cross-validation

K-Fold cross-validation is a data splitting technique that lets you train and test the model on all subsets of the data.

In this book till now, normally, you divide the data into 80 percent training and 20 percent test set. However, it means that only 20 percent of the data is used for testing and that 20 percent of data is never used for training.

For more stable results, it is recommended that all the parts of the dataset are at least used once for training and once for testing. To do so, the K-Fold cross-validation technique can be used. With K-fold cross-validation, the data is divided into K parts. The experiments are also performed for K parts. In each experiment, K-1 parts are used for training, and the Kth part is used for testing.

For example, in 5-fold cross-validation, the data is divided into five equal parts, e.g., K1, K2, K3, K4, and K5. In the first iteration, K1–K4 are used for training, while K5 is used for testing. In the second test, K1, K2, K3, and K5 are used for training, and K4 is used for testing. In this way, each part is used at least once for testing and once for training.

Scikit-learn library contains built-in `cross_val_score()` function from the `sklearn.model_selection` module, which you can use to perform cross-validation.

In this section, you will see two scripts. In the first script, you will see model training without cross-validation. In the second section, the same dataset will be used for the model training with cross-validation.

9.1.1 Prediction Without Cross-validation

You will be using the winequality-red.csv file from the Datasets folder to import the dataset, as shown in the following script. The following script also prints the first five rows of the dataset.

Script 1:

```
1.  import pandas as pd
2.  import numpy as np
3.
4.  # importing the dataset
5.  wine_data = pd.read_csv("E:/Datasets/winequality-red.csv",
    sep =";" )
6.
7.  #printing dataset header
8.  wine_data.head()
```

Output:

	fixed acidity	volatile acidity	citric acid	residual sugar	chlorides	free sulfur dioxide	total sulfur dioxide	density	pH	sulphates	alcohol	quality
0	7.4	0.70	0.00	1.9	0.076	11.0	34.0	0.9978	3.51	0.56	9.4	5
1	7.8	0.88	0.00	2.6	0.098	25.0	67.0	0.9968	3.20	0.68	9.8	5
2	7.8	0.76	0.04	2.3	0.092	15.0	54.0	0.9970	3.26	0.65	9.8	5
3	11.2	0.28	0.56	1.9	0.075	17.0	60.0	0.9980	3.16	0.58	9.8	6
4	7.4	0.70	0.00	1.9	0.076	11.0	34.0	0.9978	3.51	0.56	9.4	5

The following script divides the dataset into features and labels sets.

Script 2:

```
1. #extracting features
2. X = wine_data.drop(['quality'], axis=1)
3.
4. #extracting labels
5. y = wine_data["quality"]
```

The script below divides the dataset into 80 percent training set and 20 percent testing set using the `train_test_split()` function from the `sklearn.model_selection` module.

Script 3:

```
1. #dividing data into training and test sets
2. from sklearn.model_selection import train_test_split
3.
4. X_train, X_test, y_train, y_test = train_test_split(X, y,
   test_size=0.20, random_state=0)
```

The script below uses the `StandardScaler` class to normalize the training and test dataset.

Script 4:

```
1. # feature scaling using standard scaler
2. from sklearn.preprocessing import StandardScaler
3. sc = StandardScaler()
4. X_train = sc.fit_transform(X_train)
5. X_test = sc.transform (X_test)
```

Finally, the following script trains the model and makes predictions on the test set.

Script 5:

```
1.  #importing the random forest algorithm from Sklearn
2.  from sklearn.ensemble import RandomForestRegressor
3.  rf_reg = RandomForestRegressor(random_state=42, n_estimators=500)
4.
5.  #training the model
6.  regressor = rf_reg.fit(X_train, y_train)
7.
8.  #making predictions on the test set
9.  y_pred = regressor.predict(X_test)
10.
11.
12. #evaluating the model performance
13. from sklearn import metrics
14.
15. print('Mean Absolute Error:', metrics.mean_absolute_error(y_test, y_pred))
16. print('Mean Squared Error:', metrics.mean_squared_error(y_test, y_pred))
17. print('Root Mean Squared Error:', np.sqrt(metrics.mean_squared_error(y_test, y_pred)))
```

Output:

```
Mean Absolute Error: 0.40390625
Mean Squared Error: 0.3176339125
Root Mean Squared Error: 0.563590199080857
```

9.1.2 Prediction with Cross-validation

In this section, you will again use the winequality-red.csv dataset. But this time, the data will be trained by using the 5-fold cross-validation.

The following script imports the dataset and prints its first five rows.

Script 6:

```
1.  import pandas as pd
2.  import numpy as np
3.
4.  # importing the dataset
5.  wine_data = pd.read_csv("E:/Datasets/winequality-red.csv",
    sep =";" )
6.
7.  #printing dataset header
8.  wine_data.head()
```

	fixed acidity	volatile acidity	citric acid	residual sugar	chlorides	free sulfur dioxide	total sulfur dioxide	density	pH	sulphates	alcohol	quality
0	7.4	0.70	0.00	1.9	0.076	11.0	34.0	0.9978	3.51	0.56	9.4	5
1	7.8	0.88	0.00	2.6	0.098	25.0	67.0	0.9968	3.20	0.68	9.8	5
2	7.8	0.76	0.04	2.3	0.092	15.0	54.0	0.9970	3.26	0.65	9.8	5
3	11.2	0.28	0.56	1.9	0.075	17.0	60.0	0.9980	3.16	0.58	9.8	6
4	7.4	0.70	0.00	1.9	0.076	11.0	34.0	0.9978	3.51	0.56	9.4	5

Output:

The dataset is divided into the features and labels sets in the script below:

Script 7:

```
1.  #extracting features
2.  X = wine_data.drop(['quality'], axis=1)
3.
4.  #extracting labels
5.  y = wine_data["quality"]
```

Data Normalization is performed in the following script:

Script 8:

```
1.  # feature scaling using standard scaler
2.  from sklearn.preprocessing import StandardScaler
3.  sc = StandardScaler()
4.  X = sc.fit_transform(X)
```

Next, instead of dividing the dataset into the training and test sets as you did previously, you will simply initialize an instance of your machine learning model. The following script initializes the `RandomForestRegressor` model from the `sklearn.ensemble` class, as shown below:

Script 9:

```
1.  #importing the random forest algorithm from Sklearn
2.  from sklearn.ensemble import RandomForestRegressor
3.  rf_reg = RandomForestRegressor(random_state=42, n_estimators=500)
```

To perform cross-validation, you can use the cross_val_score method from the sklearn.model_selection class. The first parameter to the cross_val_score method is the classifier that you want to use for training. Next, you need to pass the features and labels set, which are X and y in this case. The number of cross-validation folds is specified by the cv parameter. Finally, the performance metrics that you want to use is defined by the scoring attribute, as shown here:

Script 10:

```
1.  #importing cross-validation model from the sklearn
2.  from sklearn.model_selection import cross_val_score
3.
4.  #applying cross-validation with 5 folds
5.  scores = cross_val_score(rf_reg, X, y, cv=5, scoring ="neg_mean_absolute_error")
6.  print(scores)
```

In the output, you will see five values. Each value corresponds to the mean absolute error for one of the five data folds.

Output:

```
[-0.504025  -0.51095625 -0.50714375 -0.5192125  -0.49863323]
```

You can find the average and standard deviation of the mean absolute error values for the five folds using the following script.

Script 11:

```
1.  print("%0.2f accuracy with a standard deviation of %0.2f"
    % (scores.mean(), scores.std()))
```

Output:

```
-0.51 accuracy with a standard deviation of 0.01
```

It is always recommended to use K-fold cross-validation when selecting which model performs best because one model may perform better on one subset of data, while the other model may perform better on the other subset. Therefore, dividing the data into five folds and training and testing on all the folds may give consistent results.

9.2 Hyperparameter Selection

The Performance of a machine learning model also depends upon the hyperparameters chosen to train the model. Selecting the best parameters for a model is a tricky task. However, there exist algorithms that can be used to select the best parameters from a list of parameters.

One such algorithm is the Grid Search algorithm, which searches for the best parameter set by trying all possible combinations of parameters to perform a particular task. In this section, you will see how the Grid Search algorithm can be implemented to select the best parameters using the Scikit-learn library.

You will again be using the winequality-red.csv dataset for this section. You will try to predict the quality of the wine.

The following script imports the dataset and prints its first five rows.

Script 12:

```
1.  import pandas as pd
2.  import numpy as np
3.
4.  # importing the dataset
5.  wine_data = pd.read_csv("E:/Datasets/winequality-red.csv",
    sep =";" )
6.
7.  #printing dataset header
8.  wine_data.head()
```

	fixed acidity	volatile acidity	citric acid	residual sugar	chlorides	free sulfur dioxide	total sulfur dioxide	density	pH	sulphates	alcohol	quality
0	7.4	0.70	0.00	1.9	0.076	11.0	34.0	0.9978	3.51	0.56	9.4	5
1	7.8	0.88	0.00	2.6	0.098	25.0	67.0	0.9968	3.20	0.68	9.8	5
2	7.8	0.76	0.04	2.3	0.092	15.0	54.0	0.9970	3.26	0.65	9.8	5
3	11.2	0.28	0.56	1.9	0.075	17.0	60.0	0.9980	3.16	0.58	9.8	6
4	7.4	0.70	0.00	1.9	0.076	11.0	34.0	0.9978	3.51	0.56	9.4	5

Output:

The script below divides the data into features and labels sets X and y, respectively.

Script 13:

```
1.  #extracting features
2.  X = wine_data.drop(['quality'], axis=1)
3.
4.  #extracting labels
5.  y = wine_data["quality"]
```

To perform grid search, you have to create a dictionary where dictionary keys represent the parameter name and dictionary values consist of lists, which contain items that contain values that you want to test for the attributes specified as dictionary keys.

For instance, in the following script, you want to test values 100, 300, 500, 800, and 1000 for the `n_estimators` attribute of the `RandomForestRegressor` class from the Sklearn library.

Script 14:

```
1.  # defining list of hyperparameters to be tested
2.  grid_param = {
3.      'n_estimators': [100, 300, 500, 800, 1000],
4.      'min_samples_leaf':[1,3,5],
5.      'bootstrap': [True, False],
6.      'criterion': ['mae']
7.  }
```

Next, just like you did with cross-validation, you need to specify the machine learning model whose parameters you want to select. In the script below, we select the RandomForestRegressor algorithm.

Script 15:

```
1.  #importing the random forest algorithm from Sklearn
2.  from sklearn.ensemble import RandomForestRegressor
3.  rf_reg = RandomForestRegressor(random_state=42, n_estimators=500)
```

Finally, to perform grid search, you can use the GridSearchCV class from the sklearn.model_selection attribute module. You need to pass the machine learning model whose hyperparameters you want to select, the parameter dictionary, the accuracy metrics, and the number of cross-validation folds as parameters to the GridSearchCV class. Look at the following script for reference. Here, n_jobs = –1 specifies that use all CPU cores for Grid search selection.

Script 16:

```
1.  #importing the GridSearchCV class
2.  from sklearn.model_selection import GridSearchCV
3.
4.  gd_sr = GridSearchCV(estimator=rf_reg,
5.      param_grid=grid_param,
6.      scoring ="neg_mean_absolute_error",
7.      cv=5,
8.      n_jobs=-1)
```

Finally, to train your grid search model, you need to call the fit() method, as shown below:

Script 17:

```
1.  #training with grid search
2.  gd_sr.fit(X, y)
```

Once the grid search finishes training, you can find the best parameters that your grid search algorithm selected using the best_params_ attribute, as shown below:

Script 18:

```
1.  #printing the best parameters
2.  best_parameters = gd_sr.best_params_
3.  print(best_parameters)
```

In the output below, you can see the parameter values that return the best results for the prediction of wine quality as selected by the GridSearchCV() algorithm.

Output:

```
{'bootstrap': True, 'criterion': 'mae', 'min_samples_leaf': 1, 'n_estimators': 300}
```

To see the best case mean absolute error returned by the grid search using the above parameter, you can use the best_scores_ attribute, as shown below:

Script 19:

```
1.  #printing the best results
2.  best_result = gd_sr.best_score_
3.  print(best_result)
```

Output:

```
-0.531481223876698
```

Though one model may perform better with one set of parameters, the other model can outperform the previous model with another set of parameters. Therefore, to compare two models, you should try different parameters using grid search.

9.3 Model Evaluation via Validation Curves

In chapters 5 and 6 on regression and classification, respectively, you saw some object criteria to measure the performance of a model. For instance, to evaluate the classification algorithm, you used metrics, such as confusion matrix, accuracy, F1 measure, etc. In addition to object criteria, you can use validation curves to measure the performance of a machine learning model.

Learning curves can be used to see if a machine learning model has a high bias or high variance. A machine learning model with high bias performs poorly on both training and testing data, whereas a model with high variance performs very well on training data but poorly on test data. A model with high bias is called an underfitting model, whereas a model with high variance is called an overfitting model.

Learning curves can be used to plot the performance of a machine learning model on both the training and test sets against the number of training records. Ideally, with an increase in the number of records, the performance of the model on training and test sets should become equally good.

Let's see an example. The following script imports the required libraries.

Script 20:

```
1. import pandas as pd
2. import numpy as np
3. import matplotlib.pyplot as plt
4. from sklearn.ensemble import RandomForestClassifier
5. from sklearn.model_selection import learning_curve
```

The script below imports the banknote.csv dataset from the data folder in the book resources and displays its first five rows.

Script 21:

```
1. # importing the dataset
2. banknote_data = pd.read_csv("E:/Datasets/banknote.csv" )
3.
4. #printing the dataset header
5. banknote_data.head()
```

Output:

	variance	skewness	curtosis	entropy	class
0	3.62160	8.6661	-2.8073	-0.44699	0
1	4.54590	8.1674	-2.4586	-1.46210	0
2	3.86600	-2.6383	1.9242	0.10645	0
3	3.45660	9.5228	-4.0112	-3.59440	0
4	0.32924	-4.4552	4.5718	-0.98880	0

As we did previously, the following script divides the data into the training and test sets.

Script 22:

```
1. #extracting features
2. X = banknote_data.drop(['class'], axis=1)
3.
4. #extracting labels
5. y = banknote_data["class"]
```

Next, to plot the validation curves, you can use the `learning_curve` class from the `sklearn.model_selection` module, as shown in the following script. Like grid search, you need to pass the classifier, the features and labels sets, the performance metrics, and the number of jobs to the constructor of the learning curve class. The important parameter is the train_sizes.

You need to specify the list containing the number of sets you want your data to be divided into. For instance, the following script will divide your data into 100 sets.

Script 23:

```
1.  #finding the train and test scores on 100 records
2.  train_size, train_scores, test_scores = learning_
    curve(RandomForestClassifier(),
3.      X,y,
4.      cv = 5,
5.      scoring = 'accuracy',
6.      n_jobs = -1,
7.      train_sizes = np.linspace(0.01, 1,100),
8.      verbose =1)
```

Look at the train sizes returned by the above script. Your dataset is divided into 100 sets. The first set consists of 10 records, the second set consists of 21 records, the third set consists of 32 records, and so on.

Output:

```
[learning_curve] Training set sizes: [   10 21 32 43 54 65 76 87
  98  109 120   131   142   153 164   175   186   197   208   219   230
 241   252   263   274   285   296   307 318   329   340   351   362
 372   383   394   405   416   427   438   449   460 471   482   493
 504   515   526   537   548   559   570   581   592   603   614 625
 636   647   658   669   680   691   702   713   724   734   745   756
 767 778   789   800   811   822   833   844   855   866   877   888
 899   910   921 932   943   954   965   976   987   998 1009 1020
 1031 1042 1053 1064 1075 1086 1097]
```

Since we used fivefold cross-validation, five values for accuracy are returned for each of the 100 sets. For each set, we will take the mean value of accuracy. The following script finds the mean accuracies for the training sets.

Script 24:

```
1.  #finding the mean training scores
2.  train_mean = np.mean(train_scores, axis = 1)
3.  print(train_mean)
```

The output shows that the mean accuracies for the training data are approximately 1 for all the sets.

Output:

```
[1. 1. 1. 1. 1. 1. 1. 1. 1. 1. 1. 1. 1. 1. 1. 1. 1. 1.
 1. 1. 1. 1. 1. 1. 1. 1. 1. 1. 1. 1. 1. 1. 1. 1. 1. 1.
 1. 1. 1. 1. 1. 1. 1. 1. 1. 1. 1. 1. 1. 1. 1. 1. 1. 1.
 1. 1. 1. 1. 1. 1. 1. 1. 1. 1. 1. 1. 1. 1. 1. 1. 1. 1.
 1. 1. 1. 1. 1. 1. 1. 1. 1. 1. 1. 1. 1. 1.]
```

And the following script returns mean accuracies for all the sets in the test data.

Script 25:

```
1.  #finding the mean testing scores
2.  test_mean = np.mean(test_scores, axis = 1)
3.  print(test_mean)
```

Output:

```
[0.55539217 0.55539217 0.55539217 0.55539217 0.55539217
 0.55539217 0.55539217 0.55539217 0.55539217 0.55539217
 0.55539217 0.55539217 0.55539217 0.55539217 0.55539217
 0.55539217 0.55539217 0.55539217 0.55539217 0.55539217
 0.55539217 0.55539217 0.55539217 0.55539217 0.55539217
 0.55539217 0.55539217 0.55539217 0.55539217 0.55539217
 0.55539217 0.55539217 0.55539217 0.55539217 0.55539217
 0.55539217 0.55539217 0.55539217 0.55539217 0.55539217
 0.55539217 0.55539217 0.55539217 0.55539217 0.55539217
 0.55539217 0.55539217 0.55539217 0.55539217 0.55539217
 0.55539217 0.55539217 0.55539217 0.55539217 0.55539217
 0.62244194 0.7981075  0.88192966 0.93222031 0.96720106
 0.96938553 0.96866092 0.96793364 0.97303251 0.97448441
 0.97448441 0.97448971 0.98031586 0.97740411 0.99053484
 0.99126211 0.99052953 0.99125946 0.98907498 0.99052687
 0.99198407 0.99271666 0.99052422 0.99271666 0.992714
 0.99344127 0.99490113 0.99344127 0.99198673 0.99490113
 0.992714   0.99344393 0.9897996  0.992714  0.99198938 0.99271666
 0.992714   0.9941712  0.99417386 0.99344127 0.99489847
 0.99344127 0.99344127 0.99343862 0.99344127]
```

Next, you can plot the mean training and test accuracy scores against the number of records in the training data.

Script 26:

```
1.  #plotting learning curves
2.  plt.plot(train_size, train_mean, label = 'Training Score')
3.  plt.plot(train_size, test_mean, label = 'Cross-Validation
    Score')
4.
5.  plt.title('Learning Curve')
6.  plt.xlabel ('Number of Training Samples')
7.  plt.ylabel ('Accuracies')
8.  plt.legend(loc = 'best')
```

The output below shows that the performance on the training data remains constant, i.e., 100 percent on all the sets. Hence, the model has no bias. For the test data, the model performs poorly up to 600 records, and we can say that our model is overfitting till the 600th records. After the 600th record, the model performance on the test data starts improving and becomes very close to the model performance on the training data at around 800 records.

Output:

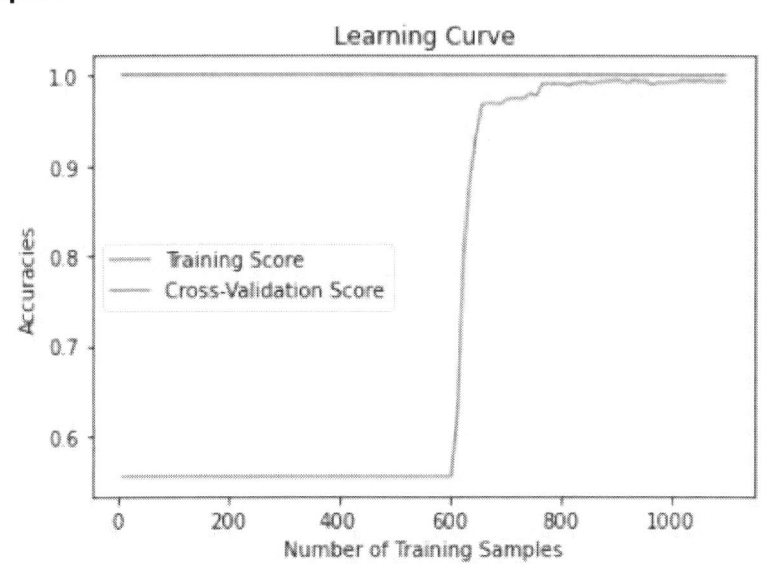

9.4 Saving Models for Future Use

Training a machine learning model can take a lot of time. Once you achieve optimal performance with a machine learning model, you can save model weights and parameters, and you can reload them to make predictions on a dataset without having to train the model from scratch. To do so, you can use the `pickle` module from the Sklearn library.

Let's see an example of how you can save and load a machine learning model with pickle. Execute the following script to import the required libraries.

Script 27:

```
1. import pandas as pd
2. import numpy as np
3. import matplotlib.pyplot as plt
4. from sklearn.ensemble import RandomForestClassifier
5. from sklearn.model_selection import learning_curve
```

The following script imports the banknote.csv dataset and displays its first five rows.

Script 28:

```
1. # importing the dataset
2. banknote_data = pd.read_csv("E:/Datasets/banknote.csv")
3.
4. #printing the dataset header
5. banknote_data.head()
```

Output:

	variance	skewness	curtosis	entropy	class
0	3.62160	8.6661	-2.8073	-0.44699	0
1	4.54590	8.1674	-2.4586	-1.46210	0
2	3.86600	-2.6383	1.9242	0.10645	0
3	3.45660	9.5228	-4.0112	-3.59440	0
4	0.32924	-4.4552	4.5718	-0.98880	0

The script below divides the dataset into the features and labels sets.

Script 29:

```
1. #extracting features
2. X = banknote_data.drop(['class'], axis=1)
3.
4. #extracting labels
5. y = banknote_data["class"]
```

Division of data into the training and test sets is done using the following script.

Script 30:

```
1.  #dividing data into training and test sets
2.  from sklearn.model_selection import train_test_split
3.
4.  X_train, X_test, y_train, y_test = train_test_split(X, y,
    test_size=0.20, random_state=0)
```

The following script performs data normalization.

Script 31:

```
1.  # feature scaling using standard scaler
2.  from sklearn.preprocessing import StandardScaler
3.  sc = StandardScaler()
4.  X = sc.fit_transform(X)
```

Next, you initialize an object of the RandomForestClassifier class and train the model in scripts 32 and 33, respectively.

Script 32:

```
1.  #importing the random forest algorithm from Sklearn
2.  from sklearn.ensemble import RandomForestClassifier
3.  rf_clf = RandomForestClassifier(random_state=42,n_
    estimators=500)
```

Script 33:

```
1.  #training the model
2.  classifier= rf_clf.fit(X_train, y_train)
```

After you have trained the model, you can save it. The process is simple. You need to call the `dump()` method of the pickle module. The first parameter to the `dump()` method is the trained classifier, and the second parameter is the file path where you want to save the classifier. You also need to pass the file permissions, which should be written binary (wb) for saving the model. Look at the following script for reference.

Script 34:

```
1.  #saving the model using pickle
2.  import pickle
3.  filename = "E:/Datasets/banknote_model.sav"
4.  pickle.dump(classifier, open(filename, 'wb'))
```

Finally, you can load the saved model using the `load()` method from the pickle module. You need to pass the file path for the saved classifier along with the read permission (r), as shown in the following script. The following script also makes a prediction on the test set using the loaded classifier.

Script 35:

```
1.  # loading the model using pickle
2.  loaded_classifier = pickle.load(open(filename, 'rb'))
3.  y_pred = loaded_classifier.predict(X_test)
```

Finally, you can evaluate the model by comparing the predicted values with the actual values. Look at the following script for reference.

Script 36:

```
1.  #evaluating the algorithm on test set
2.  from sklearn.metrics import classification_report,
    confusion_matrix, accuracy_score
3.
4.  print(confusion_matrix(y_test,y_pred))
5.  print(classification_report(y_test,y_pred))
6.  print(accuracy_score(y_test, y_pred))
```

Output:

```
[[155   2]
 [  2 116]]
              precision    recall  f1-score   support

           0       0.99      0.99      0.99       157
           1       0.98      0.98      0.98       118
    accuracy                           0.99       275
   macro avg       0.99      0.99      0.99       275
weighted avg       0.99      0.99      0.99       275
```
0.9854545454545455

Further Readings – Model Selection with Scikit-Learn

1. To know more about cross-validation with sklearn, check this link: http://bit.ly/3caOlei
2. To study more about hyperparameter selection, check out this link: http://bit.ly/3iGPxr9
3. To find out more about validation curves, look at this link: http://bit.ly/39OfDEw

Exercise 9.1

Question 1:

With grid search, you can _____

    A. Test all parameters for a model by default

    B. Test only lists of specified parameters

    C. Test three parameters

    D. None of the above

Question 2:

Learning curves can be used to study the:

    A. Bias of a trained algorithm

    B. Variance of a trained algorithm

    C. Both of the above

    D. None of the above

Question 3:

Which pickle method can be used to save a trained machine learning model?

    A. save()

    B. register()

    C. load()

    D. dump()

Exercise 9.2

Use the Grid Search to find parameters of the RandomForestClassifier algorithm, which return the highest classification accuracy for classifying the banknote.csv dataset:

```
1.  grid_param = {
2.  'n_estimators': [100, 300, 500, 800, 1000],
3.  'criterion': ['gini', 'entropy'],
4.  'bootstrap': [True, False]
5.  }
```

10

Natural Language Processing with Scikit-Learn

10.1 What Is Natural Language Processing?

Humans interact in natural language. Natural languages contain a lot of information. For example, the choice of words, the tone, and the context of a sentence can be used to the exploit mood, intention, and emotion of a human.

Furthermore, text documents, such as books, newspapers, and blogs, are full of information that can be exploited to perform various tasks. For humans, it can take a huge amount of time to understand and extract useful information the from text and make decisions based on the information provided in the text. This is where natural language processing (NLP) comes into play.

Natural language processing is defined as "a field of artificial intelligence that enables computers to read, understand, and extract meaning from natural languages spoken by humans."

Like other machine learning tasks, the Scikit-learn library contains functions that can be used for a variety of natural language processing tasks. In this chapter, you will see two applications of natural language processing with Scikit-learn. First, you will see how you can automatically classify spam emails. In the second application, you will see how to find public sentiment from text reviews about different movies.

10.2 Spam Email Detection with Scikit-Learn

If you have used Gmail, Yahoo, or any other email service, you would have noticed that some emails are automatically marked as spam by email engines. These spam email detectors are based on certain rules and statistical machine learning approaches.

Spam email filtering is a natural language processing task where based on the text of the email, we have to classify whether or not an email is a spam email. Supervised machine learnings are commonly used for classification, particularly if the true outputs are available in the dataset.

The Naïve Bayes Algorithm is one of the supervised machine learning algorithms that have been proven to be effective for spam email detection. In this project, you will see how to detect spam emails using the Naïve Bayes algorithm implemented via Python's Sklearn library.

Why Use Naïve Bayes Algorithm?

Naïve Bayes algorithm is particularly useful because it:

1. Performs brilliantly when there is no relationship between attributes in a feature vector.

2. Requires a very small amount of data for training.
3. Very easy to implement and understand.

Disadvantages of Naïve Bayes Algorithm

Following are the disadvantages of the naïve Bayes algorithm.

1. Unable to capture the relationships between various features in a dataset.
2. If a category exists in the test set but not in the training set, the probability of prediction for that category in the test set will be set to 0.

To install the libraries required for this project, execute the following pip command on your command terminal.

10.2.1 Installing Required Libraries

```
pip install scikit-learn
pip install numpy
pip install pandas
pip install matplotlib
pip install seaborn
pip install nltk
pip install regex
pip install wordcloud
```

10.2.2 Importing Libraries

The second step is to import the required libraries. Execute the following script to do so:

Script 1:

```
1.  import numpy as np
2.  import pandas as pd
3.  import re
4.  import nltk
5.  import matplotlib.pyplot as plt
6.  import seaborn as sns
7.  from sklearn.naive_bayes import MultinomialNB
8.  from wordcloud import WordCloud
9.  %matplotlib inline
```

10.2.3 Importing the Dataset

The dataset that we are going to use to train our naïve Bayes algorithm for spam email detection can be downloaded from this Kaggle link: https://bit.ly/3j9Uh7h.

The dataset is also available by the name: *emails.csv* in the resources folder of this book. Download the dataset to your local file system and use the `read_csv()` method of the `Pandas` library to read the dataset into a Pandas dataframe, as shown in the following script. The following script also prints the first five rows of the dataset using the `head()` method.

Script 2:

```
1.  # https://www.kaggle.com/karthickveerakumar/spam-
    filter?select=emails.csv
2.  data_path = "E:\Scikit-Learn- Specialization\Datasets and
    Source Codes\emails.csv"
3.
4.  #reading the CSV dataset file
5.  message_dataset = pd.read_csv(data_path, engine='python')
6.
7.  #printing the dataset header
8.  message_dataset.head()
```

Output:

	text	spam
0	Subject: naturally irresistible your corporate...	1
1	Subject: the stock trading gunslinger fanny i...	1
2	Subject: unbelievable new homes made easy im ...	1
3	Subject: 4 color printing special request add...	1
4	Subject: do not have money , get software cds ...	1

The above output shows that our dataset contains two columns: text and spam. The text column contains texts of emails, and the spam column contains the label 1 or 0, where 1 corresponds to spam emails and 0 corresponds to non-spam or ham emails.

Next, we can plot the shape of our dataset.

Script 3:

```
1.  #printing dataset shape
2.  message_dataset.shape
```

The output shows that our dataset contains 5,728 emails.

Output:

```
(5728, 2)
```

10.2.4 Data Visualization

Data visualization is always a good step before training a machine learning model. We will also do that.

Let's plot a pie chart, which shows the distribution of spam and non-spam emails in our dataset.

Script 4:

```
1.  #inreasing default figure size
2.  plt.rcParams["figure.figsize"] = [8,10]
3.
4.  #plotting pie plot for spam and ham email messages
5.  message_dataset.spam.value_counts().plot(kind='pie',
    autopct='%1.0f%%')
```

Output:

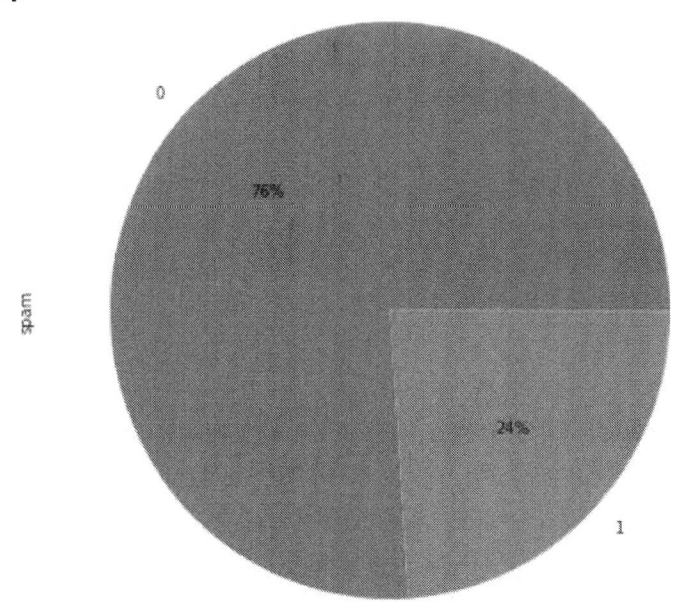

From the above pie chart, you can see that 24 percent of the emails in our dataset are spam emails.

Next, we will plot word clouds for the spam and non-spam emails in our dataset. Word cloud is basically a kind of graph, which shows the most frequently occurring words in the text. The higher the frequency of occurrence, the larger will be the size of the word.

But first, we will remove all the stop words such as "a, is, you, i, are, etc." from our dataset because these words occur quite a lot, and they do not have any significant classification ability. The following script imports all the stop words from the dataset.

Script 5:

```
1.  #importing english stop words
2.  from nltk.corpus import stopwords
3.  stop = stopwords.words('english')
4.
5.  #removing stopwords from email messages
6.  message_dataset['text_without_sw'] = message_data
    set['text'] .apply(lambda x: ' '.join([item for item in
    x.split() if item not in stop]))
```

The following script filters spam emails from the dataset and then plots word cloud using spam emails only.

Script 6:

```
1.  #filtering spam messages
2.  message_dataset_spam = message_dataset[message_
    dataset["spam"] == 1]
3.
4.  #increase figure size
5.  plt.rcParams["figure.figsize"] = [8,10]
6.
7.  #joining words in the dataset containing spam messages
8.  text = ' '.join(message_dataset_spam['text_without_sw'])
9.
10. #generating word cloud using spam messages
11. wordcloud2 = WordCloud().generate(text)
12.
13. #plotting word cloud
14. plt.imshow(wordcloud2)
15. plt.axis("off")
16. plt.show()
```

The output below shows that spam emails mostly contain a subject, and it also contains terms like money, free, thank, account, program, service, etc.

Output:

Similarly, the following script plots a word cloud for non-spam emails.

Script 7:

```
1.  #filtering non-spam messages
2.  message_dataset_ham = message_dataset[message_
    dataset["spam"] == 0]
3.
4.  #increase figure size
5.  plt.rcParams["figure.figsize"] = [8,10]
6.
7.  #joining words in the dataset containing non-spam messages
8.  text = ' '.join(message_dataset_ham['text_without_sw'])
9.
10. #generating word cloud using non-spam messages
11. wordcloud2 = WordCloud().generate(text)
12.
13. #plotting word cloud
14. plt.imshow(wordcloud2)
15. plt.axis("off")
16. plt.show()
```

You can see that non-spam emails contain mostly informal words such as thank, work, time, need, vince, etc.

Output:

10.2.5 Cleaning the Data

Before we actually train our machine learning model on the training data, we need to remove special characters and numbers from our text. Removing special characters and numbers creates empty spaces in the text, which also need to be removed.

Before cleaning the data, let's first divide the data into email text, which forms the feature set (X) and the email labels (y), which contains information about whether or not an email is a spam email.

Script 8:

```
1. #creating feature set
2. X = message_dataset["text"]
3.
4. #creating label set
5. y = message_dataset["spam"]
```

The following script defines a **clean_text()** method, which accepts a text string and returns a string that is cleaned of digits, special characters, and multiple empty spaces.

Script 9:

```
1.  #cleaning feature set (email messages)
2.  def clean_text(doc):
3.
4.  #removing everything except capital and small letters
5.  document = re.sub('[^a-zA-Z]', ' ', doc)
6.
7.  #removing single characters
8.  document = re.sub(r"\s+[a-zA-Z]\s+", ' ', document)
9.
10. #removing multiple empty spaces
11. document = re.sub(r'\s+', ' ', document)
12.
13. return document
```

The following script calls the **clean_text()** method and preprocesses all the emails in the dataset.

Script 10:

```
1. X_sentences = []
2.
3. #creating list of sentences
4. reviews = list(X)
5.
6. #cleaning all sentences using clean_text() function
7. for rev in reviews:
8.     X_sentences.append(clean_text(rev))
```

10.2.6 Convert Text to Numbers

Naïve Bayes algorithm is a statistical algorithm. Statistical algorithms work with numbers. Therefore, you need to convert the text of emails into numeric form. There are various ways to do so, e.g., Bag of Words, TFIDF, Word Embeddings, etc. In this section, you will use the TFIDF technique for converting text to numbers.

To use the TFIDF scheme, the **TfIdfVectorizer** class from the **sklearn.feature_extraction.text** can be used. You have to first call the **fit()** and then **transform()** method on the text features. Also, you can pass **"stop_words = 'english'"** as an attribute to automatically remove stop words from your text. Look at the following script.

Script 11:

```
1.  #importing stopwords and TFIDF vectorizer
2.  from nltk.corpus import stopwords
3.  from sklearn.feature_extraction.text import TfidfVectorizer
4.
5.  #converting email messages to text via TFIDF vectorizer
6.  vectorizer = TfidfVectorizer (max_features=2500,min_df=5,
    max_df=0.7, stop_words=stopwords.words('english'))
7.  X= vectorizer.fit_transform(X_sentences).toarray()
```

In the above script, the **max_features** attribute specifies that a maximum of 2,500 most occurring words should be used to create a feature dictionary. The **min_df** attribute here specifies to only include words that occur in at least five documents. **Max_df** defines not to include words that occur in more than 70 percent of the documents.

10.2.7 Training the Model

The data is now ready for training a machine learning model. But first, we need to divide our data into the training and test sets. Using the training data, the naïve bayes algorithm will learn the relationship between email texts and the email label (spam or not) since both email text and corresponding labels are given in the training dataset.

Once the naïve Bayes model is trained on the training set, the test set containing only email texts is passed as inputs to the model. The model then predicts which of the emails in the test set are spam. Predicted outputs for the test set are then compared with the actual label in the test data in order to evaluate the performance of the spam email detector naïve Bayes model.

The following script divides the data into training and test sets.

Script 12:

```
1. #dividing the data into the training and test set
2. from sklearn.model_selection import train_test_split
3. X_train, X_test, y_train, y_test = train_test_split(X, y,
   test_size=0.20, random_state=42)
```

To train the machine learning model, you will be using the MultinomialNB() class from sklearn.naive_bayes module, which actually implements the naïve Bayes algorithm in Sklearn. The fit() method of the `MultinomialNB()` class is used to train the model.

Script 13:

```
1. #training Naive Bayes algorithm on the training data
2. spam_detector = MultinomialNB()
3. spam_detector.fit(X_train, y_train)
```

10.2.8 Evaluating Model Performance

Once a supervised machine learning model is trained, you can make predictions on the test set. To do so, you can use the **predict()** method of the `MultinomialNB()`.

Script 14:

```
1. y_pred = spam_detector.predict(X_test)
```

Once you have trained a model and made predictions on the test set, the next step is to know how well your model has performed for making predictions on the unknown test set. There are various metrics to evaluate a classification method.

Some of the most commonly used classification metrics are F1, recall, precision, accuracy, and confusion matrix. The methods used to find the value for these metrics are available in `sklearn.metrics` class. The predicted and actual values have to be passed to these methods, as shown in the following script:

Script 15:

```
1.  #evaluating model performance
2.  from sklearn.metrics import classification_report,
    confusion_matrix, accuracy_score
3.
4.  print(confusion_matrix(y_test,y_pred))
5.  print(classification_report(y_test,y_pred))
6.  print(accuracy_score(y_test,y_pred))
```

Output:

```
[[849   7]
 [ 18 272]]
              precision    recall  f1-score   support

           0       0.98      0.99      0.99       856
           1       0.97      0.94      0.96       290
    accuracy                           0.98      1146
   macro avg       0.98      0.96      0.97      1146
weighted avg       0.98      0.98      0.98      1146

0.9781849912739965
```

The output shows that our model is 97.81 percent accurate while predicting whether a message is a spam or ham, which is pretty impressive.

10.2.9 Making Predictions on Single Instance

In addition to making predictions on the complete test set, we can also make predictions on a single sentence. Let's fetch an email randomly from our dataset.

Script 16:

```
1.  #printing sentence at index 56 in the dataset
2.  print(X_sentences[56])
3.
4.  #print label for the sentence at the index 56
5.  print(y[56])
```

The text of the email is as follows.

Output:

```
Subject localized software all languages available hello we
would like to offer localized software versions german french
spanish uk and many others all listed software is avail able
for immediate download no need to wait week for cd delivery
just few examples norton internet security pro windows xp
professional with sp full version coreldraw graphics suite
dreamweaver mx homesite including macromedia studio mx just
browse our site and find any software you need in your native
language best reqards kayieen
1
```

The actual output, i.e., 1, shows that sentence number 56 in the dataset is 1, i.e., spam.

Let's pass this sentence into our spam detector classifier and see what it thinks:

Script 17:

```
1.  #making prediction for the label for the sentenceat index
    56
2.  print(spam_detector.predict(vectorizer.transform([X_
    sentences[56]])))
```

Output:

```
[1]
```

The model correctly classified the message as spam.

10.3 IMDB Movies Sentimental Analysis

The second application of natural language processing that you are going to study in this chapter is IMDB movies sentimental analysis. The dataset will consist of public reviews on IMDB (www.imdb.com), and the task will be to classify reviews as having positive or negative opinions regarding movies. So, let's start.

The first step is to import the required libraries.

10.3.1 Importing Libraries

Script 18:

```
1.  import numpy as np
2.  import pandas as pd
3.  import re
4.  import nltk
5.  import matplotlib.pyplot as plt
6.  import seaborn as sns
7.  %matplotlib inline
```

The dataset for this task is available by the name *imdb.reviews.csv* in the *Resources* folder. The following script imports the CSV file into your application and prints the first five rows of the dataset.

10.3.2 Importing the Dataset

Script 19:

```
1.  data_path = "E:/Datasets/imdb_reviews.csv"
2.  #reading the CSV datafile
3.  movie_dataset = pd.read_csv(data_path, engine='python')
4.
5.  #printing the dataset header
6.  movie_dataset.head()
```

Output:

	SentimentText	Sentiment
0	first think another Disney movie, might good, ...	1
1	Put aside Dr. House repeat missed, Desperate H...	0
2	big fan Stephen King's work, film made even gr...	1
3	watched horrid thing TV. Needless say one movi...	0
4	truly enjoyed film. acting terrific plot. Jeff...	1

From the output, you can see that the dataset contains two columns *SentimentText* and *Sentiment*. The former contains the text reviews about movies, while the latter contains user opinions for corresponding movies. In the sentiment column, 1 refers to a positive opinion, while 0 refers to a negative opinion.

Let's see the number of rows in the dataset.

Script 20:

```
1.  #printing the dataset shape
2.  movie_dataset.shape
```

The output shows that the dataset contains 25,000 records.

Output:

```
(25000, 2)
```

Next, we can print the distribution of positive and negative user reviews using a pie chart, as shown below:

Script 21:

```
1.  #increasing default plotsize
2.  plt.rcParams["figure.figsize"] = [8,10]
3.
4.  #printing pie chart that displaying distributionof sentiment
5.  movie_dataset.Sentiment.value_counts().plot(kind='pie', autopct='%1.0f%%')
```

Output:

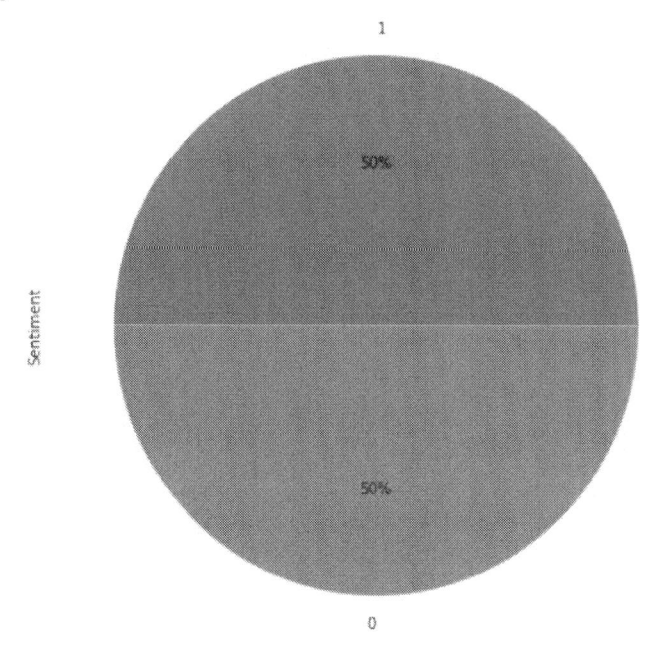

The pie chart shows that half of the reviews are positive, while the other half contains negative reviews.

10.3.3 Cleaning the Data

Before we actually train our machine learning model on the training data, we need to remove the special characters and numbers from our text. Removing special characters and numbers creates empty spaces in the text, which also need to be removed.

Before cleaning the data, let's first divide the data into text reviews and user sentiment.

Script 22:

```
1. #creating feature set
2. X = movie_dataset["SentimentText"]
3.
4. #creating label set
5. y = movie_dataset["Sentiment"]
```

The following script defines a **clean_text()** method, which accepts a text string and returns a string that is cleaned of digits, special characters, and multiple empty spaces.

Script 23:

```
1.  #cleaning feature set (email messages)
2.  def clean_text(doc):
3.
4.  #removing everything except capital and small letters
5.  document = re.sub('[^a-zA-Z]', ' ', doc)
6.
7.  #removing single characters
8.  document = re.sub(r"\s+[a-zA-Z]\s+", ' ', document)
9.
10. #removing multiple empty spaces
11. document = re.sub(r'\s+', ' ', document)
12.
13. return document
```

The following script calls the **clean_text()** method and preprocesses all the user reviews in the dataset.

Script 24:

```
1.  X_sentences = []
2.
3.  #creating a list of sentences
4.  reviews = list(X)
5.
6.  #cleaning all sentences using clean_text() function
7.  for rev in reviews:
8.      X_sentences.append(clean_text(rev))
```

10.3.4 Convert Text to Numbers

In the previous section, you studied that we need to convert a text document to numbers before we can apply machine learning techniques to the text document. You used the TFIDF scheme to convert your text to numbers. In this section, you will again use the TFIDF technique for converting text to numbers.

The following script converts text to numbers. Here, the **max_features** attribute specifies that a maximum of 2,000 most occurring words should be used to create the feature dictionary. The **min_df** attribute here specifies to only include words that occur a minimum of five times across all documents. **Max_df** defines not to include words that occur in more than 70 percent of the documents.

Script 25:

```
1.  #importing stopwords and TFIDF vectorizer
2.  from nltk.corpus import stopwords
3.  from sklearn.feature_extraction.text import TfidfVectorizer
4.
5.  #converting email messages to text via TFIDF vectorizer
6.  vectorizer = TfidfVectorizer (max_features=2000,min_df=5, max_df=0.7, stop_words=stopwords.words('english'))
7.  X= vectorizer.fit_transform(X_sentences).toarray()
```

The text data has been processed. Now, we can train our machine learning model on the text.

10.3.5 Training the Model

We will be developing a supervised text classification model since, in the dataset, we already have the public sentiment. As we did for spam and non-spam email classification, we will divide our data into the training and test sets. Using the training data, the algorithm will learn the relationship between text reviews and the opinion since both text reviews and corresponding opinions are given in the training dataset.

Once the machine learning model is trained on the training data, the test data, including only the text reviews, will be given as input to the model. The model will then predict the unknown sentiment for all the text reviews. The predicted sentiment is then compared with the actual sentiment in the test data in order to evaluate the performance of the text classification model.

The following script divides the data into training and test sets.

Script 26:

```
1.  #dividing the data into the training and test sets
2.  from sklearn.model_selection import train_test_split
3.  X_train, X_test, y_train, y_test = train_test_split(X, y,
    test_size=0.20, random_state=42)
```

To train the machine learning model, you will be using the **RandomForestClassifier** (https://bit.ly/2V1GOkO) model, which is one of the most commonly used machine learning models for classification. The **fit()** method of the **RandomForestClassifier** class is used to train the model.

Script 27:

```
1.  #training Random Forest Classifier on the training data
2.  from sklearn.ensemble import RandomForestClassifier
3.
4.  clf = RandomForestClassifier(n_estimators=250, random_
    state=0)
5.  clf.fit(X_train, y_train)
```

10.3.6 Evaluating Model Performance

Once a supervised machine learning model is trained, you can make predictions on the test. To do so, you can use the **predict()** method of the **RandomForestClassifer.**

To compare predictions with the actual output, you can use the confusion matrix, accuracy, recall, and F1 measures. The following script evaluates the model performance.

Script 28:

```
1.  #making predictions on the test set
2.  y_pred = clf.predict(X_test)
3.
4.
5.  #evaluating model performance
6.  from sklearn.metrics import classification_report,
    confusion_matrix, accuracy_score
7.
8.  print(confusion_matrix(y_test,y_pred))
9.  print(classification_report(y_test,y_pred))
10. print(accuracy_score(y_test,y_pred))
```

Output:

```
[[2078  405]
 [ 420 2097]]
              precision    recall  f1-score   support

           0       0.83      0.84      0.83      2483
           1       0.84      0.83      0.84      2517
    accuracy                           0.83      5000
   macro avg       0.83      0.84      0.83      5000
weighted avg       0.84      0.83      0.84      5000

0.835
```

The output shows that our model achieves an accuracy of 83.5 percent on the test set.

10.3.7 Making Predictions on Single Instance

Now, we are ready to make predictions on new text. The text is first converted into the numeric form using the same `TfidfVectorizer` that is used to convert text to numbers for training the model. The numeric form of the text can then be passed to the "predict()" method of the classifier object to make predictions. In the following script, we try to find the sentiment of a random sentence: "The movie was really good, I liked it."

Script 29:

```
print(clf.predict(vectorizer.transform(["The movie was really good, I liked it"])))
```

Output:

```
[1]
```

The output shows a sentiment of 1, which means our model thinks this is a positive review, which it actually is. Hence, we can say that our text classification model is doing a good job.

> **Further Readings – Text Classification**
> To know more about natural language processing with Scikit-Learn, check this link: http://bit.ly/3blb2q3.

Exercise 10.1

Question 1:

Which attribute of the TfidfVectorizer vectorizer is used to define the minimum word count:

    A. min_word

    B. min_count

    C. min_df

    D. None of the above

Question 2:

Which method of the RandomForestClassifier object is used to train the algorithm on the input data:

    A. train()

    B. fit()

    C. predict()

D. train_data()

Question 3:

Sentimental analysis with `RandomForestClassifier` is a type of _____ learning problem

    A. Supervised

    B. Unsupervised

    C. Reinforcement

    D. Lazy

Exercise 10.2

Import the "spam.csv" file from the resources folder. The dataset contains ham and spam text messages. Write a Python application that uses Scikit-Learn to classify ham and spam messages in the dataset. Column v1 contains a text label, while column v2 contains the text of the message.

11

Image Classification with Scikit- Learn

Image classification is the task of assigning a class or label to an image. For instance, if you are given a set of images of animals, you need to identify the name of the animal in an image. Similarly, identifying digits in images is another example of image classification. Neural networks, particularly convolutional neural networks, are often used for image classification tasks.

However, the use of neural networks for simple image classification tasks is a bit of overkill. You can also use Python's Scikit-learn library for simple image classification tasks, which you will see in this chapter. You will see how you can classify images of handwritten digits from 0-9 using the random forest classifier in Scikit-learn. So, let's begin without much ado.

11.1 Importing the Dataset

The dataset that you will be using to train your image classifier is the MNIST dataset. The MNIST dataset consists of 70,000 greyscale images of 28 x 28 pixels. A greyscale image has two dimensions, whereas a color image has three dimensions (width-height-color channels). Scikit-learn algorithms require data records to be in the form of one-dimensional row vectors, where each item in a vector corresponds to one of the feature values.

Since greyscale images have two dimensions, they are required to be converted into a one-dimensional array. To do so, you can use the reshape() function of the numpy array. However, luckily with `fetch_openml()` method from the `sklearn.datasets`, you can import the MNIST dataset where each record is, by default, converted into a row vector of size 784 (28 x 28). Therefore, you do not need to reshape the images in the MNIST dataset in this section.

The following script imports the MNIST dataset into your application.

Script 1:

```
1.  #importing the dataset using fetch_openml function
2.  from sklearn.datasets import fetch_openml
3.  mnist = fetch_openml('mnist_784')
```

Images are stored in the `data` attribute of the imported MNIST dataset, whereas the labels are stored in the `target` attribute. The following script prints the shape of the dataset and the unique labels in the dataset.

Script 2:

```
1.  #printing the shape of the dataset
2.  print(mnist.data.shape)
3.
4.  #printing unique labels in the dataset
5.  import numpy as np
6.  np.unique(mnist.target)
```

The output shows that the dataset consists of 70,000 records, where each record has 784 features. The number of unique labels is 10, i.e., digits from 0 to 9.

Output:

```
(70000, 784)
                         Out[32]:
array(['0', '1', '2', '3', '4', '5', '6', '7', '8', '9'],
dtype=object)
```

The following script displays the image at index 0 in the MNIST dataset. You can see that first, you converted the image back to a two-dimensional array of size 28 x 28 using the `reshape()` function. Next, the image is displayed using the `matshow()` function of the `pyplot` module from the Matplotlib library.

Script 3:

```
1.  #printing the first image
2.  image_0 = mnist.data[0].reshape(28,28)
3.  import matplotlib.pyplot as plt
4.  plt.gray()
5.  plt.matshow(image_0)
6.  plt.show()
```

The output below shows that the image at index 0 is the image of digit 5.

Output:

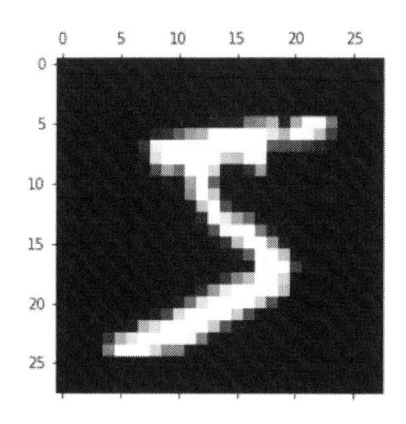

Let's now print the label for the image at index 0 to see if the label is actually 5.

Script 4:

```
1.  #printing the label for the first image
2.  label_0 = mnist.target[0]
3.  print(label_0)
```

The output shows that the label of the image at index 0 is actually 5.

Output:

```
5
```

11.2 Dividing the Dataset into Features and Labels

The next step is to divide the image dataset into features and labels sets. The features for all the images, i.e., the one-dimensional arrays of sizes 784, are stored in the `data` attribute, whereas the corresponding labels are stored in the `target` attribute. The following script divides the data into X features and y labels attributes.

Script 5:

```
1.  #creating feature set
2.  X = mnist.data
3.
4.  #creating label set
5.  y = mnist.target
```

The rest of the process is familiar. You need to divide the data into training and test sets, as shown in the following script.

11.3 Dividing Data into Training and Test Sets

Script 6:

```
1.  #dividing data into the training and test sets
2.  from sklearn.model_selection import train_test_split
3.
4.  X_train, X_test, y_train, y_test = train_test_split(X, y,
    test_size=0.20, random_state=0)
```

You can scale your image data just like any other data, as shown in the following script.

11.4 Data Scaling/Normalization

Script 7:

```
1.  #applying standard scaling to the dataset
2.  from sklearn.preprocessing import StandardScaler
3.  sc = StandardScaler()
4.  X_train = sc.fit_transform(X_train)
5.  X_test = sc.transform (X_test)
```

11.5 Training and Making Predictions

You can use any of the Scikit-learn classifiers to train the machine learning models on the image training data. However, in this section, you will be using the Random Forest classifier.

In the following script, the Random Forest classifier is trained on the training data, and then the trained model is used to make predictions on the test set.

Script 8:

```
1.  #importing random forest classifier from sklearn
2.  from sklearn.ensemble import RandomForestClassifier
3.  rf_clf = RandomForestClassifier(random_state=42,n_
    estimators=500)
4.
5.  #training the random forest classifier
6.  classifier = rf_clf.fit(X_train, y_train)
7.
8.  #making predictions on the test set
9.  y_pred = classifier.predict(X_test)
```

11.6 Evaluating the Algorithm on Test Set

Finally, to find the accuracy of your trained model for image classification of the MNIST test dataset, you can run the following script.

Script 9:

```
1.  #evaluating the algorithm on test set
2.  from sklearn.metrics import classification_report,
    confusion_matrix, accuracy_score
3.
4.  print(confusion_matrix(y_test,y_pred))
5.  print(accuracy_score(y_test, y_pred))
```

Output:

```
[[1367    0      1      0      2      4      7      0
  6      0]
 [
  0 1560    6      4      3      0      2      2
  2      1]
 [  2
  2 1409    5      3      1      5      8
  7      1]
 [         1      1     23 1364      0     15      0     11
 14      6]
 [         3      0      0
  0 1314    0      4      5
  3     21]
 [         1      3      4      9
  1 1185   12      1
  9      6]
 [         5      2      1      0      4
  7 1364    0
  4      0]
 [         3      5     20      1      9      0
  0 1399
  2     19]
 [         0      9      5      5      4      4      3
  0   13
 18     20]
 [         4      2      3     18     12      5      2     13
  8 1294]]
0.9695714285714285
```

The output shows that your model can predict digits in the images in the MNIST dataset with 96.95 percent accuracy.

> **Further Readings – Image Classification with Scikit-Learn**
>
> 1. To know more about image classification with sklearn, check this link: http://bit.ly/3pbYR92

Exercise 11.1

Question 1:

A colored image has _____ channels:

    A. 1

    B. 2

    C. 3

    D. 4

Question 2:

You need to convert an image into a _____ dimensional array before you can use Scikit-learn to train models on image data?

    A. 1

    B. 2

    C. 3

    D. 4

Question 3:

To convert a one-dimensional numpy array into a two-dimensional array or matrix, which method can be used?

    A. np.tomatrix()

    B. pd.convert2d

    C. pd.reshape()

    D. None of the above

Exercise 11.2

Divide the following image dataset into 80 percent training and 20 percent test sets. Train the model on the training set and make predictions on the test set. Print the accuracy and confusion matrix for the model performance.

```
1.  #importing the dataset using fetch_openml function
2.  from sklearn import datasets
3.  import numpy as np
4.
5.  digits = datasets.load_digits()
6.
7.  n_samples = len(digits.images)
8.  X = digits.images.reshape((n_samples, -1))
9.  y = digits.target
```

From the Same Publisher

Python Machine Learning
https://bit.ly/3gcb2iG

Python Deep Learning
https://bit.ly/3gci9Ys

Python Data Visualization
https://bit.ly/3wXqDJI

Python for Data Analysis
https://bit.ly/3wPYEM2

Python Data Preprocessing
https://bit.ly/3fLV3ci

Python for NLP
https://bit.ly/3chlTqm

10 ML Projects Explained from Scratch
https://bit.ly/34KFsDk

Python Scikit-Learn for Beginners
https://bit.ly/3fPbtRf

Data Science with Python
https://bit.ly/3wVQ5iN

Data Science Crash Course for Beginners
Fundamentals and Practices with Python

Statistics with Python
https://bit.ly/3z27KHt

Statistics Crash Course for Beginners
Theory and Applications of Frequentist and Bayesian Statistics Using Python

Exercise Solutions

Exercise 2.1

Question 1

Which iteration should be used when you want to repeatedly execute a code specific number of times?

    A. For Loop

    B. While Loop

    C. Both A & B

    D. None of the above

Answer: A

Question 2

What is the maximum number of values that a function can return in Python?

    A. Single Value

    B. Double Value

    C. More than two values

    D. None

Answer: C

Question 3

Which of the following membership operators are supported by Python?

    A. In

    B. Out

    C. Not In

    D. Both A and C

Answer: D

Exercise 2.2

Print the table of integer 9 using a while loop:

```
1. j=1
2. while j< 11:
3. print("9 x "+str(j)+ " = "+ str(9*j))
4. j=j+1
```

Exercise 3.1

Question 1

Which of the following techniques can be used to remove outliers from a dataset?

    A. Trimming

    B. Censoring

    C. Discretization

    D. All of the above

Answer: D

Question 2

Which attribute is set to True to remove the first column from the one-hot encoded columns generated via the get_dummies() method?

    A. drop_first

    B. remove_first

    C. delete_first

    D. None of the above

Answer: A

Question 3

After standardization, the mean value of the dataset becomes:

    A. 1

    B. 0

    C. -1

    D. None of the above

Answer: B

Exercise 3.2

Replace the missing values in the *deck* column of the Titanic dataset with the most frequently occurring categories in that column. Plot a bar plot for the updated *deck* column.

Solution:

```
1.  import matplotlib.pyplot as plt
2.  import seaborn as sns
3.
4.  plt.rcParams["figure.figsize"] = [8,6]
5.  sns.set_style("darkgrid")
6.
7.  titanic_data = sns.load_dataset('titanic')
8.
9.  titanic_data = titanic_data[["deck"]]
10. titanic_data.head()
11. titanic_data.isnull().mean()
12.
13. titanic_data.deck.value_counts().sort_
    values(ascending=False).plot.bar()
14. plt.xlabel('deck')
15. plt.ylabel('Number of Passengers')
16.
17. titanic_data.deck.mode()
18.
19. titanic_data.deck.fillna('C', inplace=True)
20.
21. titanic_data.deck.value_counts().sort_
    values(ascending=False).plot.bar()
22. plt.xlabel('deck')
23. plt.ylabel('Number of Passengers')
```

Exercise 4.1

Question 1

Which of the following feature types should you retain in the dataset?

    A. Features with low Variance

    B. Features with high Variance

    C. Features with a high standard deviation

    D. Both B and C

Answer: D

Question 2

Which of the following features should you remove from the dataset?

    A. Features with high mutual correlation

    B. Features with low mutual correlation

    C. Features with high correlation with output label

    D. None of the above

Answer: A

Question 3

Which of the following feature selection method does not depend upon the output label?

    A. Feature selection based on Model performance

    B. Feature selection based on recursive elimination

    C. Feature selection based on mutual feature variance

    D. All of the above

Answer: C

Exercise 4.2

Using the \winequalit-white dataset from the \Dataset and Source Codes folder, apply the recursive elimination technique for feature selection.

Solution:

```
1.  from sklearn.linear_model import LinearRegression
2.  from sklearn.feature_selection import RFE
3.
4.  import pandas as pd
5.
6.  # importing the dataset
7.  wine_data = pd.read_csv("E:/Datasets/winequality-white.csv", sep =";" )
8.
9.  #printing dataset header
10. wine_data.head()
11.
12. # dividing data into features and labels
13. features = wine_data.drop(["quality"], axis = 1)
14. labels = wine_data.filter(["quality"], axis = 1)
15.
16. # feature selection using RFE
17. lr = LinearRegression()
18. rfe = RFE(estimator=lr, n_features_to_select=4, step=1)
19. rfe.fit(features, labels)
20.
21. attributes_to_retain =  rfe.get_support(1)
22.
23. filtered_dataset = features[features.columns[attributes_to_retain]]
24. filtered_dataset.head()
```

Exercise 5.1

Question 1

Which of the following is an example of a regression output?

- A. True
- B. Red
- C. 2.5
- D. None of the above

Answer: C

Question 2

Which of the following algorithm is a lazy algorithm?

    A. Random Forest

    B. KNN

    C. SVM

    D. Linear Regression

Answer: B

Question 3

Which of the following algorithm is not a regression metric?

    A. Accuracy

    B. Recall

    C. F1 Measure

    D. All of the above

Answer: D

Exercise 5.2

Using the \Diamonds dataset from the Seaborn library, train a regression algorithm of your choice, which predicts the price of the diamond. Perform all the preprocessing steps.

Solution:

```
1.  import pandas as pd
2.  import numpy as np
3.  import seaborn as sns
4.
5.  diamonds_df = sns.load_dataset("diamonds")
6.
7.  X = diamonds_df.drop(['price'], axis=1)
8.  y = diamonds_df["price"]
```

```
9.
10. numerical = X.drop(['cut', 'color', 'clarity'], axis = 1)
11.
12. categorical = X.filter(['cut', 'color', 'clarity'])
13.
14. cat_numerical = pd.get_dummies(categorical,drop_first=True)
15.
16. X = pd.concat([numerical, cat_numerical], axis = 1)
17.
18. from sklearn.model_selection import train_test_split
19.
20. X_train, X_test, y_train, y_test = train_test_split(X, y, test_size=0.20, random_state=0)
21.
22. from sklearn.preprocessing import StandardScaler
23. sc = StandardScaler()
24. X_train = sc.fit_transform(X_train)
25. X_test = sc.transform (X_test)
26.
27. from sklearn import svm
28. svm_reg = svm.SVR()
29. regressor = svm_reg.fit(X_train, y_train)
30. y_pred = regressor.predict(X_test)
31.
32.
33.
34. from sklearn import metrics
35.
36. print('Mean Absolute Error:', metrics.mean_absolute_error(y_test, y_pred))
37. print('Mean Squared Error:', metrics.mean_squared_error(y_test, y_pred))
38. print('Root Mean Squared Error:', np.sqrt(metrics.mean_squared_error(y_test, y_pred)))
```

Exercise 6.1

Question 1

Which of the following is not an example of classification outputs?

    A. True

    B. Red

    C. Male

    D. None of the above

Answer: D

Question 2

Which of the following metrics is used for unbalanced classification datasets?

    A. Accuracy

    B. F1

    C. Precision

    D. Recall

Answer: C

Question 3

Which of the following function is used to convert categorical values to one-hot encoded numerical values?

    A. pd.get_onehot()

    B. pd.get_dummies()

    C. pd.get_numeric()

    D. All of the above

Answer: B

Exercise 6.2

Using the iris dataset from the Seaborn library, train a classification algorithm of your choice, which predicts the specie of the iris plant. Perform all the preprocessing steps.

Solution:

```
1.  import pandas as pd
2.  import numpy as np
3.  import seaborn as sns
4.
5.  iris_df = sns.load_dataset("iris")
6.
7.  iris_df.head()
8.
9.  X = iris_df.drop(['species'], axis=1)
10. y = iris_df["species"]
11.
12.
13. from sklearn.model_selection import train_test_split
14.
15. X_train, X_test, y_train, y_test = train_test_split(X, y,
    test_size=0.20, random_state=0)
16.
17. from sklearn.preprocessing import StandardScaler
18. sc = StandardScaler()
19. X_train = sc.fit_transform(X_train)
20. X_test = sc.transform (X_test)
21.
22. from sklearn.ensemble import RandomForestClassifier
23. rf_clf = RandomForestClassifier(random_state=42,n_
    estimators=500)
24.
25. classifier = rf_clf.fit(X_train, y_train)
26.
27. y_pred = classifier.predict(X_test)
28.
29.
30. from sklearn.metrics import classification_report,
    confusion_matrix, accuracy_score
31.
32. print(confusion_matrix(y_test,y_pred))
33. print(classification_report(y_test,y_pred))
34. print(accuracy_score(y_test, y_pred))
```

Exercise 7.1

Question 1

Which of the following is a supervised machine learning algorithm?

    A. K-Means Clustering

    B. Hierarchical Clustering

    C. All of the above

    D. None of the above

Answer: D

Question 2

In K- Means clustering, the inertia tells us?

    A. the distance between data points within a cluster

    B. output labels for the data points

    C. the number of clusters

    D. None of the above

Answer: C

Question 3

In hierarchical clustering, in the case of vertical dendrograms, the number of clusters is equal to the number of _____ lines that the _____ line passes through?

    A. horizontal, vertical

    B. vertical, horizontal

    C. none of the above

    D. All of the above

Answer: B

Exercise 7.2

Apply K-Means clustering on the banknote.csv dataset available in the Datasets folder in this GitHub repository (https://bit.ly/3nhAJBi). Find the optimal number of clusters and then print the clustered dataset. The following script imports the dataset and prints the first five rows of the dataset.

```
1.  banknote_df = pd.read_csv(r"E:\Hands on Python for Data
    Science and Machine Learning\Datasets\banknote.csv")
2.  banknote_df.head()
3.
4.  ### Solution:
5.
6.  # dividing data into features and labels
7.  features = banknote_df.drop(["class"], axis = 1)
8.  labels = banknote_df.filter(["class"], axis = 1)
9.  features.head()
10.
11. # training KMeans on K values from 1 to 10
12. loss =[]
13. for i in range(1, 11):
14. km = KMeans(n_clusters = i).fit(features)
15. loss.append(km.inertia_)
16.
17. #printing loss against number of clusters
18.
19. import matplotlib.pyplot as plt
20. plt.plot(range(1, 11), loss)
21. plt.title('Finding Optimal Clusters via Elbow Method')
22. plt.xlabel('Number of Clusters')
23. plt.ylabel('loss')
24. plt.show()
25.
26. # training KMeans with 3 clusters
27. features = features.values
28. km_model = KMeans(n_clusters=2)
29. km_model.fit(features)
30.
```

```
31. #print the data points with predicted labels
32. plt.scatter(features[:,0], features[:,1], c= km_model.
    labels_, cmap='rainbow' )
33.
34. #print the predicted centroids
35. plt.scatter(km_model.cluster_centers_[:, 0], km_model.
    cluster_centers_[:, 1], s=100, c='black')
```

Exercise 8.1

Question 1

Which of the following are the benefits of dimensionality reduction?

    A. Data Visualization

    B. Faster training time for statistical algorithms

    C. All of the above

    D. None of the above

Answer: C

Question 2

In PCA, dimensionality reduction depends upon the:

    A. Features set only

    B. Labels set only

    C. Both features and labels sets

    D. None of the above

Answer: A

Question 3

LDA is a _____ dimensionality reduction technique

    A. Unsupervised

    B. Semi-Supervised

    C. Supervised

    D. Reinforcement

Answer: C

Exercise 8.2

Apply principal component analysis for dimensionality reduction on the customer_churn.csv dataset from the Datasets folder in this GitHub repository (https://bit.ly/3nhAJBi). Print the accuracy using two principal components. Also, plot the results on a test set using the two principal components.

Solution:

```
1.  import pandas as pd
2.  import numpy as np
3.
4.  churn_df = pd.read_csv("E:\Hands on Python for Data
    Science and Machine Learning\Datasets\customer_churn.csv")
5.  churn_df.head()
6.
7.  churn_df = churn_df.drop(['RowNumber', 'CustomerId',
    'Surname'], axis=1)
8.
9.  X = churn_df.drop(['Exited'], axis=1)
10. y = churn_df['Exited']
11.
12. numerical = X.drop(['Geography', 'Gender'], axis= 1)
13. categorical = X.filter(['Geography', 'Gender'])
14. cat_numerical = pd.get_dummies(categorical,drop_first=True)
15. X = pd.concat([numerical, cat_numerical], axis =1)
```

```
16. X.head()
17.
18. from sklearn.model_selection import train_test_split
19.
20. X_train, X_test, y_train, y_test = train_test_split(X, y,
    test_size=0.20, random_state=0)
21.
22. #applying scaling on training and test data
23. from sklearn.preprocessing import StandardScaler
24. sc = StandardScaler()
25. X_train = sc.fit_transform(X_train)
26. X_test = sc.transform (X_test)
27.
28. #importing PCA class
29. from sklearn.decomposition import PCA
30.
31. #creating object of the PCA class
32. pca = PCA()
33.
34. #training PCA model on training data
35. X_train = pca.fit_transform(X_train)
36.
37. #making predictions on test data
38. X_test = pca.transform(X_test)
39.
40. #printing variance ratios
41. variance_ratios = pca.explained_variance_ratio_
42. print(variance_ratios)
43.
44. #use one principal component
45. from sklearn.decomposition import PCA
46.
47. pca = PCA(n_components=2)
48. X_train = pca.fit_transform(X_train)
49. X_test = pca.transform(X_test)
50.
51. #making predictions using logistic regression
52. from sklearn.linear_model import LogisticRegression
53.
54. #training the logistic regression model
55. lg = LogisticRegression()
```

```
56. lg.fit(X_train, y_train)
57.
58.
59. # Predicting the Test set results
60. y_pred = lg.predict(X_test)
61.
62. #evaluating results
63.
64. from sklearn.metrics import accuracy_score
65.
66. print(accuracy_score(y_test, y_pred))
67.
68. from matplotlib import pyplot as plt
69. %matplotlib inline
70.
71. #print actual datapoints
72.
73. plt.scatter(X_test[:,0], X_test[:,1], c= y_test,
    cmap='rainbow' )
```

Exercise 9.1

Question 1:

With grid search, you can_____

    A. Test all parameters for a model by default

    B. Test only lists of specified parameters

    C. Test three parameters

    D. None of the above

Answer: B

Question 2:

Learning curves can be used to study the:

    A. Bias of a trained algorithm

    B. Variance of a trained algorithm

    C. Both of the above

    D. None of the above

Answer: C

Question 3:

Which pickle method can be used to save a trained machine learning model:

    A. save()

    B. register()

    C. load()

    D. dump()

Answer: D

Exercise 9.2

Use the Grid Search to find the parameters of the RandomForestClassifier algorithm, which return the highest classification accuracy for classifying the banknote.csv dataset:

```
6.  grid_param = {
7.  'n_estimators': [100, 300, 500, 800, 1000],
8.  'criterion': ['gini', 'entropy'],
9.  'bootstrap': [True, False]
10. }
```

Solution:

```
1.  import pandas as pd
2.  import numpy as np
3.  import matplotlib.pyplot as plt
4.  from sklearn.ensemble import RandomForestClassifier
5.  from sklearn.model_selection import learning_curve
6.
7.  # importing the dataset
8.  banknote_data = pd.read_csv("E:/Datasets/banknote.csv" )
9.
10. #printing the dataset header
11. banknote_data.head()
12.
13. #extracting features
14. X = banknote_data.drop(['class'], axis=1)
15.
16. #extracting labels
17. y = banknote_data["class"]
18.
19. grid_param = {
20.     'n_estimators': [100, 300, 500, 800, 1000],
21.     'criterion': ['gini', 'entropy'],
22.     'bootstrap': [True, False]
23. }
24.
25. #importing the GridSearchCV class
26. from sklearn.model_selection import GridSearchCV
27.
28. rf_clf = RandomForestClassifier(random_state=42, n_estimators=500)
29.
30. gd_sr = GridSearchCV(estimator=rf_clf,
31.     param_grid=grid_param,
32.     scoring ="accuracy",
33.     cv=5,
34.     n_jobs=-1)
35.
36. #training with grid search
37. gd_sr.fit(X, y)
38.
```

```
39. #printing the best parameters
40. best_parameters = gd_sr.best_params_
41. print(best_parameters)
```

Exercise 10.1

Question 1:

Which attribute of the TfidfVectorizer vectorizer is used to define the minimum word count?

    A. min_word

    B. min_count

    C. min_df

    D. None of the Above

Answer: C

Question 2:

Which method of the RandomForestClassifier object is used to train the algorithm on the input data?

    A. train()

    B. fit()

    C. predict()

    D. train_data()

Answer: B

Question 3:

Sentimental analysis with RandomForestClassifier is a type of _____ learning problem.

A. Supervised

B. Unsupervised

C. Reinforcement

D. Lazy

Answer: A

Exercise 10.2

Import the "spam.csv" file from the resources folder. The dataset contains ham and spam text messages. Write a Python application that uses Scikit-Learn to classify ham and spam messages in the dataset. Column v1 contains a text label, while column v2 contains the text of the message.

Solution:

```
1.  import numpy as np
2.  import pandas as pd
3.  import re
4.  import nltk
5.  import matplotlib.pyplot as plt
6.  import seaborn as sns
7.  %matplotlib inline
8.
9.  data_path = "E:/Datasets/spam.csv"
10. movie_dataset = pd.read_csv(data_path, engine='python')
11.
12. X = movie_dataset["v2"]
13.
14. y = movie_dataset["v1"]
15.
16. def clean_text(doc):
```

```
17.
18.
19.     document = re.sub('[^a-zA-Z]', ' ', doc)
20.
21.     document = re.sub(r"\s+[a-zA-Z]\s+", ' ', document)
22.
23.     document = re.sub(r'\s+', ' ', document)
24.
25.     return document
26.
27. X_sentences = []
28. reviews = list(X)
29. for rev in reviews:
30.     X_sentences.append(clean_text(rev))
31.
32.
33. from nltk.corpus import stopwords
34. from sklearn.feature_extraction.text import TfidfVectorizer
35.
36. vectorizer = TfidfVectorizer (max_features=2000, min_df=5, max_df=0.7, stop_words=stopwords.words('english'))
37. X= vectorizer.fit_transform(X_sentences).toarray()
38.
39. from sklearn.model_selection import train_test_split
40. X_train, X_test, y_train, y_test = train_test_split(X, y, test_size=0.20, random_state=42)
41.
42.
43. from sklearn.ensemble import RandomForestClassifier
44.
45. clf = RandomForestClassifier(n_estimators=250, random_state=0)
46. clf.fit(X_train, y_train)
47.
48. y_pred = clf.predict(X_test)
49.
50. from sklearn.metrics import classification_report, confusion_matrix, accuracy_score
51.
52. print(confusion_matrix(y_test,y_pred))
53. print(classification_report(y_test,y_pred))
54. print(accuracy_score(y_test,y_pred))
```

Exercise 11.1

Question 1:

A colored image has_____channels:

    A. 1

    B. 2

    C. 3

    D. 4

Answer: C

Question 2:

You need to convert an image into a_____dimensional array before you can use Scikit-learn to train models on image data?

    A. 1

    B. 2

    C. 3

    D. 4

Answer: A

Question 3:

To convert a one-dimensional numpy array into a two-dimensional array or matrix, which method can be used?

    A. np.tomatrix()

    B. pd.convert2d

    C. pd.reshape()

    D. None of the above

Answer: C

Exercise 11.2

Divide the following image dataset into 80 percent training and 20 percent test sets. Train the model on the training set and make predictions on the test set. Print the accuracy and confusion matrix for the model performance.

```
10. #importing the dataset using fetch_openml function
11. from sklearn import datasets
12. import numpy as np
13.
14. digits = datasets.load_digits()
15.
16. n_samples = len(digits.images)
17. X = digits.images.reshape((n_samples, -1))
18. y = digits.target
```

Solution:

```
1.  #dividing data into the training and test sets
2.  from sklearn.model_selection import train_test_split
3.
4.  X_train, X_test, y_train, y_test = train_test_split(X, y,
    test_size=0.20, random_state=0)
5.
6.  #applying standard scaling to the dataset
7.  from sklearn.preprocessing import StandardScaler
8.  sc = StandardScaler()
9.  X_train = sc.fit_transform(X_train)
10. X_test = sc.transform (X_test)
11.
12. #importing random forest classifier from sklearn
13. from sklearn.ensemble import RandomForestClassifier
14. rf_clf = RandomForestClassifier(random_state=42, n_
    estimators=500)
15.
16. #training the random forest classifier
17. classifier = rf_clf.fit(X_train, y_train)
18.
19. #making predictions on the test set
20. y_pred = classifier.predict(X_test)
```

```
21.
22. #evaluating the algorithm on test set
23. from sklearn.metrics import classification_report,
    confusion_matrix, accuracy_score
24.
25. print(confusion_matrix(y_test,y_pred))
26. print(classification_report(y_test,y_pred))
27. print(accuracy_score(y_test, y_pred))
```

Printed in Great Britain
by Amazon